MISNEACH

The Story of

FLORA MACDONALD

by

K. L. Huntley

1

2023 K.L.Huntley   Hope, Idaho

Cover Design: Brett Batchelor
        Sandpoint, Idaho

Printed in the United States of America

Text Font: Palatino

Library of Congress Control Number: 2023931926

ISBN: 979-8-9889400-0-5
Imprint: Independently published

Dedicated to the Howie Women

Admirable Women of Strength & Fortitude

Role models before their time

&

Whom I Loved Dearly

Lilian Rose Howie-Johnston-Rennie

Maggie Howie-McGregor

&

A Special Thank You

to

Michele Howie

Who carried on the Family Tradition

with

Loving Illumination

Religion has played and continues to play, a huge role in governments globally. So has hierarchy; who succeeds whom in the halls of power whether it be King, Queen, or Dictator. Mix them together and you frequently have a volatile concoction.

England, Scotland, and Ireland were all different countries until 1603 when Queen Elizabeth I of England died childless and her heir to the throne was James Charles Stuart VI of Scotland, Mary Queen of Scot's son. To the English, he became King James I.

Things did not go smoothly with King James' heirs. The English Parliament, afraid they would revert to Catholicism, passed a series of acts in 1688 and 1701 specifically excluding Roman Catholics from succeeding the throne. The Scots did not share that viewpoint.

The dissent reached a fever pitch when the last Protestant Stuart died without heirs and the succession went to distant cousins from Hanover, Germany, ones who also shared the Protestant faith. Resentment grew, as the Highland Scots felt strongly the Stuart house should continue, regardless of religion. Thus formed the Jacobites, a name derived from the Latin version of the name James, Jacobus.

There were multiple undertakings of armed insurrection over the years attempting to restore the Catholic Stuarts to the throne. This story begins after the last fatal one, the Battle of Culloden on April 16, 1746, when Charles Edward Stuart and his Jacobite supporters were defeated. The events following have been researched by the author and are accurate.

Only one character was invented and that is of Lewa, the mixed-race woman who helps Flora MacDonald when she immigrates to the colonies.

It is important to note that Queen Elizabeth II and Parliament amended the Succession to the Crown Act in 2013 and ended the provision which stated Roman Catholics were disqualified from the line of succession.

It appears to this writer that the Scots rarely find an issue with someone's religion, but rather what they value most is quality of character and integrity in an individual.

<u>Alexander MacDonald</u> of Boisdale - frequently called Boisdale was Ranald MacDonald's half-brother. (This one stayed neutral, feeling the cause was doomed to failure.)

<u>Alexander MacDonald of Kingsburgh</u>, Skye. Factor to the Sleat Chief. Referred to as Kingsburgh to distinguish him from the other Alexander MacDonalds. He was Allan MacDonald's father.

<u>Sir Alexander MacDonald, Chief of Sleat</u> - Owned part of the Islands of Skye and North Uist. He raised troops for King George. 1710-1746

<u>Allan MacDonald:</u> Flora's husband and son of Alexander MacDonald of Kingsburgh, Skye. b. 1720 - Sept 20, 1792

Angus MacDonald - Flora's older brother who inherited their childhood home called Milton on South Uist. Angus' wife was Penelope.

Annabella MacDonald - b. 1732 - Flora's half-sister. Daughter of Hugh and Marion MacDonald. Married to Alexander MacDonald of Cuidreach.

Anne MacDonald-MacAlister: Allan's sister. Daughter of Lady Florence and Alexander MacDonald of Kingsburgh.

Anne MacDonald-MacLeod 1754-1834 Flora's daughter. Married Alexander MacLeod of Glendale, Skye. Emigrated to Colonies. She had five children.

Donald Roy MacDonald *Dòmhnall Ruadh*, (b 1708) was the son of Ranald MacDonald

Ranald MacDonald - called "Old Clanranald" to distinguish him from his heir Ranald. He was Captain of his clan and controlled an extensive estate in Eriskay,

South Uist, Benbecula: and the small isle of Eigg, Rum, and Canna.

Hugh 'One Eyed' MacDonald: Flora MacDonald's step-father who married her mother Marion MacDonald after she was widowed. Hugh's home was at Armadale on Skye.

Marion MacDonald: Daughter of Rev. Angus MacDonald and Elizabeth MacDonald. She married Ranald MacDonald of Milton and had three children. Angus, Ranald, and Flora

Ranald died and Marion re-married Hugh MacDonald of Kingsburgh at Armadale. They had four more children… Annabella, James & two younger boys.

Lady Florence MacDonald: Wife of Kingsburgh (Alexander MacDonald) and Mother of Allan MacDonald (Flora's husband).

<u>Lady Margaret MacDonald:</u> Married to Sir Alexander MacDonald and a Jacobite sympathizer. Referred to as Lady Clanranald or Lady Clan for short.

<u>Neil MacEachen:</u> Flora's cousin. Born in 1719 - Howbeg, South Uist, Inverness Deceased in 1788 - Sancerre, France. aged 69 years old. Changed his last name to MacDonald.

Lady Catherine Bruce of Clackmannan

Ceitie (Katie) MacDowal - Flora's dear friend.

<u>Children of Flora & Allan MacDonald.</u>

Charles - b. Oct. 22, 1751

Anne - b. Feb 18, 1754

Alexander - Sandy - b. Feb 21, 1755

Ranald - b. Aug 16, 1756

James - b. Nov. 30, 1757

John - b. Oct. 30, 1759

Francis - b. May 6, 1766. Francis is known as Fanny

- Flora is 44 at the time of her birth.

<u>Gaelic translations/pronunciations:</u>

arisaid	cloak
Aye	Yes
bairns	children
birlinn	boat used in the Hebrides
blootered	drunken
bonxies	rapacious seabird
Cabock	Cheese
Ceitie	Katie
close	narrow street or alley
Dinna fash	Don't worry
Gaelic	Gah-lick
gòrach	Foolish
Jacobite	Latin for James - James VII of Scotland - their last monarch.
maistir	urine
misneach	courage - (mish-nock)
sheiling	small rock hut
taibhse	tieb-sha / ghost
Uist	Yew-ist
Unasary	Un-asary
ya ken	you understand/know

CHAPTER 1

The Meeting

Full Moon - Friday, June 20, 1746

It was close to midnight when Flora was awakened by her brother's dog Kelpie shoving his nose urgently into her face without a sound. Blinking awake from her deep sleep, she plainly heard the gentle tapping on the door of her sheiling at Unasary. Instinctively Flora clasped her fingers gently around Kelpie's muzzle signaling silence while looking directly into his eyes. Her own heart was beating fearfully and for a split second, she briefly entertained the wonder if it could be heard. Moving quietly Flora sat up and reached toward the knitting basket near the end of her bed. She plunged her hand deep into the soft wool yarn feeling for the bottom and the hard surface of her dirk. The tapping on the door became slightly more insistent.

Holding tightly to the small but sharp dagger Flora grabbed her arisaid which just seconds ago she had been sleeping peacefully under and wrapped it tightly around herself concealing the weapon in the folds.

Clearly, she was frightened. This was just the very reason her brother Angus and wife Penelope had wanted her to hide up in these mountains, far from the thousands of the King's troops scouring the Isle looking for Charles Edward Stuart.

A familiar voice from the past whispered hoarsely from outside the Sheiling, "Flory, it is I, cousin Neil—Neil MacEachen."

Flora silently moved across the dirt floor to the door, still slightly suspicious, and leaned against the rough wood separating the two. "Neil—what are you doing here? I thought you were in France." She spoke quietly in Gaelic and when reassured it was truly her cousin, she slid the door latch to the side and opened it to the full moon illuminating her beloved cousin. There stood Neil in front of her with a pile of weapons and provisions dropped casually at his feet. His familiar handsome face appeared slightly worn for the wear and a few years older than when she had seen him last, yet the twinkle in his eyes and the slight grin remained the same.

"Are you alone?" He inquired peering about the tiny room.

Flora smiled, still slightly groggy, "Aye, alone with the coos you silly lad."

The two cousins enveloped each other with a long hearty hug, Flora holding her wrap tightly along with her dirk with her free arm. "How did you know I was here? It has been so long. When did you leave France?" Her questions were coming at a rapid pace.

"One question at a time lassie. Your kin made me aware you were up here visiting your brother Angus, and I remembered the paths from when we ran these hills as bairns." Neil's face took on a more serious note as he met her eyes. "I have someone with me that needs your help."

Flora quickly covered her open mouth and her astonished eyes widened as she looked knowingly into Neil's, reading his thoughts. "The Prince? You have brought Bonnie Prince Charlie here—to an Unisary Sheiling?"

Neil's answer came as a quiet whistle and out from the shadows appeared a tall slender figure.

"Aye, and Fora, we need your help. Hugh believes you can assist us greatly in getting him to Skye safely."

As Charles Edward Stuart stepped into the doorway, Flora fell to her knees and took his hand. "Your Royal Highness."

Charles, flattered at her response, pulled her to her feet as Neil began to explain to her in French that the Prince did not speak Gaelic, and they would have to communicate in French.

Flora, confounded, answered Neil again in Gaelic. "He doesn't speak our Mother tongue? How is he to lead Caledonia and our people?"

Neil shrugged and Flora, still holding Charles' hands continued her questions in Gaelic. "Neil, he smells! Where have you two been all this time?"

"On the run Flory, on the run. It has been fifty-seven days since Culloden. I've counted them. We have slept in caves, on the heather and under rocks. We moved at night—in every way imaginable. Now we are here and needing your help. The pitiful man has had more to drink than eat for far too long. We are weary lassie. Weary to the bone."

Flora, now fully awake and cognizant of the urgency of the situation was overcome by trepidation. She wanted to talk to her brother Angus about the already dangerous situation in which they were plunged. She felt she was in a thickening quagmire. Would Neil and the Prince's arrival bring searching troops upon them? Culloden, whose battle seemed so distant and far away was suddenly standing on her moonlit threshold, along with a Prince who had a £30,000 bounty on his head instead of a crown.

Charles, not comprehending a word she said, clearly understood her tones and respectfully looked into her face with haunted, pleading eyes. His body filled the low doorway and it was noticeable that even under these circumstances he held himself regally, a true prince and rightful heir to both the crown of England and Scotland.

Flora was rapidly putting it all together in her mind fully realizing they were here explicitly for her help. But why? "Neil why me? How can I help? I am gathering you need to get him back to France and out of Britain quickly, but how do I figure in the scheme? I can not comprehend why you have brought him to me."

Neil switched to French to include the Prince. "Your stepfather, One-eyed Hugh, felt strongly that you could help. He said you ken every trail, nook and nanny in the Hebrides and, as we all know my dear, you have been traversing them since a young lassie. You have a detailed map etched in that pretty little brain of yours. You are a top-notch guide even in the dark."

Flora gave a short laugh and rolled her eyes. "That old fox! When I was young and came home early in the mornings from rambling he would look at my rosy pink cheeks and call me his 'Highland Rose'. And now, as you know, he is wearing a mask. His heart is with our Bonnie Prince here, yet he holds the position of a Commanding Officer of the local troops." Flora's eyes twinkled revealing a bit of merriment. Her only recollection of her birth father was watching from an upstairs window as he was carried out of the house in a box and her mother's frightening keening wails.

Realizing she was still in her sleeping gown with a tartan cloak wrapped around herself, standing in front of a man who could be king someday, Flora stepped back, slightly embarrassed. She then gently requested both men step outside again while she dressed.

The Prince was the first to leave and Flora faced Neil again in Gaelic. "How many of you are here? Just the two?"

"Just one other, besides the Prince. We have a man named Felix O'Neil with us."

Flora sucked in her breath. "Felix O'Neil?"

"Aye, he is a Colonel. He's been with us since we left France."

Flora rolled her eyes again. "I know him Neil, and I'm not a fond of him. The only thing Irish about him is his name and his attentions toward me at Nunton were a bit unwelcome." With that, she gently shoved Neil's back out the door. "Give me a minute to dress."

With the men safely out of the sheiling Flora took less than a few minutes to lace her front stays and throw on a skirt. She was still plaiting her hair when the Prince stepped in a second time, his face clearly showing exhaustion, a stubble of beard, and sunken eyes. Directly behind him stood an equally weary Felix O'Neil who smiled meeting Flora's eyes.

Flora straightened up and aware Felix also could not speak Gaelic, greeted them in her finest French and a slight curtsey. "You are all welcome here and I am honored to be of service." Without asking if they were hungry she reached for some fresh Caboc rolled in oats handing the men a healthy portion. Bringing out a bucket of fresh milk from its covering in the corner, she proceeded to share her food, passing out the left-over bannocks she had brought from Angus' home.

The men stood about the small dwelling talking in hushed tones and eating as if it had been the first solid food in days. As they discussed and discarded various ideas of smuggling Prince Charles off this island of South Uist and onto the Isle of Skye, he paced about the small shelter nervously. Could they get him to Skye and safely onto the rescue ship en route from France? A heavy desperation hung about each word they spoke knowing, if not successful it would mean death for them all. One idea after another was presented and discarded.

"He stands out the way he is." Flora stated looking at the prince's physic, then half-jokingly mentioned he would draw less attention if he were a woman.

"That is it!" Neil MacEachen exclaimed slapping his knee. "We will disguise him as a woman. Flora me lassie he can pose as your handmaiden and besides, a beauty like yourself would never be suspect of smuggling anything, let alone the Prince." Neil was smiling broadly from his epiphany while gazing at his charming cousin.

"We will have to make you a dress Prince Charles. How do you feel about that?"

Charles Edward Stuart pulled out a flask, took a long pull then laughed. "I like the scheme." He passed his flask to Neil and added, "If it is ever our good fortune to get free of these troubles I will see to it that you live well for the rest of your life Neil MacEachen."

Flora suggested they hurry while they still had the cover of darkness. Even though the moon was full she figured those searching for the Prince should rightfully be asleep by now. They would have to move north to the Island of Benbecula quickly and up to Nunton where she was sure she could get help from Lady Margaret MacDonald, the one known as Lady Clanranald, or lovingly Lady Clan for short. Lady Clanranald was the wife of the chief and a known Jacobite sympathizer. Flora gathered up a few things, stuffed them in the pockets tied about her waist then slipped on a pair of pampooties over her heavy knit stockings. As they headed into the night she made a low whistle and Kelpie instantly heeled. She reached down and gave the dog a rewarding pat and scratch behind the ears then, switching to her native Gaelic she turned to Neil MacEachen.

"We've got to cover as much ground as we can before daybreak. I need to get Kelpie home to Angus and let him know I'm safe."

Flora mulled over the word *safe*. No one had felt safe from the British before nor after Culloden. This land she loved so dearly, a land she felt deeply rooted to was being turned inside out by sassenachs, strangers with no connection to the sea, the ebbs and flows of the seasons, or to the ground so many considered hallowed. They failed to understand the people, the language, or their customs.

With thoughts swirling through everyone's mind, the small party moved stealthily yet purposely down the moonlit stony path.

CHAPTER 2

Benbecula

Flora guided the men a slight half-mile down a barely discernible trail, pushing a few cows out of her way with a long stick and Kelpie trotting faithfully by her side. When she could see the outline of Angus' home in the distance she knelt down to the border collie and wrapped her arms around him. Then she pointed to her brother Angus' house and commanded the dog home with one word. Assured Kelpie was trotting off as directed and not following them, she took a turn to the right and onto another branch of the pathway, with Prince Charlie, Neil, and Felix all following her closely.

After walking on treacherous and uneven ground for most of what was left of the short night, the straggly party skirted the head of Loch Eynort. The waking barks and grunts of the seals could be heard signaling dawn was close, so Flora led the group up a steep climb into the Glenn of Corodale. There Flora located a familiar rock outcropping she had used in the past as shelter. The wind and rain had eroded a small cave underneath which was barely detectable in the rugged terrain. From here they had a natural lookout providing a scan of the sea, the moors, and hills of the area without being detected.

The Prince took some long pulls from his flask again and moved to the back of the cave where he spread his plaid and laid down, falling instantly asleep. Felix O'Neil and Neil MacEachen agreed to take turns watching guard with MacEachen taking the first shift. Sitting side by side at the mouth of the cave he and Flora watched the sun come up, revealing the Isle of Skye in the distance and appearing as a small rise in the ocean. Had the circumstances been different they both would have felt tranquil in this setting. As it was they were comfortable in the warmth of just sitting next to each other.

The cousins slipped into their native tongue in quiet, hushed tones. "You surprised me, Neil. Last I heard you were at Douai studying to be a priest at

Scot's College. Sounds like you traded the bible for a sword?"

Smiling Neil put his arm around Flory's shoulder. "I couldn't take those vows of celibacy sweet cousin. It was thoughts of women like yourself that made wearing the robes inconceivable in the end."

Flora looked into her cousin's smiling eyes and replied that he knew full well she had given her heart, long ago to her best friend's brother, Allan MacDonald. But where was Allan?

"Flory, I joined the Jacobite's cause some time ago, when I first met Charles Edward in France. I've been with him ever since." Neil paused for a minute and when he did the two could hear tossing and moaning from inside the small cave.

The Prince's sleep was troubled and the two could hear him plainly in the back of the cave, suddenly cry out. Flora flinched realizing it was Charles Edward in the throws of a harrowing nightmare and hoping they weren't detected by his moans.

"What in the world ails him, Neil?"

"He's been disturbed like that since Culloden. He weeps of wounds that chan urrainn be seen. The screams of our countrymen, wounded in battle continue in his mind and he is unable to silence them even when he attempts sleep. I doubt he ever saw a chicken butchered before." Neil shook his head as he continued. "Now he has seen and heard thousands dying and smelled their blood as it oozed into the soil across Drumossie Moor." Anger darkened Neal's face like an unexpected storm. "That damned butcher Cumberland ordered his men to finish off every man which lay wounded. Those poor souls were clubbed and stabbed to death laying in the dirt screaming. My heart clutched my soul in horror as I dragged Prince Charles off the battlefield. Those hapless lads were murdered in cold blood. It was a carnage of epic proportions Flora, and the Prince knows the bloody outcome was mostly his fault. Some of his faithful were yelling curses at him as we fled."

The cousins sat again in silence lost in their thoughts for a long time looking out at the ocean until

Flora asked about Allan. "And Allan? Where is my Allan?"

"Flory, bad news travels fast on a wicked wind. I'm sure he is alive and probably hiding in a cave similar to this one. Go lie down lassie and take your rest. We have got much to accomplish. You are safe with me."

"Am I Neil? Am I? We are far from the dances, laughter, and the music at Armadale in more ways than one. Here we are hiding like mice in our own land with a big mean puss and her kittens lurking behind every heather bush. The King's troops are crawling across our land like flies in the coo's eyes. Will we make it?"

He was quiet for a minute. How could he reassure her? Neil felt he lacked the second sight so many in his family possessed. He had a rare premonition that Culloden would be a disaster, but today, nothing. He just smiled at Flora, patted her shoulder, and repeated his wish for her to rest.

CHAPTER 3

On Her Own

Saturday, June 21 - Summer Solstice

For a few hours, Flora was able to slide into a restful sleep and felt refreshed when she woke surprised to find Neil's warm body curled up beside her. Felix was sitting guard at the entrance and the Prince was starting to move about. She rose waking her cousin in the process. As they divided the provisions they had brought along among themselves she told everyone that she thought it best if she moved north to Benbecula by herself. She could head for Nunton and Lady Clan's on familiar trails then gather supportive Jacobites to help Prince Charlie escape. Night again would supply some safe cover. Everyone agreed with the plan and Neil decided to join her for a short distance on the trail.

The two set out sure-footed and down the steep incline with Neil carrying Flora's small bag. An hour or so out he stopped at a wide spot in the path and motioned her to rest on a big sitting rock before they parted. "Flory, you must be ever so careful. We haven't told you all about King George's men and what they are capable of." Neil's eyes misted over and he ducked his head for a moment wiping them with the sleeve of his shirt. He spoke in a low mournful voice. "All the way from Culloden to Inverness Scots have been slaughtered—men, women, and children. Innocent bairns." He paused recalling the horror. "Anyone in Highland clothing was butchered and the troops showed no mercy. Men with weapons of any kind were hung and Flory…" MacEachen took her hand gently looking into her pale face. "The women raped—all ages —young and old alike." He halted momentarily, again finding it a difficult tale to relate. "Their homes, their barns, hundreds—burned on the spot. They've been left without shelter, without food, and some without husbands, wives, sons, or daughters. Whole families Flora—whole families! Our people are wretched, hearts and spirits broken. They are desperate and hungry with all their livestock stolen by the soldiers. Herded off to be sold."

Flora's heart sank to her feet. She felt devastated. She knew she was sent to Angus' for protection but this news was far worse than she could have imagined. She had not been exposed to the whole story. Struck with the tragic news she sat for a moment breathing deeply to calm herself.

"It appears the British are deaf to every voice of humanity."

Standing up and putting her arm on Neil's she continued. "We have no alternative at this point cousin. We are safer right now without each other—alone. I will be ever so careful not to show myself until I am out of harm and on Benbecula. I know the way where so many do not, however, I need to get going because of the lunar tides." Neil too was on his feet and reached for Flora giving her a long hug. Handing her the lightweight bag all he could whisper was, "Godspeed cousin. Godspeed."

Flora turned, pulled herself up to her full diminutive stature, and struck out heading down the trail without looking back. She was afraid this man, who had known her since she was a toddler, would read her face like the books in which he had taught her.

It was late the following afternoon when Flora found herself at the ford connecting the two islands, South Uist to Benbecula. Between the two points, there was the wee island of Creagorry. Flora watched the foamy ocean water carefully as it lapped in and slid quietly across the sand. Luck was on her side, the tide was still moving out. She had gone this treacherous way many a time before and knew where the path started by the standing stone. She had been born here and as a young lassie had been guided and taught to be aware of the tides, taught which direction was secure and where to avoid the treacherous quicksand of the ford. Flora wasted no time taking off her foot coverings and proceeded slowly into the ankle-deep water, conscious of each step.

The crossing was successful and as she sat on the long sandy beach pulling her stockings back on, she heard the muffled sound of horses and men in the distance. Flora looked up from where she was seated to gaze at the one thing she was trying to avoid, and that was a militia galloping down the beach heading straight for her. Clearly, despite all her precautions, her trip to Nunton had not gone unnoticed. As soon as the riders reached where she was sitting they ordered her, in harsh English tones to see her passport, which of course she had none.

With the confidence of a queen and in an indignant tone, Flora pulled herself up regally and demanded to know the name of their Captain and who was it they answered to? They told her their commanding officer was Captain Hugh MacDonald. With that knowledge Flora with a firm stance requested they take her directly to him, then staunchly refused to say anything else while inside her heart was greatly cheered.

The commanding officer allowed her to finish putting on her shoes, then ordered the men to flank her with their horses, forcing her to march on foot back to their unwelcoming militia guard house. The weary militia arrived near dusk and the soldiers, irritable and wanting to end their day, hastily locked her in their guard room for the night. The hair on the back of Flora's neck stood straight up as she heard the metal bolt slide ominously across the thick wooden door locking her in. However, her nerves quickly rallied and she inwardly smiled at the secret of which the Englishmen were unaware. Their commander was her beloved stepfather Hugh. Yet, she wondered if she was really secure here this night. In her mind, she reluctantly recalled cousin Neil's dire warnings and the horrible events he shared that had occurred from Culloden to Inverness. With a pit in her stomach both from nerves and hunger Flora curled up on the dirt floor once again pulling her arisard tight about her. For now she was trapped like an animal. The morrow would tell another tale.

CHAPTER 4

Breakfast with Hugh Sunday, June 22

As daylight was breaking Sunday morning, two of the English militia men banged loudly on the guard room's heavy door waking Flora before unbolting it. They roughly grabbed her from the floor and marched her dirty, exhausted, and hungry to their commanding officer Hugh MacDonald, her plaid thrown carelessly across her shoulders.

Unbeknownst to them, Hugh MacDonald, or 'One-eyed Hugh' as he was called, held a special affection for Flora. Once commissioned in the French army he returned home to the Hebrides Islands where he fell in love with Flora's mother Marion, an attractive widow managing her farms on South Uist. Flora was slightly over two years old when Hugh married Marion, taking Marion, Flora, and her brothers to his holdings in Armadale on the Isle of Skye. He was the only father Flora had ever known or at least remembered.

Hugh may have been the commanding officer of the local militia, but deep down he too was a Jacobite supporter, one who felt Scotland should be ruled by the Stewarts and not the German line of King George II. The arrest of Flora put him temporarily in an awkward position but one which he handled craftily.

Looking at Flora's disheveled state and commenting that she looked like a drenched rose after a storm, he dismissed the men holding her arms, explaining to them she was simply distressed over the events in the Isles with all the armies moving about. Offering a further explanation, he stated that basically, Flora was simply a foolish lassie trying to get home to her mother. He intentionally left out the fact that Flora's mother was also his beloved wife.

After Hugh discharged the troops, he ordered his loyal servants to help Flora clean up and serve her a hearty breakfast. Within an hour Flory, as he too affectionately called her, was seated across from him, freshly dressed and her hair brushed. Ravenous she was trying desperately to take lady-like bites, where in reality she wanted to pick up the oatmeal bowl and empty it like a starving wench.

The two quickly resorted quietly to Gaelic while Flora explained her situation, her commitment to Prince Charlie, and the plan to disguise him and sail to Skye. Hugh thought it brilliant and began to pen her mother a letter when a second group of militia arrived with yet another prisoner.

Hugh, quick wittingly stood up when he saw who it was, his large muscular body dwarfing the room, and thundered as the guards brought in Neil MacEachen. Without pause, he strode over to Neil in giant steps and shouted, "You Glaikit! You were supposed to stay with Flora!" Then, much to Flora and Neil's shock, he smacked hard him across the face with his open hand almost knocking Neil off his feet.

The soldiers stood stoically observing their Captain's reaction. Hugh looked at them and loudly explained that Neil was Flora's servant and somehow had lost himself and that he intended to send them both to Skye as soon as he located Flora's dim-witted maid from Ireland. Hugh excused the men with a wave of his hand then sat down again at the head of the table.

In the meantime Flora kept her head down and held her hands in her lap, fearing her face might betray her feelings or that she would be recognized as the woman troops they had brought in earlier. She also was trying desperately not to laugh at Hugh's performance even though she was puzzled that Neil was here and not with the Prince, yet at the same time relieved how Hugh so expertly and deceivingly handled both situations.

No sooner had Hugh dismissed the militia back into the field and the men were far from the house and earshot, he ordered another breakfast for Neil. The ruse had been successful for the time being. All three put their heads together whispering in a buzz of questions, answers, and smiles.

Neil rubbed his reddening face looking at Hugh. "You pack a good wallop man."

The men embraced and laughed. Neil had been a second son to the MacDonalds, coming and going in their home and frequently staying while tutoring the growing family. Hugh grinned. "It's a good thing I was only pretending laddie. But why are you here? Tis my understanding you were guarding the Bonnie Prince."

"The Prince became anxious, impatient and demanded I come to Benbecula to find out how things were going. He was nervous to know if the arrangements had been made. I assured him everything would be all right and that we barely had given Flora any time, but he insisted. So, after making sure he was safe in his hiding place I set out. When I got to the ford at Carnana it was more closely guarded than I imagined. I was quickly discovered and arrested for not having any papers. And here I am." He opened his hands on the table and smiled then reached for a slice of pie.

Everyone thought it quite the tale. Hugh explained to Neil how he and Flora had streamlined the plan to smuggle the prince out and that he was writing a letter for Flora to show to anyone asking that she was permitted to travel to her mother's house in Skye with her servant Neil MacEachen and maid Betty Burke. He set the letter on the table for all to read.

Dear Wife,

I have sent your daughter from this country, lest she should be anyway frightend with the troops lying here. She has got one Betty Burke, an Irish girl, who she tells me is a good spinner. If her spinning pleases you, you may keep her 'till she spins all your lint' or it you have any wool to spin, you may employ her.

I have sent Niel M'Eachan along with your daughter and Betty Burke, to take care of them.

I am your dutiful husband,

Hugh M'Donald

June 22, 1746

All were fully cognizant of the danger they were in and equally aware the Prince and Felix should not be left alone for long. Neither those two knew the surrounding country and worse yet, the language. They would be identified quickly. It was a hazardous enterprise for multiple players with Felix and Charles left to their own naive devices.

It was decided that Flora was to move on quickly to her destination of Lady Clanranald's at Nunton. "Neil you must return to the Prince. It is imperative. It is going to take the ladies and me a few days to make his disguise. I will meet you at Rossinish. Do you remember how to get there?"

Neil sighed and shook his head affirmative. "We were there at the end of last April, the 27th I believe. At times it feels like we are going in circles and metamorphosing into nocturnal beasties. Rossinish is flat, open, and grassy. It is going to be a hard place to hide along those white sand beaches, but I will get him there again Flory—I promise. And you my dear cousin, continue to be wise as a serpent and harmless as a bonnie dove."

With the ink dried on the letter to Marion, Hugh set Flora's confiscated dirk on top with a thump. "If anyone asks for your papers again show them this letter Flory, along with your passport—and lassie, slip that dirk back in your stocking. You may need both." Then, placing his hand on her shoulder he lowered his head in a blessing prayer. "May the everlasting Father

shield you east and west wherever you go."

CHAPTER 5

Lady Clanranald

Scotland and her people were divided at this time as to whether support Prince Charles Edward Stuart's claim to the British throne or not. The clans were divided inside themselves and Lady Clan and her beloved husband, Chief Alexander MacDonald, were no exception. They each took an opposite position on the matter. Alexander was loyal to England's King George II, whereas Lady Clan was a quiet, yet a staunch Jacobite supporter of Charles Stuart. It was a subject they agreed not to approach often.

Few in Scotland held personal ill-will against the Bonnie Prince. It was just that all were justifiably in fear of King George's third and youngest son, Prince William, the Duke of Cumberland. The Scots frequently referred to him as 'the butcher' and with good cause. Everyone would be more comfortable when both major players, Cumberland and Stuart, were out of Scotland and off her islands.

Walking to Lady Clan's, Flora's mood lifted and she experienced a rush of nostalgia sighting the MacDonald's stately Nunton home with its countless chimneys reaching up to the sky in greeting. Behind the house rose the solitary hill of Rueval, a navigational beacon on the flat landscape. Flora considered this place a second home having spent weeks and occasionally months here as a young girl. She was especially close to Lady Clan who had taught her so many things, grooming her for an eventual high position within their clan. Flora not only spoke four languages she also was literate in them.

Conveniently Sir Alexander was not home the afternoon Flora arrived on foot. Lady Clan had just returned from a late Mass and embraced her kin warmly putting down an extra plate for tea. As she rested and was fed, Flora began relating her tale. Margaret praised her repeatedly for being so clever along with applauding the actions of the delightfully deceitful One-eyed Hugh. After some fresh baked shortbread, the two women laid out plans on how to dress the Prince as the fictional Betty Burke. They would enlist the help of a local elderly woman whose stitching and eyesight still proved straight and strong. Sizing was also critical. The prince must appear as a woman and the dress genuine, not something quickly thrown together.

"He is a skinny malinky longlegs!" giggled Flora, explaining the Prince's body physique. "My head barely came to his chin." Together the ladies measured out the fabric, Flora's height, and added the length to the skirt they felt necessary. They used a light-colored, quilted material with tiny purple flowers on it for the petticoat, a large white apron would be made, and a dun-colored mantle on which they could attach to the hood. The hood was cut extra large to draw over 'Betty's' face. In addition, Lady Clan sewed a cap with a broad flapping border to further obscure Prince Charlie's features. With the help of the elderly woman, the seamstresses took the better part of the week constructing the disguise. They could stitch into the late evenings as the summer sun hung long in the Hebrides Islands of Scotland this time of the year.

The women gossiped throughout the days about the Prince, the community, and the eclectic collection of everyone's affairs and emotions. When Flora inquired about Allan everyone shook their heads. It was Lady Clan who tried to comfort her growing anxiety by saying, "Evil news flies faster still than good."

It was late the second evening that a local lad arrived telling them that Neil and party had made it to Rossinish, cold and wet. Lady Clanranald ordered parcels of food to be sent back with the boy along with a bottle of brandy. There was food enough for the Prince, his party, and the lad's family too. This became the new routine for the next few days. Sewing throughout the long days accompanied by chatter and gossip.

"I read that the Prince had a thirty-thousand-pound bounty on his head." the lady of the house loudly proclaimed.

"And where pray tell, did the thirty-thousand come from? That is a lot of money." Flora asked.

Lady Clan chuckled. "It is French money! Prince Charles arrived here with several ships from France.

According to the paper, they were the '*Le Mars*' and '*La Bellone*'. Both were laden with a huge quantity of gold, weapons, and men to assist him in the cause. These two vessels never reached Charlie. They were intercepted and damaged in a skirmish with three English navy ships." Lady Clan continued stitching slightly more furiously. "The French ships limped back home I suppose. I am sure you heard about that. All his supporting troops went back to France leaving him here with only seven men." She shook her head and continued. "One of those seven, the Colonel from *Barrisdale* proceeded to get totally drunk and accidentally blew up a barrel of gunpowder. In the melee after the explosion, the gold went missing—£30,000. The identical sum offered for the Prince's capture!"

Lady Clanranald lowered her voice and sounded discouraged. "This has been an ill-fated endeavor from the get-go."

Flora felt uncomfortable, a cold feeling of dread throughout her body. Were they cursed? All of them? Could she actually get Charles Edward Stuart to Skye?

She put the last stitch in Charlie's hood and broke the thread with her teeth.

Tuesday night, in the dark and during a wild gale, Neil also arrived at Nunton. He had a more hair-raising tale to relate. After the encounter with Hugh's militia where he and Flora were released, he had to return to the Isle of South Uist again, crossing the water and heading straight back to Charles and the watchful Felix. He was cognizant that his challenge would be getting all three of them to Rossinish with the English military scouring under every bush in the area. Fortunately, Neil found four local fishermen who agreed to row them across in their small yawl for a price. Neil fictionalized a story for the men that they were from the Campbell clan and with a look, admonished Felix and Charlie not to utter a word. However, as there was a cloud cover that night, and even though they thought they had landed on the Isle of Benbecula, they were actually on a wee skerry. The men, miserable and wet from a downpour were additionally cold and hungry. Adding to the dilemma the Prince was drunk once again, and infuriated by their error. After the yawl departed he began yelling and accusing Neil of marooning him intentionally. Words got ugly with Neil stripping off his shirt telling him he'd swim across the water and bring him another boat if they weren't discovered by all his loud French profanities! It was then Felix and Neil noticed the tide ebbing and could see that within an hour they'd be able to walk the short distance. It was a sullen Neil who redressed and put his boots back on questioning his loyalties and wondering if it was all in vain. Who was this pretender to the throne? Was Charles Edward Stuart even capable of leading, of being a monarch? He shook his head sending water droplets everywhere. Maybe he could shake out his misgivings.

Gratefully the weather broke and dawn came quickly when the party crossed to the other side of the inlet and onto Benbecula. It would be too easy to discover the three men moving in the encroaching daylight and across the treeless landscape. They desperately needed a place to hide and there was no time to lose. Fortune was on their side when they spotted a rock sheiling a short distance away and when inquiring at the door who the occupants were, discovered it was occupied by two MacDonald clan members. Food and brandy were shared, then Neil and Felix took turns standing guard while Charlie slept.

Neil was unfamiliar with this particular route going further up the Isle to Rossinish. The clansmen informed them that two days earlier militia had also arrived on the island and were presently camped less than a quarter of a mile away. Too close for comfort. Neil could feel the warm breath of the royal lion on their necks and knew they had to move out as soon as it was dark again, thankful they had walked into friendly clan folks in the sheiling rather than the King's military encampment.

Their wish for darkness came in the form of a cloud cover and additional rain. One of the men offered to show them the way across the trackless moor to Rossinish and around the military force. The sodden ground below their feet quickly became a slippery mire and in the dark Charlie continually slipped and fell, his shoes being sucked down in the mud. Neil, again and again, helped him up, groped in the slimy slush with his hands until he found the man's shoes, and continued to follow their guide pulling, dragging, and carrying Charles most the distance. The almost five-mile journey took the better part of the night. At last, they stumbled into a hut near Rossinish looking a sorry muddy mess and startling the sleeping couple inside. Neil quickly told them in Gaelic that they were harmless and on their way to Sir Alexander MacDonald's home when they were caught unprepared in the storm. Fortunately, the old couple were silent and did not openly question why they would be traveling in such conditions and at night!

Their guide made excuses to leave quickly and Neil MacEachen gifted him a half guinea for his troubles before the man disappeared into the remaining dark. Felix stoked the occupant's fire with a poker before tossing in a bit of peat as Charlie threw off his rain-soaked plaid mumbling something in French that Neil hoped the residents did not hear. The man seemed oblivious way too often as to the danger he was in nor the precautions he should take to hide his identity.

CHAPTER 6

Tuesday, June 24, 1746

The startled occupants of the hut were befuddled as Neil told them how they had landed in Rossinish late. At daybreak in the sheiling, after their stormy ordeal, the tenant's wife warned Neil it was unsafe to remain. She explained the military had been in the habit the last few days of coming early in the morn to buy milk. Not knowing fully who the other two men were, her eyes widened as Neil apprised her of their precarious situation rapidly in Gaelic. Prince Charlie begged Neil MacEachen to quickly go to Nunton by himself and tell the household there that he had arrived, but Neil was uncomfortable leaving him and Felix alone again like defenseless goslings out in the open of the island. Felix spoke and understood only a spattering of English and less Gaelic. In addition, neither man was acquainted with the area nor the customs. It was a recipe for disaster and if they encountered anyone at all, their mere language barrier would finger them as suspicious in an area where everyone was rapidly becoming distrusting of everyone else, not kin and possibly even then.

Thanking the herdsman's wife the men departed swiftly locating a rocky spot near the shore where they could keep an eye on the cottage in the distance. The incessant rain began again and they had no alternative but to lie miserable in the long heather for three soggy hours just waiting. To compound their wretchedness the moisture only encouraged the midges and all of them were viciously bitten on every piece of exposed flesh. Within a short time, small, itching, and irritating bumps appeared all over their skin in the areas where they had been attacked. Relief came at last when the signal went up that the troops had left and they could return to the sheiling. Once tucked inside the warm shelter the group quickly stripped off their soggy garbs and put about warming themselves by the fire while waiting for their clothes to dry. In the meantime, they used scraps of canvas from sails to wrap themselves in like cocoons and slept with little to eat and only milk to drink.

It was Tuesday night when Charles once again became anxious and antsy. Pacing about the room he insisted, actually commanded Neil walk to Nunton house and find out how Flora was coming along. Neil was apprehensive about leaving Charles. He felt responsible for his safety yet fully realized the prince did not have a realistic grip on their situation. He did as bided however before departing admonished both Charles and Felix not to leave the confines of the shelter. Neil left them both in comfort, knowing it would take him more than two hours to reach Nunton on foot. He was muttering about the Prince, who he thought was more than a wee bit crabbit, demanding and drinking way too much of Lady Clanranald's wine. The man was entitled to the throne by birthright, however, Neil was becoming increasingly conflicted whether Charles Edward Stuart was competent to rule as king, an attribute that was rarely a consideration when it came to leaders of countries.

Neil MacEachen's thoughts and philosophies swirled about his head keeping him company as he walked. As Nunton came into view he concluded to himself that he would remain loyal to Bonnie Prince Charlie and the cause, keeping his gob shut as to his apprehensions and misgivings. Perhaps when this was over and they were safely ensconced back in France, he could help Charles mitigate his impulsiveness by taking a role as a trusted advisor.

MacEachen was greeted warmly at Nunton, but quickly informed them he could not stay long. Assured everything was in place and ready for their charade he fortified himself with some stout port and traveled back in the night to the hut that was sheltering Charles Stuart, the Pretender to the throne.

CHAPTER 7

Friday, June 27, 1746

It was Friday morning, June 27, 1746, when the three men, Charles Edward Stuart, Neil MacEachen, and Felix O'Neal left the protection of the sheiling at Rossinish and made their way across the flat moor and to the top of Rueval hill where they laid down in the grass to watch the comings and goings at the MacDonald home at Nunton. Flora had sent a message earlier with the herd boy that a boat was ready to take them to Skye. The rowers, who could be trusted, were Flora's cousins, brothers John and Roderick along with Rory MacDonald of South Uist.

Everyone at Nunton was excited including Lady Clan's seven-year-old daughter Peggy. At last, they had an opportunity to meet the man they sincerely felt held the birthright to be their King. But their current situation was complicated and they found themselves weaving a web of entangled deceit. It was decided that Rossinish would be a safer rendezvous spot and better to avoid any suspicion that Sir Alexander MacDonald might possibly be involved, a risk no one was willing to take.

The fixings for a large meal were gathered, along with the custom-made garments made to disguise the Prince. It was high noon when Lady Clanranald left Nunton house with her daughter and Flora, heading as if they were taking a leisurely stroll to the shelter at Rossinish. Even Flora's brother Angus joined them, having arrived by boat with his wife Penelope.

An impressive table was set and the Prince, who had been rather melancholy before everyone's arrival, assumed the role of honored host and king displaying a gracious manner and decorum. He insisted that Flora sit on his right and Lady Clan on his left. With spirits lightened and fortified with roasted beef, lamb, and copious amounts of wine, the merry group created quite a festive picture.

As the party continued, with everyone courteously speaking French, the young lad who had been carrying messages for them came breathlessly through the door. Cap in hand he explained that a bomb ship, christened *The Furnace* and captained by the notorious John Ferguson, had delivered Commander Campbell close to the MacDonald's home in Nunton. They were unloading a number of red coats just three miles away to search the island.

The party, still in a gay and now in a rather reckless alcohol-induced mood, grabbed various food items, including several additional bottles of wine, and dashed out of the building with Flora following after them. Fortunately in their haste, she remembered to grab the frock made for Betty Burke and stuff it in a bag as she rapidly followed the escaping group of MacDonalds.

Quickly loading into awaiting boats, Angus took the oars of one, and the cousins of another, slipping to the other side of a close-by loch where they set about finishing their party as if the military searches were a mere inconvenience. Blankets were spread on the ground, the food and wine re-laid out and the festivities continued. After consuming more wine the Prince giddily stated he wanted to try on his custom-made dress. So there, on the bank of the loch, and much to the entertainment of the party-goers Bonnie Prince Charlie quickly became Betty Burke an Irish flax spinner.

Somewhere in the early morning of the following day, a small birlinn rounded the point where the group was still laughing heartily over Betty having trouble with 'her' headdress as she pranced about pretending to be a lassie. The merry revelers sobered up instantly when they saw the somber look on the rower's face. The message was dire from the red-coated Captain Campbell. Lady Clanranald and her daughter were to return immediately to their home or he would demolish it to the foundation! He had the power to do so from the mighty cannons mounted on *The Furnace*.

Hearts dropped knowing Commander Campbell meant what he said. The entire party sobered knowing their clandestine schemes were close to being discovered. It was estimated about 1,500 red coats were being ferried to Benbecula at that very moment.

Lady Clanranald and Peggy hurriedly gathered their things, boarded the servant's birlinn, and were rowed back to Nunton taking Flora's sister-in-law Penelope with them and leaving the others on the beach. Lady Clan was worried how would she explain all this to Sir Alexander, or worse yet, what story could be fabricated for General Campbell? She could tell him she was taking care of a local child who was taken ill. Penelope fully intended to collaborate any story Lady Clan might invent and Peggy would too.

Flora exhaustingly looked around feeling a wee bit abandoned by the other women thru necessity. Remnants of the night's foolishness were strewn about the beach including the Prince's suit of clothing. There she stood, marooned in the early morning light with six men, staring at one who was dressed as a woman and still quite drunk.

What had she gotten herself into and where would this lead? Instinctively she sucked in her breath, bit her lower lip, and started tidying up their litter.

CHAPTER 8

Saturday, June 28, 1746

Saturday morning greeted the seven now very sober individuals, with an azure blue sky and a dash of fluffy white clouds. It was a promise of hope. Flora watched as a short-eared owl swooped down and picked up a rodent close to their belongings. She thought it a good omen announcing, "Aye—good luck for all of us, but we must stay here until nightfall then make our moves in the dark."

All were keenly aware that in the middle of summer in the Hebrides, nightfall would be some time and then very short. Trying to sound casual she looked at the Prince and teased. "Betty dear, you need to shave."

None of the men were clean-shaven at this conjecture of their travels. However, the prince had brought a small straight razor which he produced from his pack. He even had a wedge of French soap and immediately took to the task down at the water's edge.

"Careful not to cut yourself," Flora chided. "We might have difficulty explaining that if we are stopped."

Shortly after he shaved an argument broke out. The Prince took his pistol from the top of his clothes pile and began shoving it under the muslin apron over the skirt he was now wearing.

"You cannot carry that!" Flora stated her hands moving to her hips.

"I can and I will!" snapped Charles' equal retort.

"No! You cannot! What if you are searched?" Flora's stance was firm and unflinching.

The Prince got a slow relaxed smile across his face. "My lady Flora—if they lift my skirt to search me they are going to find more than a pistol."

Flora joined him in a smile and relaxed for a moment having two older brothers and several younger half-brothers. But she was not backing down. Looking Prince Charles firmly in the eyes she held out her hand with the other arm remaining on her hip. "Give the gun to me. Neil can carry your cudgel for you —that is all."

It was a shock to Charles to have anyone tell *him* what to do. He was an individual whose entire life was one of privilege and rank, even when it was illogical. No one had ever told him no, and the few that advised him not to do something he ignored. Even after the massacre of Culloden, where his impulsivity and commands proved disastrously wrong, men still obeyed him. Now here stood a petite young woman telling him that he was forbidden to carry his own weapon. It was incredulous!

Flora had fixed her doe-like eyes on him. She was not a threat, she was not angry, however, it was clear she was adamant about her position regarding the weapon.

After a few uncomfortable seconds Charles reluctantly placed his pistol in her outstretched hand raising his eyebrows as he did.

That is when the second argument broke out. Felix O'Neal's passion got the best of him. He had fallen in love with Flora the first night he met her months ago at Nunton. He also was more than a faithful dog to Prince Charles and reluctant to lose sight of either one of these people. Felix insisted he go with them to Skye.

Taking a deep breath at this statement Flora whirled around and simply said, "No, you must not go. The passport is explicit. It says three people, my servant Neil MacEachen and my maid Betty Burke." She paused, "It does not mention you!"

"Flora you are surrounded with men. Tis not proper you being alone with all of us. What would people think?" Then, poor Felix, in his distress proposed marriage to Flora right then and there. Her brother Angus' eyes widened, his arms folded across his chest, curious to see how his sister head-strong sister would handle this.

Flora was gentle with the man's heart, however firm in her determination to get Prince Charles to Skye. "Felix, your loyalty to the Prince is commendable. You have been with him for a very long time and a bless you for that. However, we cannot take you with us and that is final." She purposefully avoided the question of matrimony.

It was then Prince Charlie became assertive again and Angus stood by, arms still crossed and knowing his sister well, and watched for her next reaction. "If Felix doesn't go, then I'm not getting in the boat!" Charles said.

Flora was standing firm and continued enunciating slowly in French so all could understand what was being said. "We cannot have him on board. He knows not Gaelic! We are posing that we are local people which means we all speak Gaelic with the exception of Miss Betty here. If you fail to get in that boat with us tonight you will surely be caught and heads will roll—all of our heads!" At no time did Flora take her eyes off of Charles'.

Felix immediately gasped knowing that it was he who could be the cause of the Prince's demise. "No—no—I will go with Angus back to South Unst. I will take the weapons and meet you on Skye. We have a rescue ship coming from France and it is imperative we do not miss this one. There will be another day."

Finally, it was agreed, though not verbally, that diminutive Flora was in charge. The men set about making a small fire as Angus began preparing his boat and packing his passenger's items for the trip back to Unst.

In the meantime, sensing the importance of their journey, Flora's two cousins recruited another three men to help procure a larger shallop, one eighteen feet long with a mast and oars. Four would row with one at the helm.

When it was as dark as it was going to be in the northern hemisphere, the three passengers departed Benbecula, across the sea for the last time. The water was calm and all anticipated an easy sail across the Sea of the Hebrides in a narrow section referred to as the Little Minch.

Around midnight a heavy fog draped the boat conveniently obscuring their presence, but also their view of the Isle of Skye. In short order the rowers were disoriented. To compound the situation the wind came up suddenly, gusting against the sails of the shallop with such force that the masts groaned in protest. The open boat started to pitch nose up, then plunge as the turbulent swells of water rose higher and higher

seemingly angry and intent on destroying them all.
Hastily the sails were dropped and the crew began
rowing as hard as they could, spitting out the salty
water as it pelted their faces and drenched their bodies.

The Prince, dressed as Betty Burke, skirts around
his knees, began to tell them all stories to keep the
lurking fright down on the keel. It is hard to know if
the rowers even understood him. Perhaps he was
consoling himself with the endless chatter or his voice
droning on and on as they rowed.

Making conversation Charles inquired about
Flora's age, and both she and Neil MacEachen smiled.
"I have not that knowledge for sure," she told the
Prince. "My mum was frightened by an old wizard
named Auld Nicky that lived near us. She said no one
should peer into the future and Auld Nicky read the
stars and the tea leaves. She told me to see happiness in
every sphere of life and no worry about the future."
Flora further explained, "Her da, my gran-da was a
Presbyterian Minister so I know I was christened, but
she hid the certificate."

Neil chipped into the conversation. "It was calving season Flora, I remember because my mum took me with her to your house. I was about four, so that would make you about twenty-two now bonnie cousin."

The Prince muttered that he had turned twenty-six on New Year's Eve and was hoping to see twenty-seven.

To change the subject and bring himself out of a descending melancholy the Prince began to sing. It mattered little which language, he just sang to keep his and the other passengers' spirits up. Neil moved about the boat relieving different rowers giving them short breaks for sore hands and backs. Anything to help them keep going in the night.

After a few tunes from the Prince, Flora decided he might enjoy one of the songs which had stirred her and her compatriots to back him and his endeavor to gain the throne. She told him the young people had sung it together at many of their gatherings and then as she started to sing it to the Prince with the rowers joining in as a diversion keeping their minds off the

task at hand.

GEORDIE SITS IN CHARLIE'S CHAIR

Geordie sits in Charlie's chair, Bonny laddie, Highland
laddie;
Deil cock him gin he sit there,
My bonny laddie, Highland laddie!
Charlie yet shall mount the throne,
Bonny laddie, Highland laddie;
Well ye ken it is his own,
My bonny laddie, Highland laddie
Weary fa" the Lawland loon,
Bonny laddie, Highland laddie,
Wha took frae him the British crown.
My bonny laddie, Highland laddie.
But weel's me on the kilted clans,
Bonny laddie, Highland laddie,
That fought for him at Prestonpans,

My bonny laddie, Highland laddie.
Ken ye the news I hae to tell,
Bonny laddie, Highland laddie?

Cumberland's awa to hell,

My bonny laddie, Highland laddie.

When he came to the Stygian shore,

Bonny laddie,- Highland lucldie,

Tile deil himself wi' fright did roar,

My bonny laddie, Highland laddie.

When Charon grim came out to him,

Bonny laddie, Highland laddie;

"Ye're welcome here ye devil's limb !"

My bonny laddie, Highland laddie.

They ate him up baith stoop and room

Bonny laddie, Highland laddie'

And that's the gate they serve the duke,

My bonny laddie, Highland laddie.

As they all finished the last line, the gusts of wind became more intense throwing waves of cold salt water onto the pitiful men clinging to their oars. Flora scooted under the sails piled on the bottom of the boat while Neil MacEachen led some of the crew in the rosary…

Ave María, grátia plena, Dóminus tecum. Benedícta tu in muliéribus, et benedíctus fructus ventris tui, Iesus.

Sancta María, Mater Dei, ora pro nobis peccatóribus, nunc,
et in hora mortis nostrć. Amen.

Glory Be.

Flora ensconced and semi-dry under the oiled sailcloth and just as frightened as the rest, recited quietly the reassuring 23rd Psalm.

"The LORD is my shepherd; I shall not want." She felt her teeth chattering, and she could not remember some of the verses. She just repeated part of it. *"Yea, though I walk through the valley of the shadow of death, I will fear no evil: for thou art with me; thy rod and thy staff they comfort me."*

Eventually, the young woman fell asleep thinking this was her demise as she whispered the last line—*"I will dwell in the house of the LORD forever."*

CHAPTER 9

Sunday, June 29, 1746 - The Isle of Skye

The men leaned into their oars, the cold wet wind lashing relentlessly in their faces. Fatigue was creeping into every muscle and their hands were raw even with Neil's help. The crew was experienced making this particular crossing, but never at night. Without a compass on board, they could only hope the tumultuous wind was coming from the North and they needed to steer directly into her, but the question remained were they making any headway at all? In the overwhelming darkness, they were navigating now by dead reckoning and instinct. The hours melted together, time forever dragging as the shallop and her passengers were tossed about like dolls, the men trying to keep a rowing rhythm and spirits intact by their continual singing of traditional shanties.

Flora woke with a start and was disoriented for a split second until she realized she was looking at the Prince's hands spread above her face. He started to laugh as she sputtered awake realizing he was sheltering her from the rain with his body. Just then the turbulence ceased and to everyone's relief the sky lightened, dawn was approaching and they could see the welcoming cliffs of Skye at Waternish Point. They had survived.

The cousins knew of a wee cleft in the rocks where they beached the boat, made a small fire to dry themselves along with their soaked clothing, and most importantly a safe spot to rest. The Scots, although toughed by their day-to-day lifestyle, were worn to their very cores, their hands raw and their backs sore. The last remnants of yesterday's meal were shared equally, along with the wine. They were not quite at their planned destination, however, all felt confident they would all at least now live to see another day.

It was still early morn when again they pushed off slightly refreshed and began rowing back again into the sea. No sooner when they were in the open they were spotted by two red coats who had been standing close on the cliffs above them. The militia may have detected the smoke from their fire and set about to discover the source. Whatever the reason the English soldiers, seeing the small vessel full of people, shouted for them to stop, but the rowers picked up their pace with the prince yelling for them to 'pull lustfully' as they began moving out into the large bay the locals called Loch Snizort.

One soldier turned and ran for assistance while the other fired a shot at the refugees. Fortunately, the shallop had just moved out of range with the lead ball splashing harmlessly a few feet from the side of the vessel. By the time the soldier reloaded his flintlock, the crew had rowed well out of range and were heading across the loch, hiding from further detection by threading the boat through a series of small islands like prey hiding from their predators.

It was around 2:00 in the afternoon when the party completed the twelve-mile journey to the Trotternish Peninsula and landed near Monkstadt, the home of the MacDonald's Chief on Skye. Flora was anxious that they not all arrive at the house without giving Lady Margaret, the Chief's wife, some notice. She instructed the entire crew to wait with Betty Burke in the boat while she and Neil MacEachen went up to the house to announce their landing and check if their approach was safe.

In her native language of Gaelic Flora told her rowing cousins that if anyone inquired why there was a maid with them, to curse her and say she was 'lazy and not attending her mistress'. The prince was puzzled as to why everyone burst into laughter. Not wanting to openly offend, Flora assured him in French it was just an inside joke.

She and MacEachen headed off to the Monkstadt house. On the way, Flora quickly re-did her hair and straightened her skirts so she looked fresh in the afternoon sun. MacEachen went through the back entrance into the scullery and Flora, smiling knocked on the front door. When Lady Margaret saw who was standing at the threshold the color drained from her face like a soiled cloth hitting hot water.

"Flory my darling how nice to see you," she said out loud while rolling her eyes to gesture she had others in the house. "What a pleasant surprise!" she said loudly while moving her mouth down in a grimace. She took Flora by the arm and ushered her into her private chamber where she straightened her appearance further by wrapping a fresh apron about her waist. In hushed tones Flora told her who was in the boat at their harbor then Lady Margaret revealed to Flora the men who were in her parlor, one of which was none other than Lieutenant Alexander MacLeod of Bailemenach, the commanding officer of the local militia detachment looking for Prince Charles Stuart! The hunter and the hunted were less than a mile from each other with the two ladies in between.

"Flory, you have to distract the Lieutenant while I get Kingsburgh aside for advice. We have a slippery kettle of fish here." With a flimsy plan at best Flora took a deep breath, stood straight, and entered the parlor where the gentlemen were talking.

They all stood as she graciously entered.

CHAPTER 10

The Parlour at Monkstat

Sunday Afternoon, June 29, 1746

Flora blushed at the gentlemen's standing attention while Lady Margaret introduced her to Lt. MacLeod. He kissed her hand as Flora looked into the familiar eyes of Kingsburgh, a now a distinguished-looking man of 57 years. Kingsburgh was Sleat's Factor, the Property Manager of MacDonald holdings in Skye. He was also Allan's father. Her heart ached to ask him about Allan yet this definitely was not the time nor the company where such a question should or could be presented.

Lady Margaret ordered tea be prepared while explaining to the men that Flora was on her way to return to her mother's house in Armadale.

Flora went on to describe in English how anxious she had been with all the troubles. She reasoned that English might be more acceptable than Gaelic to one of King George's men. "My brother

Angus thought it was best I was with him at first, but things have gotten so dreadful it was decided it would be more fitting if I was home with my mother…" She added as if to explain further, "to help her with my younger brothers and sister. My mother is alone down south at Armadale while my step-father, Captain Hugh MacDonald is aiding the search for Charles Stuart."

Flora briefly worried about herself becoming such a skilled liar. She would have to ask for forgiveness later. Lying here was saving lives so she kept talking to MacLeod answering his almost interrogating questions and responding with coy questions herself; where he was from and did he have a family? She mentioned she had a servant and an Irish spinner for her mother along for the journey. The conversation was light, warm, and designed to beguile the Lieutenant with Flora being at her charming and entertaining best.

MacLeod was feeling he needed to get back to his troops and was about to disengage when Lady Margaret began setting a table for an afternoon meal, stalling to get Kingsburgh out of the room and form an emergency plan. Kingsburgh must be informed the prince was waiting patiently, dressed as a woman, down at the inlet.

Flora asked if anyone would like some music while the food was being prepared and really, quite before there was an answer she moved toward the spinet and ran her fingers lightly across the keys. Deliberately choosing a German composer, Flora sat down and began playing the popular harp concerto from Handel's *Alexander's Feast*. Lady Margaret's three little ones came into the parlor and sat comfortably on the floor delighting in the upbeat music filling their parlor with joy. With Flora's innocent face and her enchanting presence MacLeod, who by now was totally charmed, failed to notice Kingsburgh slip outside and rendezvous with Lady Margaret.

As soon as they were in the garden Neal MacEachen joined the conspirators from the scullery door. "What are we to do?" Lady Margaret almost cried, wringing her hands.

Several suggestions were considered and discarded by the three and then as if on cue in a timely

moment, Donald Roy MacDonald rode up on a
borrowed bay mare.

Dismounting and still holding the reins Lady
Margaret quickly explained the dilemma in her parlor
before anyone else could even greet the man properly.
She poured out her worries and concerns in rapid
Gaelic, her eyes misting as she did so.

Donald Roy and Kingsbourgh came up with a
consensus. Obvious to everyone was that the Prince
could not come any closer to Monkstadt. MacEachen
would return to the waiting Prince, keep him dressed
as a maid, and walk part of the roughly seventeen miles
towards Kingsbourgh's home meeting them down the
road a piece. MacEachen also decided to let the rowers
go and disperse as they wished. The men would be
paid for their loyalty and services.

As soon as he was able to politely slip away
from the party in the parlor, Kingsburgh would also
head to his home, hopefully with Flora in tow and then
meet Charles and MacEachen on the road heading
south.

With the plan in place, they re-entered the home just as Flora was finishing the strategically chosen work of Handel's and saw Lt. MacLeod leaning near her, obviously enchanted and hanging appreciatively on every note.

Lady Margaret announced the food was on the table and the guests moved to the dining room. Wine was poured as Donald Roy was introduced as a neighbor, relative, and supporter of King George II. Little did MacLeod suspect that Donald Roy was a survivor of Culloden and had just returned from the local physician who was examining his wound. A musket ball had gone into the sole of his left foot and luckily out the top. MacLeod did not know the smaller man had nerves of steel and actually walked five miles from the battlefield, shoeless and bleeding without stopping to get help.

The deception of loyalty to King George II continued through the meal until Kingsburgh made his excuses. He stated the need to get a pony for Flora and collect both her dull-witted Irish spinner and servant Neil. They had several miles to go and he calculated, depending on their speed, it would take well over two hours, the goal being he would be home in his own bed by nightfall.

As custom in the area Flora would ride, MacEachen would lead and the servant Betty Burke would walk alongside for those two hours.

This arrangement did not go well with Betty.

<u>CHAPTER 11</u>

On the Road to Kingsburgh

Sunday evening, June 29, 1746

The Sunday afternoon party broke up and Kingsburgh as planned headed south with a bottle of wine in hand and some Forfar Bridies wrapped in a cloth. Lieutenant MacLeod headed in the other direction, towards his troops' billet. Lady Margaret had expressed earlier her desire to meet the prince and now openly requested to travel a short distance through the settlement with Flora. Two ponies were led around the house, the ladies mounted side-saddle and a few of the MacDonald servants joined walking behind them.

It was a pleasant June evening on the Isle of Skye, the rain had stopped and all that was needed was a jacket or light wool shawl to stay warm. Many of the inhabitants were returning from late sabbath services, walking the same road to homes and inns scattered about. The strange and foreign Betty Burke drew unwanted attention as they proceeded. As Flora rode slowly along she heard loud criticisms about her maid from multiple people who saw 'her' walking earlier with Neil MacEachen. The maid's awkward strides, how she picked up her skirts too high crossing the puddles, and how she demonstrated disrespect of her mistress by walking in front of Flora, not knowing her station in life. These were just some of the loud, unsolicited appraisals along with comments saying how impudent Betty Burke was. Hearing the chatter Flora and Lady Margaret locked knowing eyes just as one of Lady Margaret's servants made the loud observation as she looked up ahead, that Betty looked like a man wearing a lady's dress.

That is when Lady Margaret reluctantly bid Flora goodbye making the excuse she was tired and needed to rest. It appeared imperative she turn her pony around and return home, preventing her servants from further observations of the attention-gaining Betty Burke. Before she left, Flora turned her pony to the group of gossips and scolded them. "You shouldn't make fun of that woman. She cannot help the way she was born— she is just awkward, and there is no avoiding it." One of the girls answered saying Betty was a daft and a gawky loon. That is when Flora informed them Betty was Irish, however an accomplished spinner of flax and that they needed to be more compassionate. "I'm taking her to help my mother."

The women parted when Flora abruptly turned her horse and headed to catch up with Kingsburgh, Neil MacEachen, and Betty Burke. It was about a mile further when she found them easily, signaled by the flock of sheep scattering up the hill away from the walking men. Prince Charles was pacing back and forth fussing with his clothes and once again arguing loudly with Neil, apparently feeling it was beneath him to carry anything, he had thrown a small fit, tossing the light bag into the dirt.

Kingsburgh, sitting on a rock with the wine uncorked, was laughing out loud at the scene in front of him. Prince Charles refused to carry the small kit and Neil was insisting it gave him more authenticity, appearing as a servant. Both were adamant facing each other with hands on their hips, eyes locked and jaws clenched. French profanity was coloring the air blue.

The argument stopped abruptly as Flora rode up. Kingsburgh got off his sitting rock, picked up the contentious bundle, and handed it to Prince Charles along with the half-finished bottle of wine. "We've got to get a move on. I want to sleep in my own bed tonight —and keep your skirts down you silly wench." Then laughing he took Flora's reins and began leading the horse down the trail with Neil MacEachen and the reluctant Betty Burke following.

As evening descended, the sky darkened and the temperatures accordingly became chilly. Neil told Bonnie Betty to open his pack and find a heavy shawl to wear. Flora took hers and crossed it over her knees. The men pulled down their caps and flipped their collars up as they trudged on cold under the starlight. It was late when they arrived at Kingsburgh's house.

Even in the dark Prince Charles could see the impressive crow-stepped entrance with a ball finial at the apex. The slate roof reached up three stories and was picking up a glint of the moon on its surface. The oak long-case clock standing in the front parlor struck ten as the four weary travelers crossed the threshold.

Everything was quiet. The lady of the house, Kingsburgh's wife Florence, had already retired upstairs for the evening, along with most of the servants. One very young girl, barely a teenager, was still about in the kitchen cleaning up the remnants of the day. Kingsburgh requested she go upstairs and wake Lady Florence telling her he was home with Flora MacDonald and a couple of 'friends'. The girl, filled with qualms waking Lady Florence, quietly hiked up to the second floor and lightly knocked on her chamber's door.

"What is it?" asked the sleepy voice.

"Your husband has returned ma'am, with Ms. Flora and two other guests. They said you should come down."

The answer from the other side of the door was not what she expected. "Tell Ms. Flora she is welcome —as well as the guests, but I'm not coming down. You just take care of everything they need tonight and can see them in the morning."

Shaking her head as she descended the staircase the young maid relayed to Kingsburgh his wife's answer. Flora, not wanting to raise suspicion in the young lass, poured a dram in a noggin hurrying Betty into one of the side rooms saying she needed to clean up and rest. "Stay here my sovereign until we get things under control."

In the meantime, Kingsburgh was taking the stairs two at a time up to Florence's bed chamber. He did not bother to knock, it was his house and his wife, but he nevertheless startled the woman as he entered rather hurriedly, slamming the door tight behind him. "Get up, get dressed and get downstairs quickly lassie! We have Prince Charles locked in the downstairs chambermaid's room. And wake up Anne, we need her help. "

Florence overcame her shock in an instant realizing she was fully awake and not dreaming. Grabbing some clothes she hurriedly dressed, woke up her daughter Anne who was staying down the hall, and together the two women went downstairs to the parlor. Kingsburgh had already sent the maid off for the

evening telling her not to return and was in the process
of making hot toddies for everyone. Betty had returned
to the parlor and was slumped in the needlepoint
armchair with his feet extending towards the peat fire
for warmth.

As soon as Lady Florence entered the room he
rose, took her extended hand and regally kissed it. She
too couldn't help but giggle when she saw the costume
he was wearing, his bonnet and cap had been removed
revealing a tall young man in a maid's dress.

In the meantime, Anne was thrilled to see Flora
and the two young ladies embraced in greeting. They
had been friends much of their lives with Flora being
an attendant at Anne's wedding. Flora introduced Anne
to the Prince and the two set about immediately setting
a table for everyone to eat. It was critical the staff not
see the strange man in a woman's dress, so the two
young ladies took to the task of rummaging through
the pantry and pulling out bread, butter, roasted eggs
and some collops. Both the Prince and MacEachen were
famished neither having been a part of the ample meal

that afternoon in Mugstot. The two jumped on the food like aggressive bonxies.

Once fed the exhausted ladies all retired upstairs, Flora choosing the small room reserved for visiting help but not before she had a small hot toddy herself. She lay down on the maid's oat chaff bed which was surprisingly comfortable considering her last night's sleep, what there was of it, was snatched on the bottom of a shallop crossing the stormy sea. The covers were warm here and Flora felt drained however, her mind stole her solace as she ran over repeatedly the events of the day. She was uneasy and tossed restlessly wondering if the boatmen had been paid enough and could they remain loyal? Should she have told them to return to Unst so quickly? Had Betty Burke aroused suspicions?

Eventually, her anxiety slipped into the background, her muscles relaxed and Flora's body succumbed to a much-needed sleep.

CHAPTER 12

Off To Portree—Monday Morning, June 30, 1746

Flora woke up refreshed Monday morning and could clearly identify the sounds of kitchen activity lilting its way up the stairs. The smell of fresh scones filled the air titillating her nose. Before she had gone to bed, Anne kindly placed a complete change of clothes for Flora on the chair in the room. A wash bowl had also been set on the table by the window along with soap and a drying cloth. She was grateful to wash and dress in fresh clothing.

Prince Charles was sound asleep in the guest room adjoining Flora's. It was critical the house staff not know these unusual arrangements since the Bonnie Prince was still posing as Betty Burke. Flora locked both adjoining doors dropping the keys into her pocket. They needed to prevent any of the staff from wandering into either room when she went downstairs.

Clean and dressed she entered the parlor where the young maid from the night before was holding a drinking cup, the handle of which was broken off. The girl was puzzled as to what had happened. Flora took the fragments into the kitchen where she placed them on the mantle over the fire. "We'll worry about that later," she told the girl.

"Why isn't your maid up and helping?" the young helper inquired innocently.

"She isn't exactly my maid, she is for my mum, but if you are to know she had a stomach ache and I suggested she stay in bed today. We have had a long journey." More lies crossed her lips.

The explanation seemed sufficient for the time being. Flora sat down at the table as MacEachen entered from the servant's quarters where he too had stayed, then a few minutes later Lady Florence and Anne joined them. Bacon, scones, cream and tea were shared liberally with eggs and everyone ate their fill.

When the hired help were out of earshot MacEachen explained the events of the evening. He, Kingsburgh, and the Prince had several hot toddies while they sat smoking, talking and generally relaxing after the ladies had retired. Charles, quite in his cups, insisted on yet another drink. However, Kingsburgh told him enough was enough and there would be no more. The two men ended up tugging on either end of the china cup when the handle snapped, precisely at the same time that Kingsburgh came to the limits of his patience with the Prince. The two men, MacEachen and Kingsburgh did, however, manage to give the Prince his first bath in way too long and put him in a proper bed in the finest guest room.

Just as MacEachen finished his explanation of the evening Kingsbourgh came in to join them. Brows furrowed and mouth down Lady Florence gave him a stern look. "We are all going to be hanged for this you ken."

Kingsburgh reached for a scone and smiled at her. "You have had the honor of the Prince's presence my dear and besides, you can only die once you know. Now we need to get rid of the help. We cannot have them get too close to Betty."

Kingsburgh's presence as Factor was commanding. He immediately ordered one of the girls to spend the day with 'Auld Maggie' up the road and assist the widow any way she could. Two of the men were directed to move the sheep to the other side of the island, stay overnight in the sheiling there and return on Tuesday. He also wanted an inventory count of the cows and how the caving was going. To the scullery maid from the night before he told her to go home, check on her mother, and come back by Tuesday evening in time to help with supper. He kept one young teenage boy with instructions to feed and groom the horses.

With most of the servant help dispersing, Kingsburgh requested Flora take a walk with him while MacEachen waited for the Prince to wake and re-dress as Betty Burke. No one could move until the cover of night again but Kingsburgh had a plan for that.

Flora was delighted to be alone with the elder factor. She wanted so badly to ask him about his sons, primarily Allan. The two could look out over Loch Snizort to the Cuillin ridge as they walked along. Flora couldn't help but laugh when she spied a group of selkies watching them intently with their large brown eyes from the beach. They seemed so human-like in their curiosity.

"We are being watched." She smiled at Kingsburgh.

"Aye Lassie, and there is no way to know if they are friend or foe. We must get the Prince off these islands as soon as possible. We cannot sustain this ruse much longer."

They walked along in silence for a bit, Flora finally asking about his son Allan. How he was faring and where exactly was he?

"A dinnae ken, but I will tell you lassie that bad news is swift. Both lads must be fine." He touched his chest. "I would know in my heart if they had come to harm. In the meantime, we must get Charles Edward Stuart to Portree tonight. Time is not on our side."

The two friends strolled for an hour or more sharing their thoughts. Kingsburgh liked the Prince, and agreed he was entitled by birth to the throne, yet also expressed concern about his leadership. "He seems unwilling to take others' advice, even those more experienced. None of us would be in this position if he had heeded the warning to go back to France as soon as his ships were turned away. And Culloden…", Kingsburgh shook his head sadly. "His impetuous decision at Culloden was a defeat Scotland may never recover from—and the dead an obvious waste of good men and women."

Flora remained quiet. It was unusual for Kingsburgh to share his thoughts, let alone his misgivings with her. No doubt they were in a complicated situation or, as Lady Margaret had said, 'A slippery kettle of fish'. She could think of all the what-might-have-beens but, decided instead to focus on the problem in front of them, and that was getting the Prince undiscovered to Portree. She was hoping that Donald Roy would meet them there and then take Prince Charles to the Island of Raasay and to safety among some of the MacLeods.

Flora suggested that she, Betty, and Neil MacEachen all be seen leaving together. Then she and Neil would ride to Portree but Betty could change her clothes down the road, then take the trail over the hill to the McNabb's Inn. The two agreed on the plan and returning to the house discovered the Prince was still asleep and it was well past noon.

Flora went to the kitchen looking for some dried heather. She was determined to make Charles, who was suffering from all kinds of ills, a cup of medicinal tea and some bread to start his day. It was in the scullery she found rows of herbs and flowers, tied neatly and hanging from the rafters as they dried. The scent in this room was warm and calming for her. She took a deep breath, feeling the infusion of tranquility, and closed her eyes briefly.

CHAPTER 13

Debacle at Portree, Monday Afternoon June 30, 1746

It was well after lunch when Flora and Lady Florence woke the Prince knowing they were in the final leg of his escape and keenly aware it was the first time he had the luxury of a proper bed in months. Had circumstances been different he would have been welcome to an extended stay. As it were, the ladies set a tray of bannocks with eggs and cheese on the console table under the window, waking the man from his deep slumber.

"Good afternoon my liege," Flora greeted Charles. "I hope you are feeling better. The tea will help settle your stomach and possibly take care of the toothache too." Flora went on to explain the day's plan, and that Charles needed to re-dress as Betty Burke for just a while longer.

With the afternoon light coming into the room, Charles Edward Stuart appeared a different man. The sleep had softened his features. His cleanly shaven face along with his washed hair gave him a youthful look. Lady Florence took Flora's arm and with a slight curtsy ushered the girl out of the room locking the door behind them.

The head housekeeper was still on the premises and there was no minimizing the importance of Charles' presence remaining a secret. Lady Florence went downstairs requesting that the housekeeper spend the rest of the afternoon in the sewing room repairing some of the garments she carried and helping her work on a new dress for her daughter Anne. From the sewing room below she could hear the Prince again begin his incessant pacing. The housekeeper remarked to Lady Florence, "Flora's maid is an idle loon for staying in bed so long, and what is wrong with her that she paces about so?" With an accelerated heart and running out of reasons to offer for everyone's curious behavior, Lady Florence said she would take care of the matter, leaving the housekeeper alone and heading back upstairs. She stopped in the parlor where Neal MacEachen and Kingsburgh sat smoking. "Neal, we must do something with our guest," she said raising her eyebrows. "Our meddlesome staff are asking too many questions."

Kingsburgh again took command of the situation. "Move Betty to my room, leave the guest doors open so they see Flora has left, and let them peer in if they need to. I will join him in a minute and see if we can find him some clothes to wear to Portree after we get away from here."

Florence was vacillating between the thrill of having the potential King in her home and the horror of hanging as a traitor. The anxiety of it all was about to overtake her better judgment. Anne went down to the sewing room with the intent of keeping the housekeeper there for the rest of the afternoon, while Flora and Lady Florence re-entered the guest room upstairs. Charles was fussing with his dress and having trouble tying the apron. In Gaelic Lady Florence asked Flora if she thought he might give her a lock of his hair as a keepsake.

Embarrassed and flustered, Flora translated the request. Hearing this Prince Charles sprawled out across the bed where Flora was sitting and put his head in her lap. With a lighthearted laugh, he told her she could cut all the locks she needed.

Flora clipped a lock of the man's hair and then playfully pushed him away. "You need to go to Kingsburgh's room and get outfitted in gentlemen's clothes." Looking at him she almost laughed again at her Bonnie Prince Charlie in a maid's dress. Leaving Florence in the guest room for a minute, Flora took Betty by the arm into the hall, this time with his cap and bonnet on, and showed him the way to Kingsburgh's quarters. Quickly returning she found Lady Florence taking the linen sheets carefully from the bed. "Shall I take these down to be laundered Florence?" she volunteered.

The woman's face turned slightly pink as she held the set close to her breast. "No—no. I want them for my winding shroud. They will never be washed again."

Flora liked the idea immediately. "There are two. We could each have one. One for me and one for you." The ladies agreed and set about storing them in a small, rarely used chest.

It was getting late and they had fifteen miles to go. Even though it was summer and still twilight at ten o'clock pm, Flora thought it prudent the four-hour ride start almost immediately. Besides, they planned to meet Donald Roy at McNabb's Inn.

The stable boy brought Flora and MacEachen's horses around to the front door and then assisted Flora in mounting. He handed her the small bag prepared by Lady Florence and the two tied the parcel on the back of the saddle. Lady Florence had already made a present to the Prince, a silver snuff box to remember her by. Charles had stuffed it in the pocket of his dress. Kingsburgh would lead the desperate party for a mile or so as they rode south with Betty Burke again walking behind, her head down and hidden by the bonnet. This time it was real. Betty was distressed to be leaving the safe haven of the MacDonald's. He felt safe, clean, and cared for. The first time in too many weeks.

Some distance from the house there was an outcropping of stunted trees and it was there where everyone stopped. Neil held Flora's pony while Kingsburgh and Betty stepped into the cover of bushes to change disguises. Betty appeared in a short time fully looking like a Scottish country gentleman. He had on a short tartan coat, a kilt, and woolen stockings. To complete his outfit he was even provided a quality wig and cap. Prince Charles' old shoes had been worn with holes in the soles and tears on the side. Kingsburgh additionally had provided him with new shoes and silver buckles. Charles handed his blue velvet garters festooned with rhinestones to Flora as a gift.

Betty's clothing was hidden under a rock with plans to retrieve them later. Prince Charles told Kingsburgh to keep his worn shoes and present them to him when he was king as he would always be indebted to the MacDonalds. After the two men bid goodbye, MacEachen gave the reins of his horse to the Prince. Dismounting he proceeded to walk, leading Flora's horse down the century-old trail.

There was no rest until they came to the two standing stones of Sornaichean Coir' Fhinn, a little less than half the distance to Portree. Flora told the Prince that at one time there had been three, and the fable was that the stones were tripods for the warrior Finn's pots.

This spot is where Finn cooked up his venison stew using the whole steed—or that is what was believed by the locals, and Flora laughed. The Prince stood looking up wondering how the stones possibly could have been placed there and by whom. MacEachen laughed too and said they were as a warning for blootered men not to fall off the bluff and into the loch.

What began as a light drizzle turned into a healthy Scottish downpour and the three travelers were quickly soaked as they picked up their pace. Not much was spoken for the next hour as each snugged their wraps tighter around themselves, keeping their heads down as much as possible. Flora sang the traditional song *Geordie* to the rhythm of the horse's cadence but lost interest after one verse.

As I walked out over London Bridge
On a misty morning early
I overheard a fair pretty maid
Lamenting for the life of her Geordie
"Saddle me a milk white steed
Bridle me a pony

I'll ride down to London town
And I'll beg for the life of my Geordie"
And when she came to the courthouse steps
The poor folks numbered many
A hundred crowns she passed around
Saying, "Pray for the life of my Geordie"

Charles' new shoes kept his feet dry, but they were spattered with mud by the time they reached McNabb's Inn. All, soaked to the gills, went inside to thankfully find Donald Roy waiting for them. The Inn was filled with rag-tag, down-on-the-heel people, and a dubious crowd it was, yet it was warm, dry and there was plenty of liquor.

Charles Stuart wasted no time ordering a dram of whiskey which he proceeded to swallow in one gulp. The Inn's whiskey was down, dirty, and lacked good distillation thus burning the Prince's throat as he swallowed. The feeling he was going to choke came rapidly, and he demanded water. As the innkeeper went to get the water, Prince Charles sat down with Donald Roy and Flora while MacEachen pulled a couple of dry shirts out of their pack. Then Neil took Flora's water-soaked arisard and hung it near the fire to dry.

McNabb, in rather a surly mood, dropped a wooden communal bucket of water on the table in front of the Prince. Just as Charles curled his nose and began to react to the filth floating on top, Flora gently kicked the startled man under the table. MacEachen said teasingly that the bucket looked like it was used to bail out a boat and without laughing Donald Roy grabbed the ladle and took a drink never taking his eyes off Charles Stuart. "Ut, cum apud Romanos faceret romam facere sir," (when in Rome do as Romans do) Then he handed the scoop to the Prince. The last thing they needed at this point was to raise suspicion as to who they were.

Charles Stuart wanted to spend the night, but that idea failed to sit well with his Scottish escorts. His foreign ways were easier to detect in a place like Portree. People would be asking uncomfortable questions and they were not to forget the ample bounty for his capture. Donald Roy told him no—that arrangements had been made and as soon as they ate he had to leave, and that was that.

The Prince then ordered two bottles of whiskey he could barely drink and threw down more coins than was necessary. Flora kicked him again and warned. "You must ask for change," she whispered in French.

Charles Stuart never appeared, after he had a few drinks, to possess the full grasp of the situations he was in, nor comprehended just how strange he appeared among the fishermen and crofters. It was Donald Roy who called out coarsely to the innkeeper demanding the money. As soon as it arrived Donald scooped it up, handed it to the Prince, and started out the inn door and back into the rain-darkened night.

CHAPTER 14

The Parting

Monday Evening, June 30, 1746

Flora MacDonald, Neil, and Charles Stuart were all taken aback at Donald Roy's sudden and unexpected departure. Instinctively they rose and followed the older gentleman outside into the night and stood talking under cover from the pouring rain. The Prince was upset and Flora couldn't tell if he was crying or if it was rain on his face, however, it was clear his nose was bleeding. She handed him a handkerchief as he explained this frequently happened to him when he was anxious and upset.

Donald Roy's mouth was tight as he loudly addressed the Prince. "I've waited hours for you sir— and rather than be inconspicuous and discreet you were drawing all eyes in that inn. Are you daft? We are unable to tell by looking who is afore and who is against you! You are putting all our necks on the block with your behavior!"

The Prince was not accustomed to being talked to in such a manner and he sputtered for words. Flora made excuses, saying Donald Roy's foot was hurting him and he was tired, but she realized the old man's words rang true. MacEachen, also knew exactly what Donald Roy was saying and chose to look down at his own feet rather than anyone's face.

To further upset the slack-mouthed Prince Charles, Donald Roy told him he couldn't go any further with him, but that two strong MacLeod lads would row him to Raasay. That he himself was suffering such pain in his foot that he would only be a liability. The Prince surprisingly embraced Donald Roy and pleaded with him, saying he only felt safe with the MacDonalds. However, the plans were set, the men hired and the boat waiting.

Turning to Flora, Prince Charles took her hands in his and looked into her eyes. "For all that has happened, I hope Madam, we shall meet at another time at St. James Palace in London and I will reward you there for what you have done." Then, the man leaned down and kissed Flora on the cheek. "May heaven reward you as you deserve."

He embraced MacEachen, put his arm in Donald Roy's and they strode off in the wrong direction as a diversion into the night— just in case anyone was watching. Neil and Flora stood side by side as the two men vanished in the darkness.

Flora and Neil were silent as they re-entered the inn posing as a couple and ordered a simple meal. As MacNabb set their plates down he questioned the two about the 'strange fellow' with them earlier. Flora explained that the gentleman was Sir John MacDonald, a distant relative from Ireland, who was on his way to the mainland. "He doesn't want to be discovered here so keep it quiet my good man." And she gave him a knowing look while discretely sliding a few coins in his direction.

"Aye!" said MacNabb stuffing the coins in a small leather bag under his shirt. "I dinna say a word. From the looks of him, I would have believed he was the very Prince himself. He looked so noble...but I'll keep that to me self."

Both Flora and Neal hoped their efforts over the last week were a success and climbed the stairs to their rented room. It was filthy, with an uninviting bed that looked as if it was the permanent home to a collection of vermin. Flora wrinkled her nose and Neal chuckled. It couldn't have been worse. The floorboards were thin and the unpleasant smells of smoke, whiskey, and unwashed bodies oozed up through the cracks. They both chose to lie down on the floor and get as comfortable as they could, misgivings about their host swirling around their thoughts. And the Prince? Did the Prince make it to Raasay?

Neal looked at his pretty cousin on the floor and thought of all the places they had been together. He even held her wailing as a child when Hugh pretended to kidnap her mother complete with bagpipes blaring some twenty years earlier. Flora was only two years old then, crying and terrified the charade was real. Now he would protect her again and get her safely home to Armadale.

It was a fitful sleep for both and barely light when they crept down the stairs, slipped around a few leftover customers sprawled on the tables, and escaped undetected into the fresh morning air. The rain had blessedly stopped and they quickly located their ponies in the stall next to the inn. Neal saddled the horses and helped Flora up onto her sidesaddle turning the beasts south to Armadale. The plan was to take two days, overnighting at Kylerhea, a familiar crossing point for the island cattle on the way to the mainland markets. There was a comfortable inn there where the drovers and others of the isle frequently stayed.

Both riders were quietly tired and downhearted that day. Had they put their entire families in peril over their politics and actions for a cause they felt just? What if all their exertions had been in vain and come to naught? Neil was thinking of his conflicting religious and political philosophies and the active part he played in its violence. The thought of all the bloodshed sickened him and he wondered about the extent of God's forgiveness.

They had gone about ten miles when they met a scruffy young lad coming their way. Stopping them he spoke in Gaelic asking if the young lady was Miss Flora

MacDonald. He handed Flora a piece of paper with a note. She read it to herself first, then switched to French for MacEachen. "It is from Castleton to warn me that Captain MacLeod of a militia company was on the lookout for a young lady in the company of Prince Charles Stewart." Flora paused feeling, but not showing the horror she felt in her heart. "Castleton further instructs me to head directly to Armadale but not to tell anyone where we have been, including my mother." Neil nodded understanding fully the gravity of the note.

Looking at the waiting face of the boy Flora switched back to Gaelic, the only language she assumed he knew. "Tell your master we will be sure to send him the parcel he wants as soon as I reach home." Smiling Flora gave the lad a coin and pushed off again down the road so no one could see her stricken and frightened face.

She and Neal decided it was best to make the grueling ride straight through to Armadale. As soon as they were out of sight of the boy Flora swung her right leg over straddling the horse and adjusting her skirt so it covered her legs. "Neil I am unable to make thirty more miles side saddle. My legs and back will never unbend and my back is already hurting. You just hush about this."

The man, lifting his chin to the sky let out a hearty laugh to see his cousin perched on her horse like a young laddie, skirts billowing on either side as she took off in a trot, her bonnet on her back and hair flowing.

CHAPTER 15

Armadale—Tuesday, July 1, 1746

It was late when the cousins arrived at Armadale to welcoming arms and one excited terrier barking and jumping around Flora's feet. She picked up the wiggling creature and cooed softly to him as he licked her face. "Aye sweet Sidger, I missed you too."

Marion embraced her eldest daughter for a long minute, assuring her what a delightful surprise it was to have her home. Ushering everyone inside and looking at the pair, she quietly poured each a noggin of whiskey to warm their bones. Mother Marion then ordered a housemaid to prepare a meal while she put another brick of peat into the fire.

Hugh and Marion's home was the center of the MacDonalds on Skye. It was huge and able to accommodate many visitors, but tonight there was just the immediate family and it felt welcoming and tranquil.

Flora's half-sister Annabella and the three younger brothers were all tucked in their beds for the night and did not hear anyone arrive, giving Flora and Neal time to relax in the big parlor chairs and unwind before also retiring.

Marion spoke softly to Neal. "What went wrong at Culloden?"

Neal had turned this very question over in his head multiple times. Facts remained facts but how to express loyalty to a monarch and admit his gross errors at the same time presented a challenge. He cleared his throat. "Our Charles Stuart was inexperienced in war tactics ma'am. We fought with loyalty for him, but his troops were exhausted having marched all night on empty stomachs. The ground was a saturated bog and we were outnumbered two redcoats to one of us. The King's troops had set up camp on the moor and were rested, fed, and well-armed. Somehow they had figured out how to avoid our broadswords. They would slash and stab the fighting highlanders in their sides then leave them mortally wounded on the ground. The scene was carnage and the screams of the wounded and dying men pierced the air." Marion silently refilled Neil's glass as he continued. "Charles, realizing his error, his head-strong desire to march triumphantly into London without a plan, without experience, was the cause of the carnage. I was with him when he landed and the clan chiefs told him to wait, that it was not the right time but oh no, he proceeded ahead, ignoring all their advice. Then, as the fight went on, Charles Stuart broke down crying—literally sobbing. Right there on the battlefield, for all to see, openly shedding tears from bewildered shock at the horror he was witnessing. I pulled him back across the battlefield as some of the men were yelling that he was a coward. It was a defeat of body and soul Marion. A defeat of hope in less than an hour. A crushing blow to his very being and the dreams of so many of us. We've been on the run ever since."

Marion sat stunned by Neal's honest and naked first-person account of Culloden. Neal, who she had known his whole life. Neal who had been a tutor to her children. The silence was heavy and Marion, stunned by his story, was additionally afraid to ask what circumstances brought Neal MacEachen and her daughter back to Armadale.

Flora, saddle sore and worn from the ride, wanted to go no further in the conversation fearing Marion would figure out too much. She had never lied or deceived her mother in her entire life. Uncomfortable in the direction the conversation was going she finished her drink, reached for a slice of cheese, and excused herself to her room with her terrier Sidger trotting faithfully along.

She could also hear Neal making his excuses and heading for the guest room wondering if the whiskey had loosened his tongue a bit too much.

They would deal with this in the morrow.

❁

Morning came to Armadale brilliantly bright blue with moist droplets still clinging to the shrubs and grass. Neil stood at the door gazing across the loch to the mountains on the other side. Above, thin white clouds glided across the sky slowly, reminding him that time was of the essence. He had to locate Charles

Edward Stuart and return him safely to France.

Marion was up and handed Neil a strong cup of

tea. "We have eggs, bacon, and oatmeal for you laddie.

It is all on the table in the kitchen." Turning to go, the

doorway filled with squeals of laughter as Annabella

and James wrapped their arms around Neal's torso. He

laughed greeting them both and tussling James' hair.

"You two are blooming like the heather." He then stood

back and took a long look at Annabella who was

fourteen. "And you my dear are looking like your

bonnie sister—two beauties in the same stable." Neil

laughed out loud at that but then, in a more serious

tone, explained he had an important job to do and had

to return north to Portree immediately. He did not want

to divulge what the commission was. The less the

household knew the safer they would all would be.

He ate quickly while Marion saw to it that he

had a bundle of food to take with him, and a fresh

horse was brought around to the door. As Neil

mounted up Marion asked what she should tell the

still-sleeping Flory.

He leaned down with a mischievous smile. "Tell her I love her."

Marion's eyes twinkled. "Neil MacEachen you'll have to get in line with the rest of the laddies."

MacEachen trotted off down the road only turning once with a wave. "I will write!" he yelled into the wind.

CHAPTER 16

The Arrest—July 12, 1746

It was well into the afternoon when Flora woke to Sidger's soft whine wanting to relieve himself outside. He had been cuddled into her side, her arm over the little dog for most of the night. She got up and let him out the bedroom door and, for a moment considered lying back down as she looked about her room. Taking it in with a deep breath she felt safe and secure for the first time in weeks. Flora took her time cleaning up, arranging her hair, and dressing before she descended the stairs to the parlor.

Much to her surprise Donald Roy was sitting casually by the fire with his pipe and a cup of tea. As soon as he saw her he looked quickly around and put his pointer finger to his lips hushing her to be discreet.

"Why Donald Roy, such a delightful surprise."

"Aye Lassie, Hugh and I ran into each other in Portree. He suggested I join him for a few days down here and we were in luck to get a boat coming this way." He winked at Flora. "Me thinks he was missing your mother up there on Benbecula with nothing but unwashed men and the endless search for the Prince."

Flora, in the absence of her mother Marion, asked Donald Roy if he needed anything and could she order him a meal. In the meantime, her stomach, not having eaten but a slice of cheese in the last day and a half, ached for some food. Doing so Donald Roy pulled out a handwritten note in French and handed it to her.

⚮

Sir,
I have parted (and I thank God) as intended. Make my compliments to all those to whom I have given trouble. I am, Sir, your humble servant, James Thompson.

After reading the note Flora handed it back to Donald Roy and their eyes locked in silent communication—both knowing the real identity of the note's author, James Thompson. Continuing to gaze steadily at her, Donald Roy crumbled the note in his hands then tossed the paper ball into the smoldering peat, destroying any incriminating evidence.

Donald Roy's presence, along with One-Eyed Hugh being home, distracted Marion and she quickly forgot to question Flora further about her late arrival with Neil MacEachen or Neil's quick departure that morning. It was a pleasant and relaxing time to have her husband home and their dear Donald Roy.

❁

Flora's half-sister, Annabella, and ginger-haired Ceitie MacDowal spent the subsequent days talking and walking about the gardens at Armadale with Sidger trotting along and rarely leaving her side for long. Ceitie was from one of the servant families and early on in Flora's life was brought daily to the big house to play with her. The two formed a tight, sisterly bond, although Ceitie never was presented with the

131

same educational opportunities as Flora and unable to master any language other than Gaelic.

It was Saturday afternoon, on July 12 that things took a turn for the worse. Ceitie, Flora, and Sidger were strolling along the seashore watching the porpoises in the bay when a party of red-coated soldiers rode up. Looking down on the slight woman he stated in English that he had a warrant to arrest, "One Flora MacDonald, a rebel lady who is to be taken on board the *Furnace Bomb*, commanded by Captain Ferguson."

Flora, pulling her shoulders back and drawing herself up flashed her eyes with indignation. "For what cause am I to be treated such?"

The officer answered, "You are charged Madam, of having aided the escape of the Pretender to the throne. Your boatmen were not bribed to silence." Then the man continued with a twisted, sinister smile, "And the threat of more torture to them brought forth their confessions and *your* pivotal role."

Ceitie understood little of what was being said but gathered a great deal from their tones and Flora's face. At that very moment, there was a clap of thunder and the sky opened up with a torrential downpour. Ceitie screamed, grabbed Sidger, and ran towards the big house for help.

Flora, maintaining her dignity along with her innocence, requested to go home first, to tell her mother and get dry clothes however, her request was denied and her hands tightly shackled behind her back. She was walked at a quick pace to a waiting row boat and subsequently delivered to the imposing *HMS Furnace*, a fourteen-gun sailing vessel appearing in the harbor. *The Furnace* was designed specifically for bombarding fixed positions on land, a lethal weapon for the British Navy. It could have easily smashed the MacDonald home at Armadale and everyone in it.

After hearing the charges from the arresting officer, Flora spoke no further. Within the hour she was locked in a cabin waiting to be interrogated by Commander John Campbell who was aboard the ship. The Campbell clan, like many clans at the time, was equally divided by their loyalties either to the Hanoverian King George II or the Jacobites supporting Charles Stuart. However, Commander John Campbell was also a highlander and had a reputation for being more than lenient with his Gaelic-speaking kin from the North. How would he treat the pretty rebel was the question?

Flora was relieved temporarily by being locked in a snug cabin. At least she was out of the rain, could warm up and dry her soaked garments. Heavy on her mind though was what to tell her dear mother who, by now, would be totally distressed as Ceitie MacDowel screamed out the news of her arrest. She could only imagine the shock and horror her family must be experiencing. Then there was Hugh and Donald Roy's welfare. What Flora did not know at that time and would only learn later, is that those two, Hugh and Donald Roy immediately went into hiding upon the news of her capture.

She sat down and began to sing Psalm 121 as a prayer in Gaelic, her voice lilting with the lines.

I will lift up mine eyes unto the hills, from whence cometh my help. My help cometh from the Lord, which made heaven and earth. He will not suffer thy foot to be moved: he

*that keepeth thee will not slumber. Behold, he that keepeth
Israel shall neither slumber nor sleep. The Lord is thy keeper:
the Lord is thy shade upon thy right hand. The sun shall not
smite thee by day, nor the moon by night. The Lord shall
preserve thee from all evil: he shall preserve thy soul.
The Lord shall preserve thy going out and thy coming in
from this time forth, and even for evermore.*

∞

Those of the crew, whether they understood her
language or not, could hear Flora's lilting voice in
lament and were unnerved. They postponed her
interrogation until the following morning.

CHAPTER 17

The Furnace

Sunday, July 13, 1746

Flora woke at dawn with the click of her cabin door unbolting. The cook came in and placed a tray of tea along with yesterday's scone on the cabin's table and left without a word. She bit into the dry food and washed it down with the tea, straightening herself up as she did so. Within minutes of making herself presentable, a guard came in and ushered Flora into the stateroom where she came face to face with Commander John Campbell in full uniform

She was seated, and before the Commander could begin questioning her, Flora's world and the reality of her predicament crashed like a landslide in her mind. Feeling abandoned and facing an unknown future she burst into uncontrollable tears.

The weeping young woman in front of him was disconcerting to John Campbell. Hardened from many battles and accustomed to confronting belligerent, angry prisoners, he was not quite prepared on how to proceed with a sobbing lassie. He handed her his handkerchief and stood quietly while Flora attempted to compose herself. She kept repeating that she wanted to talk to her mother.

It was clear to Commander Campbell he was going to get little information from Flora until she was consoled, so he ordered a crew and a few soldiers to escort her back to Armadale to see her mother, pick up a few things, and return her directly back to the *Furnace*. He admonished her not to speak Gaelic while there, only English so her guards could understand all that would potentially be said.

Coming into view of Armadale Flora almost swooned with nostalgia. The sound of seagulls crying as they danced in the sky, coupled with the waves gently rolling in against the sand and rocks was almost melodic. As they disembarked and approached the house she could see her mother waiting at the door and her younger brothers playing innocently in the paddock. It was almost too much to bear.

What Marion knew or did not know about the involvement of her husband Hugh and their good friend Donald Roy will never be known. There is no record of that. What she did know was the two men departed hastily as soon as Ceitie MacDowel told them what happened to Flora. Marion's alibi was, that the entire time she was home tending her estate and children while the rest of the players were gallivanting about the Hebrides. What Marion did know now was that her daughter was in peril in the custody of the English. Not a good position to be in at any time in Scotland.

Upon arrival, mother and daughter embraced with Flora once again bursting into tears. Marion soothed her quietly in Gaelic, telling her to be brave and that God was with her. The soldiers speaking in English admonished them both for using their mother tongue. Only English would be accepted. As the two held each other Marion slipped a few silver coins into Flora's pocket. "You may need this daughter dear." It was then that Ceitie emerged from the side door carrying two small bags of clothing announcing to the surprise of all that she was going with Flora.

One of the custodians admonished the group again about speaking in Gaelic however, Flora had to explain to him in English that Ceitie MacDowel was basically their servant and never had mastered the English language.

Marion whispered to Flora that Hugh and Donald Roy had slipped away. Then, holding her daughter for what might be the last time, she said aloud in Gaelic, "Beannachd Dia dhuit" (blessings of God be with you). Her half-sister, Annabella said nothing as stood next to her mother stoically, looking at her beloved sister Flora while tears silently streaked down her face.

As Flora and Ceitie began the walk back to the boat waiting to return them to the *HMS Furnace*, Flora's knees went out from under her in a wash of grief and dismay. If it had not been for Ceitie's quick thinking Flora would have hit the ground. The Captain of the *HMS Furnace*, Ferguson had been terrifying the Scots for weeks, burning houses and killing cattle without discrimination as to who they belonged to. Flora was unsure of her fate if left with what she considered an evil man.

Observing his mistress being dragged off, Sidger ran towards her barking and nipping the heels of the militiamen. They had already loaded Flora into the rowboat when the little dog, determined to join her, sprung into the water and began paddling furiously towards the dinghy. It was one of the MacDonald's male workers that plunged in behind him, grasping the faithful terrier and holding him tight to prevent any further attempt to follow his mistress.

Back aboard the *Furnace*, Commander Campbell did his best to make, in his words, 'the pretty rebel' comfortable, but at the same time determined to find out her role in Bonnie Prince Charlie's escape. He also intended to keep Flora away from the other prisoners on the ship to prevent any opportunity they might have to collaborate on their stories. However, as the word spread she was onboard with them, the spirits of the Jacobite rebel prisoners in the hold were raised, even though the conditions in which they were being held were deplorable.

Commander Campbell already knew some of the accomplices in the Prince's escape as the poor boatmen who had rowed to Skye had confessed under torture, a fact of which she had already been informed. Once she regained her composure Flora did her best to protect everyone involved. She assumed the face of innocence like a familiar mask and attempted to beguile the Commander. Knowing what her mother told her of Donald Roy's escape she mentioned his name, along with Felix O'Neil's whom she had not seen since Benbecula. Giving them a spattering of innocuous information was her motive while protecting Hugh and the others.

Nothing Flora MacDonald said was accurate, even though Commander John Campbell believed every lying word from the young lassie's lips.

CHAPTER 18

Dunstaffnage Castle, July 26, 1746

Conditions on the *HMS Furnace* were deplorable on multiple levels. Flora's friends, countrymen, and fellow prisoners were kept between decks in the dark with nothing but coils of rope to lie on and just enough mealy and watered-down porridge to keep them barely alive. Flora and Ceitie were better off in the wee cabin however, there was nothing for them to do to wile away the long hours. The two lassies mostly talked about the shared memories of their childhood on Skye and avoided any speculating conversation as to what might happen to Flora. As they ran out of memorabilia there were lengthy times of silence with the girls arranging and then rearranging each other's hair. Whatever Flora's fate might be, Ceitie would go free having no knowledge or involvement in the events that landed her childhood friend in these dire conditions. Ceitie was simply there to support her life-long friend.

Captain Ferguson was ruthless. Frequently the two girls could hear the agonizing screams of tortured men being flogged with a cat of nine-tails. Scot after Scot was brought aboard the prison ship and cruelly interrogated as the search for the Prince continued. The Duke of Cumberland was still ensconced at Fort Augustus where his hate for all of Scotland and its inhabitants fermented. Cumberland's yearning to return to London catapulted sending troops scouring every inch of Scotland for Charles Edward Stuart and Captain Ferguson was in lock step with Cumberland.

It was, however, beyond John Campbell's sense of morality to watch his kin being treated so ruthlessly. Ferguson began burning homes about the area, terrorizing the inhabitants, and needlessly slaughtering sheep and cattle. Commander John Campbell made the decision to go home to Dunstaffnage Castle for a needed break and take Flora MacDonald and Ceitie with him. This meant the *Furnace* would have to sail to Scotland's west coast to the entrance of Loch Etive. There perched on a rocky promontory stood his 500-

year-old castle, the home, and stronghold of the Campbell clan.

Before the ship could set sail more prisoners were brought on board. Flora and Ceitie were standing on the upper deck ready to depart with Campbell when none other than Felix O'Neal was marched up the plank right in front of them. Flora, taken aback by his appearance, pretended to be angry in order to get closer. She walked up, struck him across the face, and loudly said, "To that black face do I owe all my misfortune!"

A tall seaman standing close to Flora gently took hold of her arm pulling her back as whispered words of encouragement, "Hold fast me lassie, hold fast."

Felix held steady, ready to protect her in any way he could. Leaning toward her he whispered advice. "Flora never pretend to repent or be ashamed of what you have done." He went on to advise her a bit more adding that he thought England would not be so barbarous or cruel to take her life.

Felix O'Neil had more he wanted to tell her, however seeing him speak to the young woman,

Ferguson became enraged and ordered that the man be stripped and tied to the rack. The seaman whose arm was still around Flora's shoulders introduced himself quietly as Nigel Gresley. At this point, Nigel stepped forward stating to the Captain that O'Neil was a French Officer and thus should not be mistreated. To her grateful consolation, Felix O'Neal was unbound and ushered to the deck below.

It was a relief for John Campbell and the Scottish lassies to eventually disembark *The Furnace* and be beached close to the decaying castle. It was the same seaman, Nigel Gresley who saw to their landing. As he helped Flora onto shore he whispered in Gaelic, "Your Allan is safe lassie". There was no time nor inclination to say more. She and Ceitie stood on the beach as the wherry shoved off again towards the bomb ship where they had had the misfortune of living for the last two weeks. The news of Allan buoyed her spirits, but she knew nothing of this messenger nor if his statement was true. Yet she also knew that she had not spoken Allan's name to anyone onboard the ship, so why would he tell her that?

It was a short walk from the shore to the Dunstaffnage Castle. Commander John was relieved to be in his own comforting home and to his wife and new babe. He, along with his father, had built an imposing new home inside the crumbling walls of the old castle and on part of the original foundation.

John Campbell saw to it that the two girls were set up in their own room, given soap, warm water, and fresh clothes. He thought both were close to his wife's size. Being home also gave him time to attend his own wounded shoulder bandaged and hidden underneath his uniform. A shoulder wound that John Campbell incurred at Culloden. He introduced his 'pretty rebel' to his wife that evening at supper and explained Flora's position, along with Ceitie's. His wife was more than sympathetic to the girls and told them she would help them with some of their clothing by supplying them with thread and needles.

It was a lovely respite for a short time with the exception that Mrs. John Campbell came to their room a few days later swooping up their plaids and informing them apologetically that a Dress Act had been passed prohibiting anyone from wearing Highland Dress. "You know this includes us do you not? We cannot wear them either." The woman genuinely appeared distraught and wanted her guests to fully realize the Act also included her family. "And the bagpipes. The bagpipes too have been banned. We are loyal to King George here, but really, the bagpipes?" She shook her head back and forth. Mrs. Campbell had already dropped some tweed wraps on the bed for the speechless Flora and Ceitie. As she departed their room she turned with apologetic eyes. "The British government wants to control all of Scotland and this is only the beginning. No tartans, no kilts, no Gaelic, and definitely no pipes." Mrs. Campbell was again shaking her head in disbelief as she exited into the hallway.

Ceitie burst out in Gaelic, "So what will they do with us? What can they do?"

The commander's wife turned and with sympathetic eyes told the young woman the truth. "They will transport you lassies. Transport and sell you in the colonies." Then she left leaving the air heavy with silence.

Their few days at Dunstaffnage were pleasant however their last night, around 2:00 am, hours after the young ladies had retired to bed, a spectacular electrical storm hit Western Scotland. Lightning arched across the sky illuminating the stone walls of their room and the surrounding areas followed by claps of booming thunder. Leaping from their beds they watched in their night clothes as the loch and hills lit up in a flash, then the sound of rolling cannons, bouncing and echoing off the castle walls. It was truly thrilling and frightening at the same time. Near the conclusion of the spectacle, Ceitie let out a scream.

"Ceitie, what is it?"

Alarmed Ceitie had covered her mouth with her hands. "I saw her," she gasped.

"Saw who?"

"The ghost of Ell-Maid. I saw her wearing the green dress." Ceitie pointed to a section of ruined castle walk outside their window. Then the distraught country girl slumped to the floor sobbing outlaid, "She is always seen before there are tidings of some kind ye ken."

Flora believed her peasant friend and shivered, but openly refused to support her in her disturbing apparition. She had to keep a clear head even though the incident gnawed at her the next morning as they sat down to breakfast.

It was still storming outside with gales lashing the coastline, whipping up waves, and tossing the boats carelessly about as if they were toys. After the meal, Commander John Campbell kindly but firmly informed Flora that she was to be moved to *HMS Eltham* that morning, the vessel which would sail her to London.

With small bags and departing gifts of threads and needles from Mrs. Campbell, the two lassies wrapped tightly in their new tweeds walked to the pier. To their surprise, the wherry had only one boatman waiting for her and Ceitie. Knowing the ocean's moods Flora felt a cold chill run down her spine a chill deeper than that of the wind. She was keenly aware this was a set-up for failure, they would never make their destination in gales of this intensity to the brand new 24 gunship waiting for them.

As she approached the wherry a familiar strong arm reached out to help her in and she recognized the dancing eyes of Nigel Gresley. He winked and his smile swept over her with encouragement. Then he helped Ceitie MacDowel, telling her how he fancied lassies with ginger-colored hair.

Nimbly, Nigel jumped from the boat and spoke with Commander Campbell. "You are sending your pretty rebel and her ginger-haired servant out on a day like this? You couldn't postpone it?"

Flora did not catch all of John Campbell's answer, the wind sweeping most the words out to sea, but she did hear him tell Nigel that drowning was better than a public execution of beheading or hanging. That it might be a blessing for all.

Nigel laughed, shook his head, loosened the dock line pushing the boat away, then jumped in and quickly raised the sail nosing the boat and its two precious passengers into the churning waves.

CHAPTER 19

The *HMS Eltham*   July-August, 1746

A vicious gust off the ocean came up just as Nigel tacked the small wherry and its two passengers into the wind. Flora sensed instantly that he needed assistance as the force increased and he lept to grab the flailing sails. She jumped to the vacant tiller seat and grabbed it with both hands, no stranger to the powers of the ocean and having sailed frequently with her brother Angus. Ceitie was quiet, biting her lips and clasping her arms tightly about herself, her face draining of all color.

The *HMS Eltham* was anchored not far from shore, but nevertheless, it was a challenge for Nigel to bring the small craft to her side taking much longer than it normally would. As the gales howled and the *Eltham* rocked in the choppy water, a rope ladder, aptly named Jacob's, was tossed over its side where Nigel Gresley grabbed it and held on for dear life as the two vessels lurched back and forth. Quickly another crewman scurried down the spliced steps and tied the small vessel tightly to the *Eltham's* side then proceeded to help the two ladies up, skirts billowing in the wind.

Flora went first and as soon as she was on deck reached back to grab Ceitie's hand as she also ascended to the railings. Nigel followed with their bags thrown over his back as he nimbly scaled up. Relieved that all were on deck, the two young ladies looked about at the 40-gun frigate and its huge masts. It was impressive as was Commodore Thomas Smith strutting towards them. He greeted the two referring to Flora again as 'their lovely rebel' giving her his arm in order to guide her to her cabin with dignity. Ceitie was trailing behind as the crew looked respectfully on with awe at their captive female celebrity.

On the way, Commodore Smith explained they would be heading through the Pentland Firth and on to the Northeast corner of Aberdeenshire with their final destination being Leith, Edinburgh's seaport. It would be his responsibility to get her to London where she would testify to her involvement with Charles Edward Stuart, the Pretender to the crown.

As he spoke Flora was thinking of the advice Felix O'Neil had given her aboard the *HMS Furnace*. He told her she had many good friends of whom she was unaware, though she should be careful and not be frightened by thoughts of her present circumstances. He warned her not to say or do anything that may, in the least, tend to contradict or sully the character of she was now mistress, and which she could never be robbed of, but by herself. She drew herself up proudly, wrapped her arm tighter in Commodore Smith's, and walked to her awaiting cabin with Ceitie following.

The Commodore was immediately impressed by Flora's demeanor and began treating her like his daughter. Though the cabin was small he ordered a new bed brought in and inquired if she or Ceitie needed anything else.

Flora was unaware fully of the fate of so many other prisoners of the English. The conditions in the prison ships were dire and word was that 157 in-prisoned men had already died before charges were even formally made against them.

It was Nigel who let her know that Alexander MacDonald of Kingsburgh, Allan's father was also arrested, but that Donald Roy had escaped that fate. Flora often wondered how he knew what he knew and where he got his information, but when she inquired he'd whispered the less she knew the better they both would be, and then he'd smile and wink at Ceitie. He did answer Flora though when she asked where he learned Gaelic. Again, with an impish grin, he answered that it was his nanny, a lass from the Isle of Skye.

It would be six weeks of good sailing before the *Eltham* anchored at Leith Road. Flora and Ceitie had no complaints during that time, pretty much having been allowed to roam the ship's decks at will with few constraints. Both ladies were thrilled to see the great black and white sea mammals they called Mada-chuain swimming and breaching in small groups and the feel of fresh air filling their lungs. The Commodore frequently invited the young ladies for tea and, for their enjoyment, occasionally provided a baked delicacy.

They were beginning to think imprisonment was not all that bad.

It was the eighth of September when the *HMS Bridgewater* tied up at the dock in Leith, took on new tiller rope, six hogsheads of brandy, fifteen tons of coal, and a new prisoner, Flora MacDonald accompanied by her servant Ceitie. Interestingly for the ladies, was that also transferred aboard the *Bridgewater* was Commodore Thomas Smith along with midshipman Nigel Gresley.

The mood about the *HMS Bridgewater* was different though, and the air surrounding Leith unmistakably stagnant. The first thing the girls thought unusual was that Commodore Smith had a lovely riding outfit made for Flora and also saw to it that Ceitie was given enough linen to make whatever she needed. When he was out of earshot Flora looked at the gifts of apparel and laughed. "Good lord Ceitie, what am I do with a riding outfit? Where is the steed to mount that I might ride back home? What in the world was the Commodore thinking?"

Flora and Ceitie's movements were more restricted on the *Bridgewater* and they were limited where they could exercise. Both became increasingly aware that other prisoners were being loaded daily to the decks below. And though the living conditions were much better than the *HMS Furnace*, the *Bridgewater* was quickly becoming a floating brig or gaol as some called it.

Captain Knowler was also kind to the two ladies assigning them to a small cabin next to his in the stern's quarter gallery. He even extended his generosity by allowing them both to use his private toilet. The ladies had to acclimate to the unpleasant odor of so many ships in one location, all dependent on the ocean and tides to wash away the daily human waste from hundreds, perhaps thousands of bodies. Flora and Ceitie were relieved not to share the toilet at the other end of the ship designed for the rest of the crew and lord knows where the other prisoners were relieving themselves.

Leith Street itself was the main road connecting the port to the center of Edinburgh, and within a few days of her transfer to the ship, the curious populous of the city began to form long lines down the dock wanting to get a glimpse of the infamous Flora MacDonald. Captain Knowler was tickled to play a public role associating himself with the events and would dress immaculately in his uniform each day looking forward to putting Flora, the pretty rebel, on display.

Midshipman Nigel Gresley was seen getting on and off the *Bridgewater* frequently, always asking Flora and Ceitie if they needed anything; thread, hooks, or needles? One day he came back with the sad news that Kingsburg was in chains at Fort Augustus in a dungeon along with Felix O'Neal. Hearing this news Flora buried her face in her hands and sobbed while Ceitie sat nearby, a comforting arm around her. Guilt weighed heavily on her shoulder and she wondered if they all would be hanged.

"Oh poor, poor Kingsburg," she cried. "We must pray his life be spared. And oh Ceitie, what will Allan think of me? So much of this is my fault—I brought the diabhal devil to their doorstep."

Ceitie was at a loss how to console Flora over this dire news, and a dismal mood descended on both accompanied by literal dark clouds and rain falling outside. Ceitie said she believed it was tears from heaven.

Both girls felt their spirits dampen and sink but quickly had to hide their emotions as Captain Knowler was allowing people onto the ship in small groups to meet the infamous rebel, Flora. No doubt as the shy girl was put on display and expected to be entertaining, she couldn't help but wonder if the good captain was profiting by making her a public display.

Their trusted friend Nigel came one day to Flora and Ceitie's cabin making sure he was not seen and there were no guests. He told them that on Monday, September 9th, Bonnie Prince Charlie had successfully escaped, along with Neil MacEachen on a French Man-of-war and both were safely back in France. They had left from Loch nan Uamh in Lochaber. Nigel's news delighted Flora and proved her efforts and confinement had not been in vain. There will be another day, another day to try again for an independent Scotland.

CHAPTER 20

Life on *The Bridgewater*

Captain Knowler installed a small spinet in Flora and Ceitie's cabin and began providing refreshments for the daily onlookers and sightseers. The event became more and more bizarre with a parade of Edinburgh's finest among the spectators. Each morning the young women were expected to dress nicely and entertain whoever came on board, with Flora playing and singing traditional Scottish ditties. She hated it! There was the distinct feeling that the individuals attending thought of Flora as a simple country girl curiosity. Few knew that she had spent years furthering her education in their fair city as did her beloved Allan. Edinburgh was not unfamiliar to her however, she would not be allowed this time to set one foot on the cobblestone streets.

The guests, as Captain Knowler referred to them, requested her to sing and play a variety of music and frequently begged her to dance with them. It was a party atmosphere that Flora was completely appalled by and uncomfortable in. She politely refused to dance but would, however, comply by playing dance tunes for the merrymakers in her cabin for hours. Frequently the people would bring gifts and trinkets, as if it were payment for their visit. And Flora's suspicion increased that the good Captain Knowler was profiting nicely.

One lady did bring Flora a Bible and a Book of Prayer both translated into Irish Gaelic. It was a lovely gesture and Flora felt tears welling in her eyes at the gift. Even though it was not exactly her form of Gaelic she was able to read it. She thanked the woman profusely saying she, "Had not been able to read God's blessed word since leaving home and how thankful she was for the gift." Flora shared the stockings and sachets with Ceitie knowing they could use both. In the evenings, when they were thankfully relieved to be alone, they took up their traditional habit of bible readings and prayers, which each found heartwarming. They fell into a comfortable evening routine.

A disconcerting event was the odd woman, Lady Mary Cochrane, who wanted to say she had slept with

Flora. Flora thought she was a twisted hussy who was enjoying her and Ceitie's misfortune. Then when it came time to leave, Lady Mary Cochrane pretended, with conviction, to be afraid to be rowed back to shore in a wind, thus marooning her on board. Flora explained to her nicely that she and Ceitie had very narrow berths and assured her she would be safe with experienced rowers however, the woman insisted and was resolute in her request. Captain Knowler ordered another bed be brought into the cramped cabin and set up for Lady Cochrane. The following morning after breakfast when the contentious woman left, Flora claimed she felt unwell and could see no visitors that day. She even feigned a cough to ensure her charade for privacy was convincing.

As soon as they were alone and the cabin door fastened Flora exploded. "This has been a lot of nonsense!" she spoke freely to Ceitie. "We are both caged monkeys, just objects of curiosity and not real people. I am sick and tired of playing for an audience and acting agreeable to so many strangers. Have they nothing better to do than gawk at us?"

Ceitie looked at her life-long friend. "Flory, it is going to be all right. Keep your faith."

Flora, totally distraught shared her thoughts in a quieter tone. "My faith ebbs and flows like the tide out there. Somedays I feel strong and with God as a partner and a friend. On other days I feel like a frightened tiny girl hiding under the bed with my brothers. I am at a loss to know what to think Ceitie. We have been here six weeks. Six weeks with practically every day someone staring at us as if they had never seen a young woman before. It is bizarre! Some days I am strong and hold fast and others I doubt. Are my prayers heard? Will they be answered? Am I weak when I should be strong? Then I get a surge of faith as if God himself is talking to my heart. It is hard to explain. But I want this to end. I want it over and I want to go home!"

"Flory we both are tired. No guests today, let us just rest, and this afternoon walk on the deck a bit and get some fresh air." Then Ceitie smiled, sniffing the sachet she was holding in her hand and impishly smiling, "As fresh as it gets here."

Rumors were swirling and Nigel Gresley confirmed them, that in less than two weeks they would be sailing for London. The parties were to stop, but then Nigel said he had a request himself. He wanted a portrait of Flora. Flora laughed, "Of me? Why of me?"

Nigel was serious, "You are an exquisite woman Flora MacDonald and I think we need to capture that beauty on canvas." Lowering his tone he continued, "I also want something to remember you by."

As the hoards of curiosity seekers ceased coming, a new guest arrived with his box of odiferous oil paint, one Allan Ramsay, an Edinburgh portraitist. So for days and hours on end, Flora would sit still, quietly thinking Ceitie would be by the window knitting and Ramsay would be hard at work trying to capture her likeness. It was a time of respite, a time of quietening their souls from the incessant expectations of others. It was the break Flory and Ceitie desperately needed.

Alone in the evenings, Flora would attempt to teach Ceitie some English. "Ceitie dear, are you not the least bit curious about what is being said around you?"

Ceitie was resolute. "I dinna like them Flora and I care less about what they say."

Flora sighed. "It might come in handy if you need assistance escaping or you need help getting home."

"I'm staying with you Flory, no matter the outcome. You shan't be alone in this nightmare. Never! I can find my way home when our ordeal is over. I know where Skye is."

Frustrated with the English lessons Flora would describe the grand city of Edinburgh and the castle instead. She told Ceitie how, when she was here as a child, that she would go to Saint Giles. "Ceitie, there is a huge steeple at the top of the church. It looks like a crown with an immense clock at the top. It is so large you can read the time from all over the city. The inside of the church is an experience you would never forget. You have to tilt your head back to see the vaulted ceilings they are so high and I used to think heaven might just be on the other side. The roof is held up with pillars which are bigger around than any tree you or I have ever seen and maybe, if we could put our arms around one we might be able to hold hands—just might." Ceitie looked at Flora amazed and Flora continued enjoying her own description. "And you should see the floors, they are bumpy and uneven, you have to watch your step but they are studded with memorials and carvings of all kinds." Flora was smiling recalling the Edinburgh cathedral. "It is fascinating Ceitie, you would not believe the arched windows and the lights. Oh, the light cascades into the sanctuary as if it is slowly dancing across the statues. It is beautiful my friend. When the scriptures are read the words spoken echo off the walls as if to repeat. And the singing, oh it is beyond description how beautiful it sounds. Oh Ceitie dear, how I wish we could go there one Sunday. I would thrill to take it all in again and pleased for you to see it too."

Flora did not understand what happened to the Prince's campaign to regain the throne when he arrived in Edinburgh, nor why he had not taken the castle.

They had been so close just a few months ago. Neal MacEachen told her that many of the inhabitants of Edinburgh had met in Saint Giles and agreed to surrender to Charles Edward Stuart and his army. The Jacobites had everything going for them at the time but alas, wanted more, decided not to take the castle, and continued marching toward London. Their support simply dwindled as winter was approaching and the promised support ships from France, carrying money and supplies were again thwarted. Finally, there was the disastrous battle of Culloden, the death knell to the campaign.

As he finished Flora's portrait Allan Ramsay took a wee bit of artist's license. Flora's MacDonald tartan had been taken from her at Dunstaffnage Castle by Captain John Campbell's wife, yet Ramsay wrapped her in a plaid on his painting. Then, as a final symbolic touch, he painted several white roses on her bodice, the floral symbol of Prince Charles Stuart.

As the portrait was completed, and the last details painted on the canvas, orders arrived that the *Bridgewater* should set sail immediately. However, the skies opened up once more and the ensuing weather conditions postponed weighing anchor another week. It was the 7th of November that the *Bridgewater* sailed away from the port in Leith to loud Edinburgh crowds waving and cheering Flora on from the docks.

Flora stood on the ship's deck fighting back tears and trying to maintain a brave face while the ship moved slowly out to sea. Would this be the last she would see of Scotland? Then, off in the distance she heard the unmistakable sounds of the banished bag pipes as if answering her question. The haunting music rolled and tumbled down the cobblestones and into her heart saying take courage lassie, hold fast, we are with you. Fortified by the melody Flora squared her shoulders and reached for Ceitie's hand as Edinburgh slipped out of view.

CHAPTER 21

The Tower of London

November 28, 1746

It was close to three hundred miles and twenty-one days later that Captain Knowles steered the *Bridgewater* into the mouth of the River Thames and to a sandy dock called the Nore. The Thames itself was congested with trading vessels of all sizes and shapes making it difficult for anyone to navigate up or down her. It was here the *HMS Bridgewater* met the prison ship, *The Royal Sovereign* destined for London and the infamous Tower.

Captain Knowles was distressed to let Flora go and Nigel Gresley felt worse. Unbeknownst to the Royal Navy that he was a Jacobite sympathizer he soon would be promoted to Lieutenant. Both he and Captain Knowles wrote letters stating how Flora's behavior had been exemplary and pleaded that she not be sent to the Tower, stating she was fragile and it would not be agreeable to her. The letters requested she be lodged in a messenger's house as an alternative, but there were no orders or answers. Lacking directives from any higher-ups they had no choice but to deliver her to *The Royal Sovereign.*

As Flora and Ceitie prepared to move to the fetid prison ship, Nigel Gresley held her hands gently in his. "I cannot go any further with you my lady. I am sorry. The vision of your face will be forever in my heart." For the last time, Flora leaned on Nigel's strong arms as she traversed the wide plank that had been placed between the two ships. Ceitie waited on the *Bridgewater,* holding their bags until Gresley came back for her. Captain Knowles, face long with disappointment waved weakly to her as the plank was slid back in place and the two ships uncoupled.

It was the last day of November, and the world seemed endlessly grey as the two young women were rowed towards Traitor's Gate, tightly holding hands. Flora began mumbling parts of the 23rd Psalm, *"Even though I walk through the valley of the shadow of death I will fear no evil for you are with me."*

The menacing stone arch above the Traitor's Gate was wet from the rain cascading down in rivulets. The stones themselves seemed to weep the tears of the thousands who had traveled this way before. Both lassies trembled as they docked and were subsequently escorted up the stairs toward the prison. It was never the introduction to London that either had fantasized or wished for.

As they entered the Tower they could see, in the dim light that the walls were covered with names, poems, and some heralds, chiseled in the rock by the hundreds of prisoners held here over the centuries. Flora ran her hand down the cold wall as they walked, wondering if she too would be here long enough to make a mark for posterity to see. She pondered how Mary Queen of Scots must have felt being escorted down these same dim corridors not knowing, like she and Ceitie, her fate or how long she would be confined. Not a word was spoken as the entourage walked to the chilly dark chamber where they were to be detained. The only sound was the pat-pat of their own feet and the rhythmic boots of their keepers.

When the young women were left alone for the night Ceitie looked at Flora in horror. "Oh Flory dear, this place is evil. I can feel it deep in my bones. There is an overwhelming sadness piercing into my heart. It is from so many—so many." Ceitie placed her hand over her breast and then, taking a deep breath collapsed on the floor covering her face with her skirt as she began shaking her head back and forth.

Flora felt it too. Something sinister emitting from the gray rock walls. It was a sense, a feeling deep in her chest, an actual perception of unseen, overwhelming sorrow beyond description. It was a sorrow that transcended her own, not just herself, but a collective feeling of all that had been interned here before them. She could feel their anguish and their pain. The collective agony of those poor souls who too had walked these very corridors.

The first night was miserable, dank, and biting. Ceitie and Flora wrapped themselves together to stay warm. But Ceitie slept little telling Flora in the morning of the taibhse (ghosts) she saw and felt in this place, walking the passageways throughout the night. Flora did not disbelieve her, in fact, it was just the opposite, she simply had not experienced any apparitions herself.

In the morning they were given a slice of stale bread and a potato along with tepid tea. Not knowing what would be next, the two ate in silence. Formal charges had not been made against Flora other than the arrest warrant. Anxiety was born from the unknown and all she could do was pace about the cell while Ceitie recited the rosary incessantly. The days blurred one into another with Ceitie and Flora spending hours doing some needlework they had with them and attempting to ignore the grumbles from their hungry stomachs and the screams coming down the corridors. Only the food deliveries and occasional guards walking by broke up the monotony. The women would stare at the walls for hours and then doze off frequently out of boredom. Both allowed their imaginations to fill with dark, gloom and doom thoughts, running out of encouraging things to say to each other.

It seemed like months had gone by when in reality it had only been slightly over a week when Flora and Ceitie's prison door was opened and they were ordered to gather their things. They were being taken to the home of Mr. William Dick, a messenger.

"What is a messenger?" Ceitie asked.

Flora did her best to explain. "He is an official. He takes people like us from one place to another. Someone has got us a place at his home, but I think we'll have to pay him."

"I've no money!" Ceitie exclaimed wide-eyed.

"I still have the silver coins my mother gave me. Let's hope it is enough to keep us for a while."

"A while? A while? Flory how much longer? What is a while?"

CHAPTER 22

Mr. William Dick's House

December, 1746

Flora and Ceitie were escorted personally by 36-year-old, William Dick to his London house. The sky was robin-egg blue and clear as they walked out of the dungeon and neither lass complained of the chill as they squinted and held their hands up to shade the outdoor brightness as they became accustomed to the brilliant light. Crossing the Tower yard they watched the ebony ravens bouncing about squabbling over a few insects on the ground. William Dick had a waiting coach just the other side of the wall and the three were whisked away to his house a mile down the London streets. The ladies would have enjoyed the walk in the fresh air, but it was out of the question under these circumstances. Flora was still a prisoner, her prison had just been upgraded.

Much to their surprise William Dick's home was crowded with her friends and family including Flora's two cousins who had been the boatmen to Skye.

Looking at the sea of familiar faces Flora smiled. There were at least fourteen men in addition to Flora and Ceitie, all of whom stood in respect as she entered the upstairs attic where they were to be held.

There was Clanranald, but not his wife. Lady Clan had also been arrested but held at another messenger's house. Malcolm MacLeod was there with John MacLean from Iona, along with three others from the MacDonald clan. Additionally, there was a doctor from York named John Robert Burton. Flory briefly wondered why he was there but it was a relief knowing most of her close-knit family and friends were well. They were alive and in relatively good condition so far. It quickly turned into a merry band with exchanges of news and where everyone was. In addition, Mr. Dick also had the ability to send and receive letters. Flora could write home. But first, she requested that she and Ceitie be allowed to bathe somewhere and clean up. She suspected they both had head lice and that idea sent a chill down her spine. She always had taken pride in her cleanliness.

Not all was good news. Two days after arriving at Messenger Dick's house, December 8, 1746, the Scots learned that Charles Radclyffe, the 5th Earl of Derwentwater, was beheaded for his involvement with the Jacobites. Flora unconsciously put her hand up to her neck, frightened but trying not to show it, as the group talked about the beheading. The man had almost been Flora's age the summer of 1715 the first time the Jacobites seriously rose against George I. Convicted and escaping to Europe then, Radclyffe was returning to Scotland when arrested at sea, a thirty-year-old conviction bringing him to the executioner's block.

Mr. Dick, as with Captain Knowles, saw a good opportunity to increase his income by displaying Flora to the general and curious public. She was quickly becoming a celebrity about London as several embellished stories had been written about her in the local pamphlets. In the first line of eager 'guests' to see the 'pretty rebel' was one Anne Delincourt Primrose. Lady Primrose was widowed and had, at her disposal, inherited funds from her family in addition to her late husband's estate. She was a strong Jacobite supporter and immediately took Flora under her wing, bringing her elegant clothing to wear and seeing that the fees were paid for keeping not just Flora, but Ceitie and the rest of the inmates.

Lady Primrose was so taken with her new friend that she requested the young Richard Wilson, a beginning portraitist, to also paint Flora. Once again, Flora found herself sitting for an artist while her fellow captives whiled away the hours in the cramped quarters, playing whist. Christmas came and went with little to celebrate. Flora read aloud the Christmas story as her fellow captives sat and listened. The London fog, drizzle nor rain failed to deter the crowds flocking daily to see Flora and resumed in earnest as soon as the holidays were over.

Early spring brought yet another guest to Messenger Dick's house, this one arriving in a black carriage and attended by footmen. Flora was quickly dressed in one of Lady Primrose's finest and instructed to welcome His Royal Highness Frederick, Prince of Wales, King George II's eldest son.

It was a sunny afternoon when Frederick swept into the parlor where Flora was waiting with all of William Dick's staff, himself, and his wife. The men bowed and women curtsied as he entered while the rest of the Jacobite prisoners were admonished to remain quiet in the upstairs attic.

The Prince, even though Flora did not consider him *'her'* Prince, begged her to be seated in his thick German accent. He explained he was representing his father the King and then, with a flourish of his hand excused everyone present save for Flora. "I can easily see madam why you were named Flora. You know she was the Roman goddess of spring flowers and here you sit, looking like a flower yourself." Prince Frederick continued after smiling at her and pulling a chair opposite. "I am here madam, nevertheless, to try to understand why you would risk your friends and your relatives to take part in such a scheme against the crown of England. Why would you risk all their lives and your own to save a traitor who wanted my father's throne?" Frederick was not angry and questioned Flora with sincere curiosity.

Taking a deep breath Flora collected herself sitting as tall as she could get. In her best English, she answered. "Sir, are you familiar with the parable of the Good Samaritan? I believe it is in the book of Luke."

Flora assumed he knew his bible and did not wait for the answer, but continued with her dialogue. "Jesus told us to love our neighbors as ourselves. The story is of a traveler, a man not from the area who was lying wounded alongside a road. Many pass him by in the story, including a priest. Finally, a man from a clan that normally despised the Samaritans happens by and helps him. He basically saves his life." Flora leaned forward towards the man to make her point and looked directly at Prince Frederick. "Sir, I would have done nothing less had it been you. I do not believe in bloodshed. Charles Stuart needed help to escape." She paused, then repeated herself, "I would have done the same for you. Nothing less."

Frederick sat in silence for a moment, tapping his finger on the arm of his chair. "Madam, we offered a thirty-thousand-pound reward to anyone helping us capture Charles Edward Stuart. That sum could have set anyone up, and their heirs in comfort. I cannot grasp why you, nor any of your kinsmen rejected the opportunity for themselves and their relatives."

Flora paused thoughtfully for a moment. "Sir, the Scots are like a tightly knit family. We do not always agree, sometimes there is infighting and we have different faiths, but mostly we respect each other." She tilted her head and smiled at Prince Frederick. "And like all families, the Scots are loyal to a fault. They are not going to give up one they consider their own. We banded together as Scots Sir, not English, not British."

The Prince was rather taken aback, he had not quite experienced that sentiment in his formative years in Germany, and he had not had anyone speak to him so honestly, yet with kindness and lacking malice. However, resolute to gain some facts he continued questioning Flora. "I still need the names of those who helped you. These crimes against the King will not be ignored."

A calmness came over Flora and all feelings of apprehension and nervousness dissolved. "I appreciate your intentions Sire, however, I cannot reveal the names of anyone else involved. You see, what you consider a rebel and an enigma to the King, I consider a brave brother or sister, a patriot if you will. I dinna think I can reveal who they are. There has been enough killing and death."

Flora in one way wanted to bite back. It was Frederick's younger brother, William, the Duke of Cumberland who slaughtered so many of her kinsman at Culloden then igniting a fire of terror throughout Scotland. She bit her tongue and waited. What would happen next? Prince Frederick too sat for a moment and thought. He knew the last passage in Luke, where Jesus pointed out that the Samaritan showed mercy and felt that the point was more people needed to go and do likewise in their lives.

He got up, and quickly Flora also stood, hoping her knees would hold her up as she curtsied in respect. Prince Frederick turned, sincerely thanked her for speaking her truth, and then departed.

He was no sooner out of sight than Lady Anne Primrose came into the room rather flushed. She had inadvertently entered Dick's house just as the Prince was asking Flora to be seated. Lady Primrose ducked under the stairwell at the entrance unnoticed and unintentionally heard the entire conversation. She was pleased and felt guilty at the same time.

CHAPTER - 23

What to do? April 9, 1747

There was friction in the German family currently ruling Britain. Prince Frederick had been left in Germany for fourteen years when the rest of the family moved to England. He personally felt abandoned and remained bitter about the separation for the rest of his life. Frederick was next in line for the British throne, but his father, King George II openly favored his second son, William George, the Duke of Cumberland. Frederick and William did not get along either with both having different backgrounds and philosophies. In addition, Cumberland, 'The Butcher' was honored all over England for his bloody victory at Culloden.

Prince Frederick realized there were other viable ways of claiming victories and frequently longer-lasting ones when done through diplomacy. It was not unusual that his governing ideas conflicted with those of his father and brother when he expressed them. After visiting Flora he sought an audience with his father and presented his logic regarding the Scottish uprising. He told King George II that Flora had done them all a favor; Charles Stuart was off the Island and back in France. He also mentioned that Flora's celebrity status could bring down the royal house if they executed her and further informed him of the books and pamphlets being circulated to an adoring public who referred to her as a brave heroine, one loyal to her cause. Undoubtedly Flora, if executed, would become a martyr to the Scots possibly reigniting their fervor.

Frederick expressed to King George that he felt it would be too risky to execute any more Highlanders. They may have gotten rid of Charles Stuart for the time being but, who knew when they might organize again? He felt England should fear more anger and the possibility of a full-out revolution in the Scot's zeal for independence.

These matters would be pondered and discussed at length in the royal house with George II actually mulling over his son Frederick's logic. However, on April 9, 1747, two more Jacobite participants in

Culloden were taken from the Tower up to Tower Hill. The first to lose his head was Lord William Boyd of Kilmarnock. He was forty years old. Later that afternoon Arthur Elphinstone, the 6th Lord of Balmerino was beheaded. He was the older by eighteen years.

It was the following day when the Daily Gazetteer or London Advertiser arrived at William Dick's house and he delivered the paper up to Flora on the second floor where the inmates gathered around as she read, first in English then translated to Gaelic.

"William Boyd, Lord of Kilmarnock, guilty of high treason was executed by beheading in the early morning of April 9, 1747." Ceitie's eyes widened and Flora's misted over, yet she continued reading for everyone to hear. "Boyd was forty years old. He leaves behind a wife and three young boys. Eyewitnesses say he met his end calmly and in prayer."

Flora needed a second to regain her composure before she continued. She knew neither man personally but was aware everyone's loyalties sprang from the same source. "In the afternoon Arthur Elphinstone, 6th

Lord of Balmerino was also executed by beheading." It says here, "He met his fate with astonishing calm, talking cheerfully to friends and inquiring how Lord Kilmarnock had done. Someone loudly cried from the onlookers, 'God Bless King George' and Balmerino looked at them and said, 'No, God bless King James.'

"Oh," Flora exclaimed. I'm surprised they were allowed to print that. "Our darling King James, Mary Queen of Scot's son. Yes, bless him and both these strong men." Flora swallowed before she continued reading. "He pulled a plaid tartan cap from his pocket, put it on, and told the executioner he would detain him no longer, that he would die a true Scotsman."

Flora set the newspaper in her lap and the room remained silent for longer than required. The same fate was potentially awaiting all of them. She suggested they all say a prayer and as the group bowed their heads she opened her prayer book and read in their native tongue.

"Almighty God, our creator and redeemer, you are our strength and our hope. You have given us these two men

to know and to love in our pilgrimage on earth. Uphold us now as we entrust them to your boundless love and eternal care. Assure us that not even death can separate us from your infinite mercy. Comfort us in our anguish, that we may know your sure consolation and live in confident hope of the resurrection; through your Son, Jesus Christ our Lord."

In chorus, the mourners muttered 'Amen' together. Then John MacLean broke into singing the lament, The Fleurs the Forest (Are a' Wede Away) in Gaelic.

Dr. John Burton was writing quietly in the corner as the others began to disperse. He had been released on bail a month earlier but chose to continue staying at the Messenger's house until his trial date scheduled in July. After all, he was with trusted co-conspirators, where out on the public street there was no assurance as to who could be trusted and who could not. His curiosity and interest in facts propelled him to write, in what he thought was accurate detail, of the events as told by the other residents.

In June of 1747, the Act of Indemnity was passed in the English Parliament. In effect, all Scots who had participated in the uprising that supported Charles Edward Stuart were to be set free. It was two months too late for Lords Balmerino and Kilmarnock, but soon enough for the prisoners housed in the attic of the Messenger's house.

With the news came the screams of delightful celebration with all the Scots jumping and rejoicing including Ceitie. She was laughing, crying, and singing in Gaelic all at the same time. The house was filled with rollicking congratulations and back-slapping, everyone talking at once. After all the activity and excitement simmered down the prisoners started packing the few belongings they had and writing letters that probably would arrive home after they did. The happy chatting was an incessant sharing of plans to return to their homeland—Scotland.

Ceitie and Flora began to pack also, anticipating being picked up in the morning by Lady Anne Primrose. Neither lass planned on staying long in London. The city was rank with smells of squalor and human waste deposited directly in the Thames. Gin had become easy to make and easier to procure and with the populace referring to it as '*Madame Geneva*'. In the months of confinement, it was common to see men and women fighting, yelling, and staggering down the streets in front of William Dick's home. It was not a town that Ceitie and Flora wanted to stay in much longer. They both yearned for the fresh sea breezes sweeping the fragrance of heather across the moors and the expansive views in every direction. The young ladies wanted nothing more than to see their loved ones once again. It had been almost a year to the day when Flora was arrested at Armadale.

The following morning the orders for release came and one by one the inmates of the attic began to bid each other goodbye. Their six months at the messenger's house had bonded them together, and there were hugs, tears, and promises to stay in touch as they dispersed out the door.

That is, everyone but Flora and faithful Ceitie. Flora's order for release had not arrived with the others. Ceitie slumped to the floor completely deflated, her bags dropped to her side. One of the oarsman and distant MacDonald cousins slipped a piece of paper into her pocket and looked sad as he moved around her and out the door.

Flora, totally bewildered, had grabbed the doorknob to hold herself up and bid farewell to her fellow prisoners. "Tha amàireach ann. (There is the marrow)," she told herself.

CHAPTER 24

Lady Anne Primrose — July, 1747

It was two tediously long days before Flora's release papers arrived at Messenger Dick's house, and within an hour of their arrival Flora and Ceitie, thinking it was almost too good to be true, were driven away to Lady Anne's home on Essex Street. In a light atmosphere, they were greeted at the opulent townhouse with warm hugs and a table of food laid out which both lasses considered a magnificent feast. "Oh my dear," exclaimed Lady Primrose, "We are so happy to see you, we are going to have a small gathering of well-wishers for tea. There are some new gowns waiting for you in your room and you have time to rest and clean up."

Flora was flabbergasted that she would be thrown back into public view in only a few hours. To compound her confusion Lady Primrose was ordering her maid to take Ceitie and her bag to the servant's quarters. Finding her voice Flora requested she and Ceitie share the same room.

"But my dear, she must know her station and keep to it."

The word 'station' stung in Flora's ear. She liked Anne Primrose a great deal but felt strongly that Ceitie, who had stood by her and literally slept next to her for the last year, should be treated any different from herself. Flora spoke softly but pointedly. "Lady Anne, I so appreciate all you have done for me, I truly do, however, I must insist that Ceitie stays with me until arrangements can be made to get her home safely to Skye. I owe her that. Ceitie MacDowal is no less than I —no less."

The dowager's mouth tightened, but she acquiesced and had Ceitie and Flora's belongings sent to the same room. Ceitie was following the maid up the stairs when Lady Anne told Flora quietly that Ceitie was *not* to appear at the tea that afternoon under any circumstances. She compromised by allowing the servant to sleep with Flora, however, she would not compromise for the scheduled social event.

Clearly, Flora was trapped. This time in a setting with upholstered furniture and impressive artwork hanging on the walls. The money her mother had given her a year ago was long gone on bare necessities during their confinement. She actually lacked the means with which to get either she or Ceitie home. She would have to write her family and request they help her with funds, a prospect Flora found humiliating after all she felt she had put them through already.

Flora found her way up to her assigned room in the rather plush townhouse to discover that Lady Primrose had also purchased her a completely new wardrobe, which she explained later, was for her to 'meet people'. She stared at the assortment of silk dresses laid out across the bed. All were beautiful, especially the rose-colored one with light green and tiny brown stripes. All would fit perfectly and Flora MacDonald felt that each and everyone was opulent and not at all to her taste. Worse yet she was put in the awkward position of feeling indebted to Lady Anne Primrose both for lodging expenses and emotional support during her and Ceitie's confinement.

It was two days later that Flora received her first letter from Allan MacDonald. It was short but in his unmistakable script stating it was the fifth letter he had written her, and how anxious he was for her return home. Allan was careful not to say much, many letters were intercepted and he wanted to hint at nothing that would incriminate him or his fellow Scots. He explained the family was well, that Hugh MacDonald had returned to Armadale, and that everyone there was hoping to see her soon. She was completely relieved and sat down quickly to write him and her mother once again. She had taken to writing a small number up at the top of her letters so they would know how often she was writing. They may not get the previous letters—but know she was writing and attempting to send them. In her letters she told them that she would be relieved to leave the squalor and wretchedness of London fast behind her, however, would be detained a wee bit longer at Anne Primrose's on Essex Street.

It was that same day that Ceitie MacDowel pulled the forgotten piece of paper from her pocket. "Flory, you know I cannot read. What does this say?"

Flora looked at the note and smiled. It was from one of the oarsmen housed at Mr. Dick's. "Ceitie, this young man is waiting for you. He says he wants to escort you back to Skye. He is your ticket home!"

Ceitie's face matched the color of her hair and when she recovered and laughed. "Does he know where we are?"

"He has left us an address and I will have Lady Primrose let him know you are ready at a moment's notice."

Ceitie wrapped her arms around her dear friend. "Oh Flory, we both get to go home."

"Yes, but I have to stay here just a bit longer so I do not appear ungrateful for all Anne Primrose has done for us—for both of us. I plan to send my letters with you Ceitie, then I will know for sure they will be delivered, and I will be just a few weeks behind you. Lord knows I want to look out across the sea and breath in the enormity of it all. The heather will be in full bloom soon and you will be there. Pick a bunch for me and dry it." Flora's eyes misted. "Oh, how I wish I could go with you on the morrow."

The two friends sat on the bed side-by-side holding hands for a moment wrapped in the nostalgia of home. Then Flora put on her pleasant face as if it were a mask and went to find Lady Primrose of Dunnipace, who she knew would be more than happy to see Ceitie on her way.

Twenty-four hours later a carriage awaited Ceitie MacDowal at the door on Essex Street with a familiar young man holding the door for her and beaming. The two Scottish young ladies, life-long friends and inseparable for the last year embraced for minutes wanting and yet not wanting to let go. Flora spoke in enduring tones. "Biodh beannachd an t-solais ort. Solas às aonais agus solas a-staigh.Biodh solas na grèine beannaichte ort mar theine mòr mòine." (May the blessing of light be upon you. Light without and interior light. May the light of the sun bless you like a great peat fire). Then she slipped a gold filigree ring she had been given, onto Ceitie's finger. With another quick embrace, Ceitie was helped into the homeward-bound carriage. A slap of the reins from the driver announced their parting as the horses leaped forward.

Flora MacDonald quickly became a novelty among a variety of wealthy Londoners and Anne Primrose was equally pleased to be the facilitator of their entertainment. Once again Fora was required to represent what she was not; a happy highlander lassie with a sprig of heather in her blouse. Her schedule was full with visitors starting early in the day and staying until the wee hours. She found most of the guests and their conversation superfluous and boring and frequently had to put her fan in front of her face when she failed to stifle a yawn. The amount of money spent on visitations, plays, and operas appeared ostentatious as they drove past street urchins for another tedious, expensive night out. She was appalled at the fuss and the pedestal on which she was placed along with the days of endless visitors lining their carriages up and down Essex Street.

In no time Flora grew weary, despondent, and lethargic making excuses as to why she could not come down to the parlor and perform once again on the

Fortepiano. Lady Primrose could see her fashionable flower wilting. It was clear the young woman was overwhelmed and Anne Primrose was feeling somewhat guilty. She decided to surprise Flora by taking her to see Handel's new Opera, *Judas Maccabaeus*. Her motives were not totally altruistic though, Anne secretly relished being seen with the notorious Flora MacDonald, the beautiful rebel. Excitedly Lady Anne produced the tickets to the Covent Garden where the opera was to start promptly at six o'clock that evening.

Flora played her role, dressed in her finest, and set off with Lady Primrose arriving an hour early so her hostess could once again rub elbows with the elite and show off her trophy. It was on their way home from the performance that the air became tense in the carriage. Flora felt her neck muscles tighten and the beginnings of a headache.

"Lady Anne, did you know the opera was dedicated and written for Prince William Augustus, the Duke of Cumberland?"

"I did not.

"We Scots refer to him as *'The Butcher'* you know. He ordered men be burned alive as they hid wounded in a barn after the battle at Culloden. Some weren't even soldiers. The British soldiers just barricaded the barn door and set fire to the building." Flora paused before continuing to try and lower her voice. "I dinna care for opera Anne. Most of it is in Italian and I do not speak Italian. I do not comprehend a word and I'm forced to sit there for hours looking pleasant—when I feel far from it."

Lady Primrose fidgeted with her beaded handbag for a minute. "Flora, you aren't the only one personally affected by Culloden. One of my relatives was hung also for their involvement." The only sound in the coach came from the hooves on the cobblestone street. It was then that Anne informed Flora that her admirers had been donating quite a bit of money for her future and she was sure it was over £1,500. She continued by hinting strongly that if Flora stayed in London she could accrue more.

Flora sighed and then gasped as they passed a particular pungent pile of dung in the street.

Automatically Lady Primrose handed her a sachet of smelling salts mixed with French lavender.

"I want to go home. I need to go home. You have been more than kind, more than generous, but I will die here if I stay much longer. I dinna feel close to God here. I say my prayers and they float across the room and seemingly fall flat somewhere, as if they have not been spoken nor heard." Flora did not realize it but her cheeks were wet with tears cascading down as she wept. "And the men, good grief, I have had so many marriage proposals and they do not even know me! They simply want a decoration on their shelves, something they can display like a fine horse."

Mercifully the next morning arrangements were made for Flora MacDonald to return to Scotland via a braw post-chaise, a fast carriage, in the company of an escort, Malcolm MacLeod. Since Scots were still suspect all over England Malcolm and Flora thought it best they traveled as brother and sister. Flora suggested they use the name Robertson. And so it was, Mr. and Miss Robertson were heading north to their Scottish home, leaving London on Monday, July 27, 1747.

As he entered their shared carriage Malcolm started to laugh and said to her in Gaelic, "I went to London to be hanged and returned in a post-chaise with the famous Miss Flora MacDonald. Life can be strange."

CHAPTER 25

Heading Home - Edinburgh

The carriage ride was turbulent with a constant, clattery din of wooden wheels clattering and crashing on the variety of rough surfaces, unable to avoid the deep ruts and potholes. The saving grace was the weather was cool and a gentle rain kept the dreaded road dust down on the ground where it belonged. There were few breaks for conversation, a situation which was more than fine for Flora. She was weary of the never-ending, meaningless chatter required at Lady Primrose's. It was a relief to travel with anonymity as Malcolm's sister, and when the coach switched horses or drivers there were no stares and questions at the roadside inns. The second night found Flora and Malcolm MacLeod in York, where they were welcomed into Dr. John Robert Burton's home.

Dr. Burton was delighted to see them both, their friendships bonded during everyone's captivity together in London at William Dick's. Burton was writing a book about the rebellion and wanted to ask Flora more questions. However, by this time Flora had grown suspicious of any inquiries thrown her way and became keenly protective of all involved from her step-father Hugh to Allan's father and even Allan himself. Yes, Dr. Burton had been a prisoner with them, however, she had not known of him, nor his involvement until Mr. Dick's attic. Flora skirted most of his queries and skillfully kept the conversation flowing between the two men on multiple topics other than her involvement with Prince Charles Stuart's escape.

Dr. Burton had, as she recalled, been released three months before the others and the charges against him were always vague. Her evasiveness was intentional and calculated, sincerely feeling she could trust few. Truly exhausted from the constant jostling of the carriage, she graciously excused herself early leaving the two men enjoying a dram in Dr. Burton's parlor.

Two days later, late in the evening, Mr. Robertson and his sister happily arrived in Edinburgh.

They were both more than welcomed at the home of
Lady Catherine Bruce, a prominent figure in the city.

A year of confinement with limited exercise and
frequent hunger had left Flora weak, lacking in the
slightest energy. She was no longer the robust lass of
Skye and was now requiring a rest most afternoons.
Determined to regain her physical health Flora, once
settled into Lady Bruce's home, began walking daily
about Edinburgh exploring the streets and its shops,
and each day intentionally extending her distance. It
was also an acceptable quiet time where she could sort
out some of her conflicting emotions. She walked up
the hill to the castle one afternoon and slipped into the
crumbling interior of St. Margaret's chapel. The uphill
walk itself had winded Flora and she had already
stopped several times to rest. The chapel was
unoccupied with the exception of a few benches and
Flora slumped gratefully into a waiting pew.

Sitting still, alone in the cool room she felt, at
long last, the presence of God. How she had missed
that connection for the last year. In the surrounding
solitude, Flora could pray, listen, and talk with the

Almighty. She was relieved to be herself once again, without pretense or expectations.

She lay her burdens down one by one in prayer. First was her guilt. She was going home, virtually unscathed when so many lay buried on the moors, and hundreds more were living survivors of rape, pillage, and hunger. Everyone had lost or knew of someone who had experienced great loss and yet, here she sat in one of Lady Primrose's dresses with a pocketful of money. She felt it woefully wrong that she had financially profited when others had suffered so terribly. How was she going to explain what she considered blood money to anyone? Money that the family could probably use, but came from what she considered ill-gain? Children had been orphaned, crops and animals herded off and the people left with virtually nothing. So many of the different clan chief's homes had been burned to the ground. Yet here she sat, safely in the quiet of Saint Margaret's chapel with over £1,500 to her name.

Additionally, Fora felt responsible for the arrests of her kin and friends, Lady Clan, her step-father Hugh

MacDonald, and even Allan's father. Had she not been involved with the Bonnie Prince, she concluded, neither would they. Then the nagging question of how would they receive her when she got home to Skye? Her friends, her family? She was not sure. Would she be welcomed or scorned? Was her family honored or shunned by the community? Had she brought shame to them? No one had said any word in that direction in their letters, but she couldn't help but wonder.

Could she face Hugh MacDonald and her mother again? Because of her, he too had been imprisoned and her mother left alone with wee bairns and a tract of land to manage.

Flora sat for a long time thinking about all that occurred since that night when Neal MacEachen had knocked on her sheiling door. Should she push onward home to Skye in this condition or stay and recuperate? At least she had the funds and a place to stay and there would not be the humiliation of having to ask for additional monies from her family. That too felt shameful for she had profited from the events where her kinsmen clearly had not.

Then, there was Allan. She was nervous about her appearance. Her once shiny hair seemed to flatten limply on her head, the curl and waves gone. Her complexion was sallow lacking the pink on her mouth and cheeks and she was experiencing another, more critical medical problem.

Flora could not be sure how long she sat deep in prayer and contemplation, but the shadows lengthened and she realized it must have been hours. At one point she even imagined her Presbyterian grandfather sitting next to her. The one that had been a minister. She dragged herself up, straightening her skirt, and could at least smile knowing that it was a downhill walk to Lady Bruce's home.

As she strolled along she passed St. Giles and became aware of strings being played nearby. Approaching Niddry's Wynd Flora heard the familiar melody of Pachelbel's famous Cannon lilting in the breeze through the close and from another chapel named St. Mary's. She had been told this was the home of Edinburgh's Musical Society, but to actually be standing under their window, listening to such music made her smile within. She leaned against the rock

wall, closed her eyes and let the melody sail her away

for a few lovely minutes. It felt like decades since she

had heard such inspiration fill the air. Slightly

trembling Flora made a decision regarding her

homeward journey. She must wait—she needed to heal

her heart first and then her body, keenly aware of how

the two were connected, hand in hand.

CHAPTER 26

Edinburgh August 2, 1747

Flory was groping for words, not knowing how to explain to her family her decision to stay in Edinburgh a while longer. She did not want to appear apprehensive about returning to the Isle of Skye, nor did she want to cause any more pain or worry for her loved ones. Returning to Lady Bruce's home she sat down in the library to write her first letter and that would be to Allan. Her shoulder muscles tightened with tension knowing the need to avoid telling Allan the main reason for her delay. She could not tell him, nor anyone that her monthly bleeding had stopped as soon as she and Ceitie had been delivered to the London tower. Women just did not discuss that subject with men. It was a taboo topic to be whispered about only on occasions to other close, trusted women and never ever with the opposite sex.

Being raised with herds of breeding animals, highland girls were no strangers to normal bodily functions. Flora knew stress and diet could temporarily cause her condition, however, she also knew the painful truth. Without the monthly curse, there could be no children. If she could not fully recover, in all likelihood she would not be able to give Allan an heir. She would not marry him under those circumstances. Flora would let the man she so faithfully waited for all these years slip out of her grasp.

Desperate to give herself more time to search for an answer to her dilemma, Flora gently whispered a prayer under her breath as she sharpened the end of a quill with a pen knife. Her head spun and dark thoughts consumed her like a rock in her gut. Gaelic, their native tongue, would be the best language to use writing Allan. The reason for Flora's stall was her secret and hers alone. She wanted to work this out by herself and most importantly on her own terms. She preferred to suffer hidden in Edinburgh quietly, then under her family's watchful eye where inevitably the truth might be revealed. She missed her dear friend and confidant Ceitie.

The solution could be in her handwriting itself. Her family, including Allan, had gently teased her for some time that her letters, though always welcome, were practically illegible and they passed them around from one to another trying to decipher her scribbling. Flora, who could read and speak four languages was a novice when it came to writing script. Good penmanship was considered an essential skill for boys, yet was not taught until they were proficient at reading, around the age of twelve. Young ladies, like herself, had to learn on their own. To complicate matters, the cursive manuscript was entirely different from the print that Flory was used to reading. It was visually another whole language. Would improving her handwriting suffice as an excuse to stay away?

It would be socially acceptable to tell her loved ones she was in a fragile state and needed to regain some strength before traveling further. She would tell them that to occupy her time she desired to improve her handwriting. Her letter to Allan would explain that one David Beatt, a schoolmaster with Jacobite sympathies, was living in Edinburgh and highly recommended as a tutor. The catch was he was out of town and she needed to wait for his return. Flora dipped her newly sharpened quill into the ink and began.

Dearest Allan…

It was then that a single salty tear slid down Flora's cheek creating a catastrophe on the still-wet ink. Allan's name unfurled and swirled into an indescribable blot. Quietly she looked at the wet smudges and folded the paper onto itself before sliding it off the table. She would have to start over.

❈

It was the middle of September before Flora could meet with David Beatt and begin her daily writing lessons. He of course had heard of her and was deeply honored to be engaged as her tutor. Her notoriety in Edinburgh had cooled some and unlike her stay on the *Eltham* while anchored on Leith Road, the visitors were kept at bay by the wise Catherine Bruce. Malcolm MacLeod was one who was allowed to come to the home frequently and often would escort Flora down the streets to her manuscript training. Flora found Malcolm easy to talk to and mentioned how kind he was in several of her letters to her mother back home at Armadale.

Then there was the problem of Robert Forbes, or as he was more correctly referred to as Reverend, the rector of the Episcopal Church in Edinburgh. Reverend Forbes was also a Jacobite supporter and for his efforts had been duly arrested, being held first in Sterling Castle and later at Edinburgh Castle. He had been released in May of the previous year. Forbes was intent on documenting the history of the attempt to restore Charles Edward Stuart to the throne. Centrally focused on this goal, he wanted to record as many first-person accounts as he could to preserve the events for posterity. Forbes' goal was to be scrupulously accurate in his documentation, hoping the interviews and stories would be as faultless as humanely possible. This of course included the first-person accounts of the illusive Flora MacDonald.

Lady Catherine Bruce made multiple attempts to get Flora to talk to Forbes, arranging teas and dinners, however, Flora remained uneasy and would not attend. She felt strongly that anything in writing, if the distrustful crown changed their minds, could once again incriminate hundreds of honest people. People whose only crime was siding with the Scottish house of Stuart, people who rightfully believed Charles Edward Stuart should be sitting on Britain's throne rather than the German distant cousins. Flora absolutely could not bear to be a part of anything that might implicate and harm one more innocent person.

The orange and yellow hues of autumn began to fade around Edinburgh, apples were stored and the daylight hours became noticeably shorter as one season prepared to slip into another. Flora was spending more and more time with Malcolm MacLeod and David Beatt, all the while dutifully practicing and improving her script. She wrote copious letters to her family and Allan displaying her handwriting progress, describing life in Edinburgh, but also expressing, without mentioning names, the pressure she was under to give her accounts of the rebellion and her role.

There was a cold November rain pelting down when who should appear at Lady Bruce's door, none other than Dr. John Burton. Apparently, Flora MacDonald was not the only person in the house writing letters. Lady Bruce had invited him to Edinburgh to see if he could persuade Flora to meet with Robert Forbes. Unbeknownst to Flora was the doctor and the reverend had also been in contact equally sharing the same goal of accurately documenting for history the events of 1745.

A variety of guests continued finding themselves at Lady Bruce's door as if invited. The first two weeks of December were crisp and clear. The sky was a sharp blue and the interior fires kept burning bright. Still, everyone was dressing in their warmest. It was to her surprise and delight when Flora got an extra special gift as she opened the front door to find her dear friend Donald Roy MacDonald filling up the frame. She held out both her hands with a full smile and he in turn took them in his own without saying a word, their expressive eyes laughing in merriment. Flory now had someone from home, someone whom she shared so much with, a friend for as long as she could remember. She had not laid eyes on Donald Roy since that fateful evening in Portree and now his mere presence was thrilling.

"Oh come in, come in" She couldn't wait to usher the man into the parlor taking his wrap and handing it to one of the servants. "Can we get you a cup of tea? Have you eaten? How did you get here?" Flora's questions came tumbling out without waiting for answers as she pulled him into the room and by the warming fire.

Donald Roy smiled chuckling out loud. "You look so good Flora. So much better than the drowned rat you appeared to be as you rode off at Portree." Then he commented that he just made a rhyme and laughed more.

Donald Roy was the linchpin to her relating her side of the story for posterity. The two spent the entire afternoon together before he had the opportunity to tell her that he had come to Edinburgh to give his first-person account to the Reverend Forbes. He decided not to even try to persuade Flora to do the same. He quietly shared his reasons and let her make her own choices. Donald Roy knew Flora since she was a wee bairn and knew too that she frequently balked when told what to do. She was a strong-willed lassie who definitely made up her own mind. Precisely why she had been perfect to assist Charles Edward's successful escape.

Lady Bruce returned in the afternoon and immediately requested the guest room be prepared for Donald Roy along with an extra plate for supper. She was genuinely surprised when he told her he had walked from Skye.

"Walked all that distance? On your injured foot?"

"Aye madam, and it only took twelve days. I've made a remarkable recovery and I consider it a bit of a miracle. I even wrote my foot an ode." And then he laughed heartily slapping his knee. "An ode to my foot."

With very little coaxing Donald Roy recited his ode to the ladies, first in Latin as he originally wrote it, and then repeated it to the gathered audience in Gaelic. The British government may have outlawed the language, but they were not inside the homes eavesdropping and it was a difficult law to enforce.

After supper Flora sat down to Lady Bruce's harpsichord and played the music she had been practicing, Bach's French Suite No. 3 in B minor. Flora blushed when Donald Roy and Catherine Bruce simultaneously clapped their hands and asked her to play another.

She apologized before she started playing her second selection, explaining she was still working on it and that it may be missing the string section. A minute later Catherine and Donald Roy were mesmerized as Flora's fingers glided over the keyboard and the notes circled the room like wisps of angels as she played Pachelbel's Canon in D Major. There was a long moment of silence as she finished the piece, and for a split second Flora wondered if it had been too soon to play it for anyone.

Donald Roy was the first to speak. "Flory you have moved me to my very soul. Beautifully done lassie, beautifully done."

The group moved their chairs from the harpsichord to the fire, Lady Bruce poured them each a dram and requested they tell her about their last meeting at the Inn at Portree. The two began talking at once and laughter again filled the room as Donald Roy explained Charles Stuart's reluctance to drink from the communal water bucket and how his refusal was drawing unwanted attention. "I kicked him gently under the table. Twice!" Flora confessed.

"And I told him in Latin because he does not speak Gaelic, that in he needed to act as if he was one of them." Donald Roy once again laughed heartily at the recollection of McNabb's Inn.

It was the following morning, after a generous breakfast, that Donald Roy and Flora, smiling arm in arm, walked to the Reverend Robert Forbes' Manse in Leith to give him their versions of the accounts surrounding the defeat at Culloden and Charles

Edward Stuart's eventual escape. It was the first time in too many months that Flora felt truly happy.

CHAPTER 27

Forbes, Yule & Hogmanay - 1748

The Reverend Robert Forbes, like many men before him, was immediately enchanted by Flora MacDonald. He had heard her referred to as the beautiful rebel, but seeing her in person took him aback. Donald Roy introduced the two and the unmarried Reverend almost lost his focus as he ushered them both into his rectory parlor.

Tea was brought and he began questioning Flora, but on a lighter note than his academic mind wanted. He first asked her what songs they had sung while crossing in the boat to Skye. Flora looked at the man gently but steadily and relayed that they were all frightened for their lives. They weren't singing songs at a soiree to be recalled nostalgically at a later date. And did Forbes fully realize that Charles Edward did not speak nor understand a word of Gaelic? Everything had to be painstakingly translated for him or they had to communicate exclusively in French.

Forbes quickly realized that not only was Flora beautiful, but she also had a sharp mind and was appearing to resent his superfluous questions. He wanted to ask her how she happened to meet Felix O'Neil but thought better of it and simply asked her to give her account of meeting the Prince for the first time, to their departure at Portree. As she spoke he took scrupulous notes asking only a few questions for his own clarification.

On the way back to Lady Bruce's home Flora told Donald Roy that she would write her mother and request some of the things Charles Edward had left behind. She thought she might give some to Robert Forbes then mentioned also that she received a letter from Neil MacEachen in France making a similar request. Cousin Neil wrote that in their escape they had been chased by British ships, yet were able to outrun them and deliver Prince Charlie to safety.

Flora chose not to mention that Neil had included a poem to her he had written entitled *Beautiful Virgin.*

December of 1747 found the Reverend Forbes busy with the approach of the Yule season. The Bruce household in Leith was also experiencing increased activity with friends coming frequently and a steady stream of hearty food laid out nightly along the dining table. There were platters of slow-roasted beef, pork and lamb served with plenty of potatoes swirling in butter. Fresh-caught salmon would be fried and desserts piled high including shortbread, plumb cake, and petticoat tails topped with fruit. And of course, when all was finished and cleared away good whiskey was brought out to be shared. The traditional Gaelic wishes of December filled the air behind the closed doors. "Nollaig chridheil agus bliadhna mhath ur—Merry Christmas and Happy New Year".

The month slipped by quickly and before anyone realized it they were celebrating New Year's Hogmanay. Hogmanay, with its traditional black bun bread and first foot into friends' homes. You wanted to be the first to visit friends after midnight and be the first to go into their homes in the new year. In addition, the Scots generally wanted the first person in their home to be a dark-haired man and for Flora, that would mean none other than her Allan. It would be a miracle if he came to Lady Bruce's. Flora's heart flew back to Skye and the great Hogmanay celebrations they had there lasting for days instead of hours. A deep longing settled into her heart. No the now—he would not be here now.

Donald Roy was a mentor and unofficial guardian for Flora while he was in Edinburgh, a dedicated father figure. He became increasingly concerned with her attachment to the young Malcolm MacLeod and Malcolm's inability to support her in any way, let alone pay for his own way home. With a few hints dropped heavily in the right direction, the Jacobite supporters hanging around the Bruce household presented Malcolm with a purse large enough to get him home to Brea and out of their heroine's life. The timing was impeccable, for as soon as Malcolm MacLeod left Edinburgh, Flora's brother James arrived with a trunk full of treasures.

It was a grand reunion. James had grown taller, his shoulders broader and his thick dark hair cascaded freely down his neck. It had been eighteen months since Flora had seen him and immediately felt his good luck, the new year's charm she needed.

When James opened the trunk he brought from home, Flora's eyes were treated to the clothes of Betty Burke and the garters of Charles Stuart folded neatly on the top. Her laugh escaped aloud and she smiled broadly when she saw it all again. But her face quickly faded to a wistful look as she gazed at a few of her own dresses packed lovingly by her mother. They were the ones Flora had worn in what seemed like another life and time on the Isle of Skye. Touching the dresses tenderly, she lifted one holding it to the front of herself. Closing her eyes she could feel her mother telling her, reminding her, of who she was and it was time to return to her heart, return to her roots, return home to Armadale.

Between Donald Roy and her brother James, the days slipped by rapidly with gossip from home seasoned with unbridled mirth. It was the tonic that Flora unknowingly needed. She woke up one morning to discover a small red stain on her sheets and her heart beat like a bird's wing in flight. A bit terrified she calmed herself knowing she was going to be right as rain.

The January weather was turning bitter, cold and came with some snow. There were still so many good people across Scotland left in wretched circumstances after Culloden. Many, in their desperation to feed themselves and their families, had become thieves and highwaymen. The inns nor roads crisscrossing across the land were not predictably safe. Donald Roy needed to return to North Uist where he was engaged as a tutor and James MacDonald was also greatly needed back home. The two agreed to make the journey together citing safety in numbers. They also agreed and informed Flora it would be prudent for her to wait until spring when they would send someone to escort her home.

On one hand, Flora was relieved. It would give her a few more months to make sure she was functioning normally as a woman and to also practice her handwriting. She did not relish the idea of slogging through ice, snow and sleet to return like a drowned rat to her mother's home. On the other hand, there was a strong yearning she could not deny, and that was to return to her roots much like the salmon rushing upstream to spawn.

Additional weeks in Edinburgh would afford her the time to honor Neil MacEachen's request to sell any of the Prince's relics and to send the proceeds to France. Flora sent over a bundle to Reverend Forbes which included fabric from Betty Burke's dress and a brogue. She was so proud of her accomplishment that she wrote Neil a long letter including the money she raised from sales.

CHAPTER 28

Return to Armadale - Spring 1748

It was Saturday, March 22nd that Flora MacDonald and Lady Catherine Bruce went to see Robert Forbes in the late morning. It was only Flora's second time to see the Reverend in person and little did he know it would be the last. As before, he was totally enthralled and overdid his hospitality fussing over the two women as if they were royalty. The attention made both ladies uncomfortable and they excused themselves as soon as they could politely. Later Forbes would write that Flora was illusive, when in actuality she felt suffocated in his presence. It was such a lovely spring day that after they left Rev. Forbes' the two ladies took the opportunity and walked into the outskirts of Edinburgh where they were treated to spotted bluebells growing in the spring sunshine. Flora ran her hand across them smiling and told Lady Bruce how her mother always called them Fairy Thimbles because so many folks thought the fairies lived among them.

"Lady Bruce, I need to be returning home soon and I want you to know how truly grateful and thankful I am for all your support and hospitality. You have been like a second mother to me."

The older woman hugged her affectionately and locked her arm in hers. "Flora MacDonald, it has been my pleasure and you too have seemed like a daughter. We are behind you my dear, all the way." Lady Bruce started to laugh. "You know I still have Robert the Bruce's sword. If you were a man I would knight you. We know full well who should be on the throne of Scotland."

Two weeks later the maid at Lady Bruce's opened the door to a complete stranger whose imposing presence filled up the entrance. He asked for the mistress of the house. When Flora came to the entry you could have knocked her over with a feather. There stood Allan MacDonald, immaculately dressed and smiling, and when he saw her held out both his arms. Flora paused a moment totally speechless then moved into his long-awaited embrace. Every apprehension evaporated as he held her tightly his head down to hers murmuring sweet words. They had been exchanging long letters however, this was the first time in close to two years they had actually seen each other in person. Neither could take their eyes off the other and their hands stayed clasped tightly.

By this time Catherine Bruce also appeared at the entrance and guessed immediately who the man wrapped around Flora was. She held out her hand to a laughing Allan MacDonald.

"I'm Catherine Bruce sir, and I assume you are the famous Allan MacDonald."

Allan blushed a bit, "You are correct about the name madam, however, I believe it is my love Flory here who is the celebrated one."

"Oh Allan, not you too," Flora smiled. "You know the only thing I ever wanted was to be your wife. I never wanted anything else."

"And you shall my love, you shall. But first, we must get you home to Armadale and to the Isles."

The two had a great deal of catching up to do and started chatting immediately. Flora began listing all the people she wanted Allan to meet. She felt as if some of them thought he was a fragment of her imagination and wanted to show him off.

"Aye me lassie, I will meet your friends, but we must get home soon. Spring is here, the caorach are lambing and the coos dropping their young. I'm needed back soon to lend a hand."

For the next few days there was a flurry of activity. Lady Bruce and Flora took Allan about Edinburgh additionally entertaining many guests in the home. Allan too had some friends he wanted to visit from his school days when both he and Flory had been sent to this city to further their educations so many years ago.

It was a fine mid-April day, the 19th to be exact, when Flora, escorted by the striking Allan MacDonald boarded a ship awaiting in Leith and headed north around the top of Scotland. There had been some discussion about their chosen means of transportation. Flora was understandably reluctant to board another ship in Leith, but Allan explained that the roads between Edinburgh and the Hebrides were rough, rutted, and filled with marauders of every shape and size. His da and her parents all agreed that a ship would be the safest means of transportation at this point. Besides, he said winking, it gave them time to be alone together without the heaps of fuss from the well-meaning folks of Edinburgh.

Aboard ship and at last alone, Flora was able to relate to Allan all that had happened to her; the Tower, Mr. Dick's house, and the money she felt was ill-gotten from a collection of admirers. Allan in turn confessed he was at Fort Augustus, but not as a prisoner, but rather like her step-father Hugh, wearing the red coat of the British. This was not a concern to Flora, she knew Allan's heart was that of a true Scotsman.

In the evenings, the two sat side by side on the covered hatch, gazing at the sunsets and listening to water splash against the side of the hull as they sailed silently. They would sit for long hours after the sun went down gazing at the night sky splattered with millions upon millions of twinkling stars.

Flora told Allan more about Charles Edward Stuart. How the Prince would mumble while he slept, repeating in the night, 'Poor Scotland—poor Scotland.'

She relayed that she felt the Prince would get totally confused, thinking people would betray him and frequently it was the very folks that were trying to save him, and then she told him about their Bonnie Prince's penchant for drinking to excess. She confessed her reluctance for any more attention regarding her role with Charles Edward Stuart. Her motivation then had been her Presbyterian upbringing and the story of the good Samaritan. Flora said in her heart she would have truly helped anyone.

As they sailed Flora described to Allan Lady Anne Primrose, and how kind and generous she had been. She shared the fact that Anne Primrose had set up a school for the orphaned lads of Culloden. Looking into her lap Flora thought to herself that it would have been nice to have included the girls, the poor waifs left to their own devices for survival, and could only console herself with the thought that at least some of the orphaned children were getting help, even if it was not all nor fair.

Allan also opened his heart to his future bride. "Things have changed for Scots all over Flory. There are new laws and new acts. You know we were disarmed, we are prohibited to wear our tartans or speak our language." Allan stopped here, looked at her, and grinned as he was explaining all this in Gaelic. He continued. "There is more—the clan chiefs have been stripped of their power. We are not going to have the same controls we had over our land tenants and the position of chief is no longer to be inherited legally. The English are trying to break our backs. I'm not sure how it is all going to work out. Most of us just want peace. It would be best Flory to keep our feelings about the monarchy to ourselves and only within our families at this point."

Flora spun the gold ring adorning her finger. There were tiny roses of diamonds and leaves of green enamel and emeralds. She remembered the words inscribed on the inside: *Flora, Preserver of the White Rose.* It was one of the more than generous gifts from the Jacobite admirers in London.

To their home in the Hebrides the two lovers joyfully sailed, getting reacquainted after their long separation, sharing their hearts, their hopes, and their dreams. Allan telling her how thrilled he was that his sister Anne and her husband had two young ones now and how much he enjoyed watching the wee bairns grow. He confessed that he wanted the same for he and Flora in the near future.

The ship docked in Aberdeen overnight where cargo was loaded and unloaded and where a few gentlemen disembarked. Aberdeen was a bustling port with fishermen and traders actively working the boats tied along the pier. Allan and Flora also got off for a while to stretch their legs and walk about the hilly city. They were told that the Duke of Cumberland had resided here for a short time before going after Charles Stuart. The mere thought of the butcher sent chills down both of their backs.

A spring storm bustled into the port with accompanying showers and a cutting wind blowing off the North Sea. The Captain decided to wait it out before heading further northwest and in turn, Allan and Flora chose to stay at a local inn for a few nights, a respite from their tiny cabins aboard the ship. Allan chuckled telling Flora that his roommate on board had snored so loudly he thought he was in a pig stye and that a good night's sleep would do them both good.

Eventually, the ship and its travelers, sailing again arrived where the Ness River flowed into the sea and the port of Inverness. From there Allan arranged for a smaller vessel to deliver both he and Flora home.

Docking at Armadale they disembarked and walked up the hill toward her house. It was her little terrier Sidger who spotted her first. He had been laying across the sunlit doorway, but when he lifted his head and recognized Flora he gave a welcoming bark or two before streaking like lightning toward his long-missed mistress. Sidger gained speed as he ran down the hill and Flora leaned down as the dog lept into her arms wiggling in delight and licking her face. She threw back her head and openly laughed at his loyal welcome, holding his warmth close to her chest as she spun around.

Behind Sidger her family came tumbling out of the house one by one almost crushing her with their embraces. Her mother Marion began to sob saying she thought she would never see her again. Marion would hold her, let go to see her face, and then embrace her all over again. Annabella stood back but was smiling from ear to ear waiting her turn and James came scurrying out from one of the sheds with his two younger brothers tagging behind.

Hugh's immense frame eventually filled the doorway of their home and Flora stepped back. Her mother's letters assured her Hugh held no ill will towards her and he blamed her not in the least for his arrest, nor the time he spent as a prisoner. All these trepidations which Flora held heavily for months were erased in a moment as the big man strode to her side, picking her off the ground in his considerable arms and swung her about like a doll.

Allan only stayed the night at Armadale, anxious himself to be getting home to Kingsburgh where he knew he was more than needed during the lambing and calving season. After an early morning breakfast of oats and bannocks Allan and Flora found themselves once again saying goodbye. Allan slipped his arm around her slender waist. "Not for so long this time lassie. I am in need of a wife." He kissed her gently on her forehead as she promised to wed him as soon as they could.

A few days later Flora's brother Angus arrived from their childhood home at Milton where he had taken over his father's holdings. One-eyed Hugh had managed the estate for all these years after Ranald's death so it could be bestowed to Angus intact. A banquet for he, Penelope, and Flora was set and the family, together intact for the first time in several years celebrated heartedly. Joyous laughter filled the house as they told stories on each other and included a few of the other, colorful inhabitants of the island. Sidger never left Flora's side, even when they moved to the sitting room to plan a walk and perhaps boating on the morrow.

CHAPTER: 29

Summer at Armadale — July 29, 1748

Returning to Skye after a two-year absence, Flora could see many changes in the people and the area, yet a great deal remained the same. Her mother Marion was thrilled to have her back home and she was just in time to help the local women waulking some tweeds. The summer sky brought with it a crisp breeze which would be advantageous for the long day's work. Marion cleared an immense well worn wooden table and a collection of chairs had been set around for the eight women she expected, along with their pre-soaked tweeds. There was a feeling of festivity in the air in spite of the fact the waulking was arduous work.

Flora looked forward to the activities as the kitchen filled up with familiar faces both youthful and weathered. The tweeds needed to be fulled to make them more durable and waterproof for whoever was to eventually wear them in a garment.

Much to her delight Ceitie MacDowal was one of the first to embrace her old friend with Flora feeling Ceitie's bulging belly against her. Ceitie tossed her red hair and grinned telling Flora about her happiness with Donald McNeill. "Oh Flory, we started out hand-fasting but…," Ceitie patted her stomach, "We needed to get from his croft to the kirk in short order." Ceitie and Flora both spontaneously threw their heads back and giggled.

The Scottish women arriving all hugged Flora in greeting as if she had been away just a short while. Then they reminded her that it was bad luck not to move the fabric clockwise as they worked the tweeds—in case she had forgotten. Her younger sister Annabella joined the gossipy group, a blossoming lassie of fifteen years who, much to Flory's delight, sat herself down by her sister reaching under the table and giving Flora's hand an encouraging squeeze. Sidger made his way in undetected and settled quietly between Flora's feet under her flowered linen skirt.

Marion slapped the soggy cloth, pre-soaked in maistir down on the table, where the ladies pulled it to its full length before they rolled the material. After measuring end-to-end the women, in synchronized motion, gripped the edges, and lifted the wet bundle up sightly before they slapped it down again in unison. As they developed a rhythm, they moved a small section of the fabric to their left each time, then picked it up again repeating the movements. The chanting began with one taking the lead in song. They started slowly with a cadence of a slow walk, slap, thump, slap, thump—the main singer making up words and singing gossip, with the others following each line, smiling and occasionally adding something along the way. Steeped in centuries of folklore they were intent on not repeating any verse. As the material dried and softened the cadence increased, the mood became light, and the labor cheerful.

The Scottish ladies took a break in the afternoon, fawning over Flora and teasing Annabella about her beau. Marion set out an extra glass of milk as a lucky offering to Loireag, the fairy woman who they believed came to all waulkings. A hearty lamb and barley stew was served up along with freshly baked bannocks. One of the ladies was off measuring the cloth a second time when Annabella questioned her as to how many more songs.

The afternoon session started with Marion leading the singing, but after a few songs, she coaxed Flora to start one. As Sidger shifted under her skirt Flora thought for a moment before making one up about the wee doggie under the lassie's skirts. The ladies were so tickled by her spontaneous lyrics that they could hardly sing trying to hold in their merriment.

It was the laughter, gossip and endless singing, along with the rhythmic pounding of the cloth, that erased most of Flora's anxiety and fears of returning to Skye. She was home, accepted back into the fold as one of them. No one asked her about her involvement with the Prince, an unspoken agreement among the women. Likewise, no one mentioned London or the Tower. Instead, there were hints and teases about Allan MacDonald and his escorting her back home to them unchaperoned—back home to all of them on the Isle as if she had been away for a simple extended trip.

As early evening approached Marion, Flora and Annabella strode with the waulking party out into their open yard. The women stood for a moment all gazing at the ocean's breathtaking beauty. The accumulation of dark clouds had broken into pieces with streams of sunlight cascading onto the water. The inky ocean appeared like velvet with spun silver shimmering in random patterns across her vast surface. It never ceased to amaze any of them—the constant, ever-changing moods and color of their sky and vast ocean.

Flora, lost in thought, and looking out at the scene in front of her, was totally jolted when one of the women slapped her on the backside playfully saying loudly that they did the tweed so nicely it would, "Keep anyone's arse dry on a rainy day."

Hugs were shared among the laughing women and they continued to sing as they parted, each going their separate ways.

CHAPTER 30

Wedding Bells—November, 1750

November 6, 1750, was a cool day when Flora and Allan MacDonald of Kingsburgh finally said their wedding vows and officially tied the knot. They complied with the old Scottish Nursery Rhyme that a marriage in 'bleak November, that only joys will come, remember.'

A few days before the wedding, her young lady friends and relatives gathered for a hen party. Many chickens were given as gifts to be used for the wedding feast and they needed preparation. Young and old women happily plucked the culled hens, rubbed them with salted herbs, and piled them in baskets keeping a few of the softer feathers to stuff pillows and comforters for Flora's new home. That party extended from early afternoon well into the evening. Along with keen gossip, laughter, and hilarity, there was music, some drink, and an abundance of sumptuous food.

Some may have considered their actual wedding a simple celebration by Hebrides standards, however, it was well attended. The home at Armadale was full of guests, including the beloved Donald Roy. Relatives and friends had been arriving for days ahead with many planning to stay a few days after, extending the celebration to almost a week. A great deal of planning and cooking had been done in anticipation of the nuptials and even a few extra people were hired to help. Raisins were soaked in whiskey and then folded into soft buns. Shortbread, made to break and share, was cooked along with the traditional cranachan. As Allan came through the bustling kitchen filled with clinking pans and women talking, he surveyed all the food, then chuckled saying, "We need not use all the whiskey in the baking. I can think of a better use."

Flora grabbed a broom and pretended to sweep him out of the busy kitchen. This pantomime was followed by gales of women laughing.

There were a variety of valid reasons the wedding had been postponed multiple times. Flora felt they had almost waited a decade to make their formal commitments in front of friends and family. It could have put it off again after the tragic death of her two youngest brothers, however, they decided that life, as fragile as it was, must go on and there had already been enough roadblocks to this wedding day. Flora, out of respect to her young deceased brothers, wore a black silk wedding gown with a lovely broach and earrings gifted her by one of the Jacobite sympathizers in London. Both she and Allan, as a symbol of good luck, carried a sprig of dried white heather that Marion had prepared for them with ribbons trailing.

Flora had written some of her own music for the occasion and after the brief ceremony, the guests danced to reels and strathspeys, rolling up the rugs in the main room of the Kingsburgh home. Donald McKay, Hugh's favorite piper, played on until his cheeks were ruddy, and then, played some more after a few hot toddies.

Tables were piled with spiced buns hot from an oven and plenty of fried chicken. After ample whiskey toddies for everyone the storytellers entertained the enraptured, and in some cases inebriated, guests with a few new and then some old favorite stories, always with a twist.

The Scots Magazine would later publish a small article about Flora and Allan MacDonald's marriage, not failing to mention that she was, 'the young lady who aided the escape of the young Chevalier'.

When the Reverend Robert Forbes read this in Edinburgh he immediately wrote to Donald Roy voicing his disappointment of not being invited to the affair.

CHAPTER 31

Flodigarry —1751

It was in the early spring of 1751 that the young couple, expecting their first child, moved to a large stone cottage named Flodigarry on the Northeast side of Skye. Flora spent some of her money making their new home just as she wanted, cozy and warm with windows looking out across the bay. The interior walls were whitewashed, curtains hung and her spinet installed in the parlor. She could not have been happier and more at peace with herself feeling a wee babe move inside her belly. She would wonder if it was a tiny hand or foot that occasionally pushed and when that happened a smile would creep across her face as she placed her hand in the area saying hello to the welcome bairn.

Flory and son finally met on October 22, 1751, after a relatively easy labor and with her mother Marion by her side. Breaking all tradition in the naming of the first child after its grandfather, the new laddie was christened Charles MacDonald after Charles Edward Stuart.

Word reached Flodigarry that the Prince of Wales, Frederick, the man instrumental in saving Flora's life in London had died unexpectedly of a lung injury at the young age of 44. Frederick left behind ten children, his eldest next in succession to the throne.

Time on the Isle turned like a rhythmic spinning wheel. There was a cadence, a rich daily pattern of routine events. Two years after Charles' birth Flora easily delivered another son naming him John and a short year after that arrived a small daughter on February 18, 1754. This daughter Flora named Anne. Allan thought it was after his beloved sister, but Flora was thinking of Lady Anne Primrose with whom she still exchanged letters.

Almost a year to the day, February 21, 1755, Flora delivered another son to Allan and this one they agreed should be named after Allan's father, so he was christened Alexander MacDonald, but forever was called by the nickname Sandy.

Flora was caught up in an endless cycle of hippins needing to be washed and toddlers under her feet and even though exhausted some days she relished what she referred to as the contented time. Often she would sing to the growing brood the sweet rich melodies of Scotland. Songs like *Mary Hamilton* would lilt up the stairs and fill the rooms with music accompanied by the spinet or whoever was present with a fiddle under their arm.

Word is to the kitchen gone, and word is to the Hall
And word is up to Madam the Queen, and that's the worst of all
That Mary Hamilton has borne a babe
To the highest Stuart of all
Oh rise, arise Mary Hamilton
Arise and tell to me
What thou hast done with thy wee babe
I saw and heard weep by thee

"I notice dear wife that you change the words of the song," Allan commented lovingly.

"You dinna expect me to sing them the truth, do you? Aye, she put him in a tiny boat and sent him out to sea. Goodness no!"

Allan slid his arm about her waist as they walked out into the night to watch the "mire dancers," the northern lights frolic across the black velvet of night. The magenta colors twisted and turned into bright yellow streaks then moved in an out of green columns of light as if choreographed to music. Even though both had watched the sky dance many times they never tired of the celestial event, standing in awe of the phenomenon. Allan muttered their Gaelic name under his breath, "solais tuath".

Flora reminded him that children born under the Northern Lights are blessed with good fortune. Allan bent down to kiss her and led her back to the hushed cottage wondering if children conceived would have the same benefit.

It was August 16th of that year, 1756 when Ranald was born, a healthy laddie named after Flora's birth father, Ranald MacDonald. And Flora sang…

Baloo baleerie, baloo baleerie

Baloo baleerie, baloo balee

Gang awa' peerie faeries,
Gang awa' peerie faeries,
Gang awa' peerie faeries,
Frae oor ben noo.

Baloo baleerie, baloo baleerie

Baloo baleerie, baloo balee

Doon come the bonny angels,
Doon come the bonny angels,
Doon come the bonny angels,
Tae oor ben noo.

Baloo baleerie, baloo baleerie

Baloo baleerie, baloo balee

Sleep saft my baby,
Sleep saft my baby,
Sleep saft my baby,
In oor ben noo.

Baloo baleerie, baloo baleerie

Baloo baleerie, baloo balee

The spinning years were blissful with Flora grateful for each day. Her brother Angus frequently arrived with Penelope and their children filling the yard of the Flodigarry stone home with the cousins playing tag and jump rope, infecting everyone with their squealing laughter. All hearts were aglow watching the bairns play and grow along with old Sidger running about with them across the grass.

In the evenings' Flora frequently read to the children as the family warmed by the peat fire after their supper. They giggled over Tom Thumb's adventures and gasped at Robinson Crusoe's exploits from shipwrecks to surviving the cannibals. Believing the devil finds work for idle hands Flora worked when the children slept, spinning, knitting, or making lace. She started to educate and stimulate the imaginations of her little brood during rain-dreary days from frequently ordered books. Short classes were held for the lot in English, French, and Latin with many a bible passage to be memorized.

The young MacDonald family read the Scots News when they got copies and exchanged letters frequently with their loved ones.

Neil MacEachen wrote that he was living in Sancerre in Central France, had married, and was changing his last name to MacDonald.

Marion wrote that Ceitie, now Mrs. McNeill, had gone to the colonies in America. She and Donald decided to seek a new life for themselves and their young ones. They had left on a ship sailing from Portree a month earlier.

Lady Anne Primrose wrote confessing that in September of 1750, Charles Edward Stuart returned to London in total disguise and that he had only stayed for five days, however, he had stayed with her.

Annabella wrote she was to marry Alexander MacDonald of Cuidreach and invited them to her wedding.

Then Allan's sister Anne wrote that her husband Ranald was quite ill.

CHAPTER 32

September, 1757

It was dawn, the last day of September, 1757 and the rain had been incessantly pounding the thatch roof for over a week. Threads of dim light from a lone window crept down the dark hallway of the Flodigarry house. Marion quietly closed the heavy wooden door to the bedroom speaking to Allan in the hall. Her apron was stained with Flora's blood and her white disheveled hair haloed her face.

Marion spoke in a hushed tone barely audible. "Allan, Flory has given you another son, but she is very weak. Her stamina for such things is gone." The small woman looked down at her stained clothes. "Flory isn't one of your brood mares. She will never deny your affection you ken, but dinna be gòrach—these babies are going to kill her." Her tone changed as she crossed her arms. "You need to sleep somewhere else!" There was a pause as Marion met Allan's worried eyes. "It is either that or you will have a family of wee orphans if you keep this up."

Marion continued by telling Allan he should not go in for a while, that Flora was getting much-needed sleep and that she was going to clean up and start some broth.

Allan's face was lined with worry and concern. "Aye Mum Marion, I understand, and I will be quiet, but I am going in to sit with me wife." He reached around her and soundlessly turned the knob to their sleeping chamber letting himself in.

Flora's half-sister Annabella was wrapping the sleeping newborn as he entered the room. She held the small bundle tightly against her chest brushing past her brother-in-law with a disapproving scowl.

Allen silently settled himself next to Flora's bed and gazed at her. Her skin was the same shade as the sheets she lay on, a colorless face with dark auburn hair flowing across the pillow. He couldn't help but think how fragile and small she appeared and yet how breathtakingly beautiful she was. His heart felt an overwhelming love for her as he bowed his head in prayer holding her limp hand.

The wee laddie James was christened two weeks later at the Presbyterian church in Portree. Flora was unable to attend, but feeling stronger and deeply grateful for her mother, sister, and servants who were tending her growing brood. Annabella returned home shortly after the christening to her own family at Armadale.

CHAPTER 33

1757-1766 Passel of Children

For the next nine years, life on the Isle of Skye at Flodigarry moved in a rhythmic cycle with the seasons. The crop of children grew, there were squabbles, scrapes, and a few broken bones. There were days of learning, laughter and occasional tears. Out-of-date newspapers and letters arrived, Annabella and Angus would visit and the family continued to weave itself tightly together as the patterned cloth of their looms.

Allan's mother, Lady Florence MacDonald passed away, on March 18, 1759, and as promised, Flora supervised the washing of her body, combing her hair and then tucking the sheet Prince Charles Edward Stuart had slept on under Lady Florence's chin and down her feet.

There was contentment at Flodigarry— predictable and comfortable times. There were days of toil and sacred days of celebration. The mornings began with hearty breakfasts and evenings finished in prayer.

Round and round the days spun like the wheel in the living room, turning their wool to yarn and the yarn to cloth. Primary teeth came in and then in due course fell out exposing larger teeth in the gaping holes. Mail improved with newspapers and parcels arriving more frequently.

In late October of 1760, King George II passed away. Since George II's death was proceeded by his son Frederick, the throne went to his twenty-two-year-old Grandson, George III. George II was the last British monarch to be born and raised in Germany and there was a sense throughout Scotland that his grandson, George III was a great deal more British and less Hanoverian. It helped that English was his primary tongue and he was not dashing off to Germany at every opportunity.

Sometime, in the spring of 1764, Allan noticed how quiet Flora had become in the last week. Neil MacEachen had sent her a small book from France and she had been reading it with intensity in the evenings. It was time to inquire. "Flora my love, what are you reading that has spun you into such deep thought?"

Flora looked up, got a twinkle in her eye, and mischievously answered that it was a banned book.

"Banned? What in the world did Neil send you?"

"A Treatise on Tolerance, written by Voltaire."

Now it was Allan's turn to tease. "We are banning tolerance these days?" and he laughed.

Flora's mood lightened, but then she shared the contents and philosophies on a more serious note. "He contends that it is mostly Christians who are intolerant of others, not the persecuted as they would like us to believe, but the persecutors. They are even intolerant of each other and he is citing example after example." Flora paused. "I think he is right, and it is shameful. At least we Scots do not let religion divide us."

Alan looked at her knowingly for a moment. "It has not divided us yet my dear, however, religion has driven the English to extremes. They cut off Mary Queen of Scot's head primarily because she was Catholic and you know that is the main reason and bottom line Queen Anne brought in the Hanoverians to take her throne. They were protestant!"

Flora sighed, opened the book, and read Voltaire's writing, "*In the end, tolerant has been responsible for not a single civil war, whereas intolerance has covered the earth with corpses.*" Her eyes misted. "Cannot you see Allan, have we even tried to love one another? At times we too have fallen to intolerance."

Allan melted. He knew her words carried a great deal of truth and sometimes wished she would refrain from so much reading. His feelings for her were overwhelming. He picked up the book from her lap, gently set it on the side table, and took her in his arms speaking the few words he knew in French.

CHAPTER 34

1766 - Fanny

In early May, when the bluebells were in bloom across the Isle, Flora, now forty-four, gave birth to her seventh child, a baby girl to be christened Francis and forever called Fanny by all who knew her. The birth again went well and surprisingly quick as if her body by now had practiced what it was supposed to do and did it in rapid time. Still, Flora and baby Fanny would stay in bed for the prescribed ten days while the rest of the household tip-toed about. Twelve-year-old Anne was totally captivated and thrilled to have a little sister. She would sit for hours in Flora's room rocking the baby girl's cradle gently back and forth staring at her and humming. Anne was instantly taken with the idea of being the guardian of this tiny wee lassie, a real sister, all cloistered together in her mother's quiet room. It was a restful and bonding time for both Flora and her two daughters and a delightful break from the normal clamor of the household.

Allan's sister Anne had been widowed four years earlier. The death of her husband Ranald found her in dire financial straits and with no means of support for her or her brood of children, Allan opened the doors of the Flodigarry home making her welcome along with her small clan of mostly rambunctious boys.

Nevertheless, the burden of filling the bellies of another big family was not a light one, and Allan, unbeknownst to any of the family, was incurring debts while keeping everyone's body and soul together.

It was a relief to all in the crowded house when the widower, Lachlan MacKinnon asked Anne to marry him and move to his home Corriechel. The cousins would miss their roommates and thought the move bitter-sweet, yet knowing Corriechel was not that far away and family reunions would remain frequent.

In the meantime, Allan still did not reveal to Flora that their absentee landlord had doubled, then tripled the rents on the tract where they lived. Allan felt his own crofters could not handle the additional charges and chose not to raise their rents accordingly, but covered the costs himself thus plunging the family further into debt.

Flora and Allan were using crop rotation and polyculture, new ideas they read about together. Just as they had broken tradition in naming their children, they broke tradition in managing their tract, planting three varieties of potatoes, rye, and red clover. Allan introduced the new black cows from Northern Scotland and was successful in breeding and selling them to the South. For a few seasons, their efforts were proving successful and they tried to get others to join their efforts. It was that winter a deep cold settled in across Scotland. Most of the crops in the surrounding area failed with little or no yield. Scotland as a whole dipped into a recession. With five children all under six years old Allan hired a few more servants to help Flora manage the family and put up stores when they could. Servants at this time Allan could ill afford. To make matters worse the black cows they were raising as an experiment were less than successful. Adding insult to injury the new agricultural methods they both had studied and incorporated were also floundering, a fact that did not go unnoticed by their critics.

Allan and Flory, together plodded on, taking on more debt and buying more black cattle to supplement the herd. They believed, as all farmers do, that the next season would be better, the ever-perennial farming chant of *next year*.

CHAPTER 35

Winter 1770 - 1771

The winter of 1770-1771 was bitter and devastating to all the crops and animals at Flodigarry. The temperatures dropped lower than anyone could remember and stayed miserably below freezing for over eight weeks. The icy snow froze hard on the ground, covering most of the livestock feed. With scarce food, exposure, and a bovine illness the MacDonalds lost over three hundred cattle, a huge investment gamble they could ill afford and one that did not materialize. Unfortunately, it was a fatal financial error to increase their cattle herd just at the very time there was an increased market for sheep and wool.

Yet long winters everywhere have their advantages in that they afford a great deal of time to socialize. The home-trapped residents of Skye, hungry for the company of friends and family and temporarily relieved from farming duties gathered together frequently. It was this frozen winter that Lt. Alexander

MacLeod of Glendale, a young widower, noticed Allan and Flora's young and beautiful daughter Anne at the gatherings.

Allan MacDonald was not prepared at all though when one evening Alexander MacLeod requested to speak to him alone. MacLeod confessed his love for the young Anne and then asked Allan's permission to marry her. Allan was totally caught off guard failing like most fathers to notice his little girl had turned into a young woman. Flabbergasted would be more accurate hearing the request. He could only respond that he would have to think about it and Alexander MacLeod agreed to wait in the most genteel manner.

Later that evening, when the MacDonalds were getting ready to retire Allan shared Alexander's request with Flora, admitting his surprise. Flora's reaction was different from his. Smiling at her husband she told him, "Those two have been making eyes at each other every chance they get. Besides dear, you have been talking and enjoying the other lad's company never noticing your daughter's flirtations."

"She is too young."

"We almost waited too long my love."

Allan walked around their room a bit lost in thought. "He is quite wealthy and would provide well for her—I believe he is still on half-pay with the military, but I think they should wait until she is older. There is quite a bit of difference in their ages."

Flora smiled, "Allan I just read in the Caledonian Mercury that Marie Antoinette just married the Dauphin of France. She is fourteen years old." Walking closer to her husband she embraced him. "Let's not get in their way. They truly love each other. I can see it in their faces."

And so it was that Anne MacDonald married Alexander MacLeod just as the cold winter broke and the promise of spring rose up from the soil. The young bride was whisked off to the Glendale estate where she was greeted by twenty servants, a huge furnished house, and a thriving farm.

The marriage itself was modest in attendance but MacLeod spared no expense with food, drink, and music for all that came. The pipers, fiddlers, and musicians played into the night with the domestic help keeping the cups full. MacLeod sent to France for an embroidered silk wedding dress for Anne and had a short jacket made for her of the dark blue and green MacLeod tartan. The man clearly was enamored by the young woman and spared no expense to please her.

❧

Emigration fever had reached a peak in Scotland during those years and thousands of her people were setting sail for the colonies with dreams and visions of a new land and a new more prosperous life. Whole families were moving together. The movement had become so popular an original song and dance was created and dubbed "Dot, a dh' Iarraidh am fortan do North- Carolina" (Going to seek my fortune in North Carolina). It was a dance that was performed at Anne and Alexander's wedding.

Flora's sister Annabella waited until after the ceremony and until each had a few celebratory drinks before taking her by the arm and onto the terrace. They stood contentedly gazing at the clear night sky studded with stars for a minute or two before Annabella broke the silence. "Sister dear, my love for you is boundless." She took a deep breath before continuing. "Tonight we celebrate a new life not only for our dear Anne, but we too are going to start a new life."

"What do you mean exactly—a new life? Are you with child again?"

Annabella laughed, "No, my dear Flory, we have plans to seek our fortune in North Carolina. We are leaving Scotland and immigrating to the colonies; all of us."

Flora gulped not sure how to react and echoed Annabella. "Seek your fortune in North Carolina? The colonies? You?" Annabella in spite of many misgivings was resolved in her decision with Alex.

"Yes, we will be leaving before the end of summer."

"What about our father Annabella? What is Hugh going to do without you? Who is to look after him?"

Annabella slid her arm around her stunned sister. "Flory, Hugh is going with us. We are taking the younger children. It is all planned. The eldest two will stay a while to finish their studies in Edinburgh but the rest are going with us—all together." She let that sink in for a minute. "All of us dear." Then she repeated herself, "By the end of summer. We are all going to North Carolina."

CHAPTER 36

1772-1773 Leaving and Grieving

Annabella, her husband Alexander, and their children did indeed sail for North Carolina in the fall of 1772 and somehow Flora felt as if a part of her had also set sail with them. Her beloved step-father Hugh, her nieces, nephews, and only sister—gone. There was a vast vacancy inside her now and knew not how to fill the void except for plunging herself into a flurry of activity with her own brood at Flodigarry. She and Allan's debt continued to spiral and mount, yet even so, ever hopeful, the two continued to keep a positive attitude trying new and different methods to improve their crops and livestock.

It was an unwanted sorrow, however, one they would never have chosen, that improved their financial situation considerably almost overnight. Christmas of that year had again been colder than normal and icy conditions miserable. To make matters worse they were summoned immediately to Kingsburgh where Allan's father, Alexander was failing. Arrangements were made with boatsmen post haste and Flora along with Allan arrived at Kingsburgh within a day. There they both kept vigil sitting for hours by the old man's sick bed. On January 18th, 1773 with his family by his side, Alexander MacDonald of Kingsburgh passed away quietly in his sleep.

The Scots Magazine the following month printed a lovely tribute to the old man written by none other than Bishop Forbes.

"Our readers will remember this gentleman's hospitality to the young pretender in 1746, his sufferings on that account and his bold avowal of what he had done… now let all the world say what they can, he liv'd and died an honest man."

With old Kingsburgh's death, his home and holdings went to his eldest son, Allan. Flora would soon leave her beloved Flodigarry, the place where all her babes were born, and become the mistress of the house where she once had brought Bonnie Prince Charlie. Kingsburgh, a home where she fell in love and married Allan, a home where plots were hatched and re-hatched with dear old friends who in turn became her in-laws and whose graves she would now tend.

CHAPTER 37

1773

Chicken dinner with Samuel Johnson & James Boswell

September of 1773 brought two exceptional and out-of-the-ordinary guests to Kingsburgh, a one Samuel Johnson and his companion James Boswell. The two were touring the Highlands in order to write a book. Twenty years earlier Johnson, who now referred to himself as Dr. Johnson, had compiled one of the first dictionaries in England. In addition, he was a renowned and published writer, biographer, and playwright. Dr. Johnson was accompanied by the much younger James Boswell, a Scot who also wrote and was a man of letters. Apparently, the two were intent on publishing a book about their tour of the Western Islands of Scotland and in particular the Hebrides. Also, whether they openly stated it or not, the men wanted to meet Flora MacDonald, the woman they both considered an influential celebrity.

Flora was less than enthusiastic with the prospect of meeting the two gentlemen and being, once again the object of curiosity. It had been over twenty-five years since her adventure with Charles Edward Stuart, and she was keenly reluctant to talk about the events so long ago. The tell of the long-ago history had been redundantly relayed and she was weary of the repetition. Besides, these two men were biographers and Flora wanted nothing in writing, still fearful of implications that could blemish or potentially endanger the MacDonald family.

From her chambers upstairs she heard Allan welcome the two gentlemen and usher them into their parlor. Fussing with her hair she eventually made her way down to join them and play her role of gracious hostess. Her first impression of the two was their corpulent bodies, sizes seldom seen in Scotland where food scarcity was common. She quietly thought and laughed to herself that their tour about Scotland was more culinary in nature. Smiling she reached out graciously presenting her hand. The two gentlemen practically blushed as they stood in greeting.

Allan, dressed in his tartan, the rules of which had been relaxed ten years earlier, had poured Holland Gin for the three of them. He had pulled his salt and pepper hair back and wore his favorite short coat with gold buttons. Flora thought, when she looked at him, that he was still a handsome man and her heart fluttered.

Dinner was served and was as genteel as anyone could have wished. There was an abundance of food with both roasted turkey and deep-fried chicken, washed down with port and claret. Flora began noticing that Dr. Johnson, though well-spoken, had a tick that affected his speech. Not only that but the man stopped at the entrance of each room; the parlor to the dining room, the halls, and then back again. He would step into each room with his right foot first and if he made a mistake, would step out and do it again. When she asked him what the problem was he said, "Better luck attended the right rather than the left."

Flora did not embellish or expand any new information to the tale that once again was requested she relay. She simply gave them the known and abbreviated version of her adventures with Bonnie Prince Charlie. Nevertheless, both men were taken by Flora MacDonald and when Samuel Johnson's book was published two years later he wrote, "*Her name will be mentioned in history and, if courage and fidelity are virtues, mentioned with honour.*"

Flora and Allan agreed that letting the men stay in the same guest room where Charlie had slept would thrill both of them and it was an easy, mutual decision. Johnson and Boswell, after a few drinks, opened up about their opinions on the monarchy. They said they believed in only male succession to the throne and were not sure of Mary Queen of Scots. Both men verbalized that they supported thirty-five-year-old King George III because, neither of them would involve nor support Britain in a civil war just to set the Stuarts back on the throne.

Flora remained quiet in her opinions as they were unsolicited by the pair, her being a woman and a supporter of Prince Charles Stuart. She too did not want a civil war, especially at her dinner table and God knows what the two writers might say later in print.

However, she thought they underestimated and lacked respect for intelligent women. Subsequently, Flora did not bother to refute any of their theories on monarchs or anything else and simply thought to save her breath with her hands folded politely in her lap.

In their later published writings and journals, both men spoke highly of Flora MacDonald. Boswell would describe her as, *"A little woman, of a genteel appearance, and uncommonly mild and well bred."* He undoubtedly would not have written that if she had honestly expressed her own honest opinions during their stay at her home.

Dr. Johnson felt unwell the next morning and complained of a cold. Feeling sympathy for the man Allan MacDonald himself rowed them across Loch Snizort to where there where they could get horses. That saved the ill and heavy-set man an additional eight-mile rough ride to his next destination and Johnson was more than grateful. A good meal, a night in Charles Stuart's bed, and assistance in his travels. He had a great deal of positive experiences on the Isle of Skye of which to write.

CHAPTER 38

1774 - Setting Sail

Just after Hogmanay of 1774, Allan and Flora made the final, agonizing decision to leave Skye and join Annabella, Hugh, and the rest of the family in the American colonies. They had discussed the advantages and disadvantages for over a year, with Flora objecting and saying that she simply hated to leave her homeland, the place of her birth. She was well aware of the dangers of the voyage and worried that their two youngest children could not survive the trip. Yet Annabella's letters from the North Carolina colony painted a positive picture telling them about their peach orchards, apples, and hogs. She wrote that the cattle fattened up easily eating the abundant wild pea vine and how content they were in the 'new country'.

Annabella wrote how proud she was of her husband Alexander of Cuidreach, that he had been appointed Justice of the Peace by the local governor. She also wrote to them saying that it was possible for them to get two crops a year of some things and there were so many apples that you could eat off the trees with your hands tied behind you. This made Flora laugh, as she knew full well that Annabella was exaggerating some of the merits of North Carolina.

Annabella's letters continued routinely with encouraging news for Allan and Flora and always an accompanying line pleading for them to join the North Carolina family. In reality, Flora's family ties to Skye were unraveling and buried on the hill by the kirk. Both of Allan's parents were gone along with Flora's mother Marion. One-Eyed Hugh was with his daughter in North Carolina and had purchased a farm of his own not far from hers.

Annabella's letters were shared with the entire family and then were passed onto young Anne who now had two babies of her own. Everyone laughed over Annabella's description of the mosquitos, which she wrote were pesky like the midges, but much bigger and thus easier to swat. She even told them about an odd plant that 'ate bugs' and that in itself sounded intriguing along with its strange name of tipitiwitchet which they all tried to pronounce with a great deal of laughter. No one was sure if Annabella was teasing them about the plants and insects of the colony.

Still, Flora found herself frequently waking at night with her fists clenched tightly under her pillow. How long had she held that tension she wondered? She would flex her fingers and then lay them flat trying to think of positive reasons to leave Skye. She could hear her sister's voice in her head telling her it would be like the old times, people dancing, wearing their tartans, and playing the bagpipes with abandon. North Carolina, Annabella wrote, was like a new Scotland with thousands of kinsmen settling in their community and prospering.

It was tempting, but a huge decision. Flora was anxious thinking about the future of all of her children. The two elder boys were all right and settled. Charles had secured a position with the East India Company and Ranald, with the help of Flora's old protector in 1745, Nigel Gresley, was a seventeen-year-old lieutenant with the marines. Allan thought rightfully that he would need the help of Sandy and James in establishing a plantation in the new country. They would go with them, but what to do with Fanny and Johnnie?

Flora had written inquiries the August before to her good friend John MacKenzie of Delvine. She requested MacKenzie take in her son Johnnie, that he was a good boy without any kind of vice. But her letter conveyed more to him when she wrote she saw no future left in Skye, but one of poverty and oppression not only for herself but her entire family. She wrote honestly and frankly to MacKenzie about their cattle losses and Allan's illness with chronic side pain.

She was hoping that Johnnie might learn a trade from John MacKenzie and also keep an eye on his sister Fanny who was only eight years old. The plan was to come and get them in a year or two, or perhaps arrangements could be made, once they settled, for the younger ones to join them. Her sister Annabella had also left her two eldest children behind, her son Donald and a daughter. However, they were much older than Flora's young ones and definitely more mature.

A great deal had to be done to prepare for the treacherous voyage across the Atlantic. It would take about five or six weeks from Scotland to North Carolina depending on the trade winds, and of course, they had to arrange for a ship and make reservations. When Flora told her daughter Anne that they had made up their minds to leave, it was not long before Anne and her husband Alexander MacLeod of Glendale decided to also join them in the adventure.

Each family called together their servants and crofters explaining their plans to relocate. Many, but not all, expressed a desire to join them, but of course, they too were unable to make the transport fees. A proposal was laid out that anyone who decided to accompany the family could work off the price of fare so to speak. They would be indebted to their benefactors for their passage and care, however, could work off that debt as an indentured servant. Contracts were drawn up for eight of Flora and Allan's workers who decided to go with them. There were two newlywed couples, three young single men, and a young widow with no children.

As the day of departure came closer, household items were packed in wooden crates, and much of the stock was driven south and sold, keeping a milk cow and two of Allan's best horses. The spinet, a treasure handed down from her mother had already made several journeys and would travel with them again to North Carolina. Flora had brought it with her to their Flodigarry home and then it was transported to Kingsburgh. She watched carefully as the men removed its legs, wrapping the body in quilts and putting it all in a huge custom-made box. She wondered what would the instrument say if it could sing its own history? Would it be a lament like *Barbie Allen* or an uptown reel like the new one called *America*?

Flora took the locks of hair she had clipped from Johnnie and Fanny, tied each with a ribbon, and placed them in a small silver box. She thought herself blessed. All her babies had been born healthy and had lived well, yet the idea of leaving any of them behind tore at her heart and she prayed she was doing the right thing. A cloud of melancholy descended on her like a grey mist, wrapping her in a tight cloak. Her head started to throb with pain as she packed away some of her mother's things, and the satin Christening gown all seven of her children had worn. Gently folding it, along with the matching bonnet she placed it on the sheet that Charles Stuart had slept on. The trunk was filling fast with Flora's treasures including the instructions that should she die on the journey, she would be buried in those sheets. She had fulfilled that wish for Allan's mother by sewing the shroud herself. The two women shared that desire. Flora smiled even thinking that Dr. Samuel Johnson, who she still thought quite odd, also had the pleasure of sleeping in the Prince's bed. She hoped they all would not be thought of as daft and totally silly in the future.

Flory was experiencing a convoluted mix of emotions and well aware of them all. She was eager to reunite with her sister Annabella who now had been in the colonies for three years, she had missed her so. There was also the grief of leaving Skye and especially Johnnie and young Fanny, mixed with the excitement of a new impending adventure filled with a myriad of trepidations. Her head hurt holding all these thoughts like a giant whirlpool swirling around and around.

She gave Fanny two books before handing her over to Mrs. MacLeod of Raasay. The MacLeods had laughed when Flora originally approached the idea of them keeping Fannie until she was settled in the Carolinas. They already had ten daughters and thought one more would not matter one way or another. They too were loyal to Flora for her role in saving Bonnie Prince Charlie years earlier and felt honored that she would ask them to care for one of her own. One of the books she gave her young daughter was *Gulliver's Travels* by Jonathan Swift and the other one of blank pages. "Journal in the empty book my dear. Write what you are feeling inside and let me know how the weather is each day, one thing new you learned, and what you are eating." She smiled holding her daughter's small hands for a long time. "Write and tell me about the Lilliputians and I will write and tell you about the people and plants of North Carolina." With that, she kissed her daughter who was whisked away with the MacLeod family.

Then Flora put her beloved young son Johnnie into a carriage bound for Edinburgh, kissed him gently then closed the door. She turned away so his last memory of his mother would be of her smiling and not of her face raining bitter tears. It was wretchedly heartbreaking to part with her wee bairns not knowing for sure what would become of any of them or how quickly she could get back and retrieve them.

The morning the MacDonald party left Armadale, Flora went out of the house and picked up several small stones to take along. Stones from Armadale. Stones from Skye that she could take as a silent reminder that this was her land and part of it would travel with her, even though she would live here no more. She swallowed hard as they were placed in the last wagon heading for Portree and the ship that would take them far across the Atlantic Ocean.

Flora and Anne had talked about the journey, the lengthy weeks at sea, and its confinement. In preparation, they fashioned a satchel together holding a few books, a bible, a chess set, thread, yarn, and needles to keep them busy. With a last-minute thought, they threw in a deck of playing cards for whist.

CHAPTER: 39

The Crossing - Late Summer - 1774

Boarding the majestic, three-masted merchant ship Flora was surprised to see the amount of livestock on the top deck. Crates of chickens were stacked one on top of another, small bins of pigs and even their milk cow was tied into a corner. Immediately recoiling from the stench of their excrement, Flora couldn't help but hope that once at sea they would be routinely cleaned and the sea air would dilute the foul odors. Barrels of flour and oats were loaded below with baskets of what appeared to be lemons and limes. She felt comforted that someone believed her countryman James Lind, who had been writing multiple articles on the theory that eating limes would prevent scurvy.

Their belongings had previously been stored in the hold and Allan's two fine horses lowered into the bottom deck with ropes and put in custom stalls. Flora's family met up with Anne, Alex MacLeod, and their two baby sons along with their twelve indentured servants on the docks. Together the two families and their workers made up a party of twenty-eight. Flora chuckled to herself thinking that at least there would be conversations and things to do, unlike her confinements with Ceitie MacDowal after her arrest so many years ago.

Their assigned cabins were small but clean and efficient and the servant's quarters, even though below deck, were not unpleasant. There were comfortable berths and room to walk about. She shuddered recalling the prison ships, the stench, and hoards of people laying on the wooden floors or piles of ropes with little air nor light and less to eat.

The family's eventual departure from the Isle had a festive feeling or at least the pretense of excitement to camouflage the heavy apprehension of leaving everything familiar and the sensation of being uprooted. Taking a deep breath, fifty-two-year-old Flora positioned herself next to Anne and held her hand squeezing it tightly. "We have each other lassie. We are doing this all together and soon we will be a whole family again with our darling Annabelle and Hugh."

Allan and the boys were excitedly walking the ship from stem to stern checking everything out as if they were engaged by the ship's owners as inspectors. Before the hour was up shouts went out, the lines were pulled and the sails snapped unfurling like open arms welcoming the wind. The ship moved swiftly out of the bay with all the passengers on the top deck totally engaged and watching as they sailed away from the land.

As the first day slipped into evening and the sky darkened, Flora looked in the direction she thought the Isle of Skye should be. The shadow of land she had watched for hours silently slipped from view as the craft creaked and groaned. She reached down picked up the ship's cat and began stroking her soft fur, noting its belly bulging with life. Looking out to the endless expanse of ocean she started humming her thoughts and sang just a verse.

"The water is wide, I cannot get o'er — Neither have I wings to fly."

Flora shook herself back into reality, dropped the cat, and nervously picked up her knitting remembering what her mother used to tell her. *'Idle hands were the devil's tools'*. These baby blankets she was knitting would be special, she had spun the wool herself from their own sheep and now they would be a small piece of the old country. Something to wrap the wee bairns up in the new.

Being at sea was a new adventure for most the entire party with the exception of the captain and crew. None had expected to be impacted by the complete vastness of the ocean or actually being able to see the slight curvature of the earth. They could never have imagined looking out and seeing nothing but water in every direction, the sheer vastness of it all making them feel so small. Then there were the clouded days, when the water and sky were the same color and it was difficult to distinguish where one ended and the other began. Those were the days they all retired to their cabins and played whist for way too long, drinking tea and reading. Allan and Sandy would engage in chess for hours and then erupt their silence with laughter and exclamations of who had won. Allan kept telling Sandy it was all about strategy and trying to calculate the opponent's next move.

The ship's cat somewhat adopted Flora jumping onto her lap for a good pet and showing its appreciation by loudly purring at every opportunity. The sailors would all smile when they saw her walking about with the cat in her arms. The superstitious crew felt it was good luck to have a cat come to them and that having cats on board was completely necessary for rodent control. But their attachment went further, with even a few believing there was magic in their tails and that they could predict the weather. Flora had trouble buying that fable but did notice how restless or nervous the puss might be just before a storm. For her it was the opposite, petting the warm furry critter relaxed her.

It was the nights though that they all found the most spectacular bobbing on the ocean. When void of a cloud cover, the dark velvet sky held vast amounts of what looked like sparkling jewels impossible to count. Millions upon millions of twinkling, pin-point diamond stars and planets of all sizes expansively stretched from horizon to horizon. They had seen beauty in the night sky in Scotland frequently yet here the immensity of the universe appeared exaggerated. Flora had her arm around Sandy one night as they sat on the upper deck trying to find the different constellations and recall the story behind each. Sandy let out a whoop when they were treated to an exciting burst of a meteor shower. He was thoughtfully quiet for a moment after that, then questioned Flora, "Mum, does God know we are here?" He took a deep breath. "I feel so small, so insignificant as if I am a wee dot on one of tiny those ships stuffed in a bottle, free-floating in the Atlantic."

It was a question Flora waited a minute to answer, that of the sanctity of life. "Sandy, in Matthew it says that a sparrow shall not fall on the ground without God knowing it and that the very hairs of your head are all numbered." She reached up teasingly and ruffled her hand through his hair smiling and attempting to comfort the young man.

He was quiet for a moment, rather overwhelmed by the entire concept of creation, the stars, and the firmament. All he said was, "That is a lot of counting."

They both laughed.

CHAPTER 40

Cape Fear—North Carolina - October 18, 1774

Six weeks and three storms later found every passenger along with the majority of the crew scurrying to the upper deck with the first call of, "Land ho" high from the ship's crow's nest. They followed the pointing finger then peered with naked eyes into the distance. There, everyone focused on the faint shape above the water line. As they waited the emerging land slowly appeared larger and darker taking formation as the sails fulled in the sea breeze. The ship tacked and headed steadily for its destination.

The Captain came close to Flora leaning on the railing and pointed out their heading. "That my lady is Cape Fear, your journey's end."

Flora's voice got slightly weak, "Cape Fear?"

"Aye lassie, do not be distressed though. It was named that two hundred years ago. A ship was caught in a storm there and the story goes the crew was fearful they would sink, so they named it Cape Fear. 'Tis a good port and that structure you see looming on the left is Fort Johnston. We are not far from the city of Wilmington. The fort has been there for twenty-five years." He started to walk off ordering deckhands here and there, but turned around and shouted to Flora. "No worries Mrs. MacDonald. You have nothing to fear." He chuckled, "For a parting gift take a couple of that puss' kittens. They are down in the galley."

❋

Allan insisted he and Flora dress in their finest to disembark, making their best debut into their new colonial life. Allan was adamant about creating a memorable first impression with the populace. Thus, with his finest tartan wrapped about him and a cap perched at an angle on his head, he made a dashing figure as a highland gentleman coming down the landing. Flora and Anne were too dressed, she in a satin skirt she had made for just the occasion, the color of highland heather in bloom, and a white ribbon cockade pinned to her shoulder.

The moment Allan's foot hit the solid ground he began organizing his servants and sons to gather all their belongings along with locating wagons and drivers for hire. One would have thought he was the owner of the entire fleet of ships as he took command. MacLeod was fast behind Allan after ushering Anne and their two tiny babes to a carriage while he located the rest of his awe-struck servants. In the bustle of activity, Flora was left to fend for herself. Most all of the other passengers had disembarked and were on the dockside watching and listening as the crew loudly unloaded the livestock with shouts, horses whinnying, and cows bellowing. The dirt street rapidly turned to dust, busy with wagons, livestock, and folks shouting in several different languages. Watching all the hustle and bustle Flora was not paying attention to her own unsteadiness, her body still rocking from the sea. She was looking for a place to get out of everyone's way when she unintentionally stumbled headlong into another woman. A quick reactive arm caught her and steadied her for a moment, speaking to her in clear

Gaelic that she was all right. The woman kindly helped Flora over to one of the freshly unloaded trunks sitting on the landing and inquired where she was headed, all the time brushing the dust from her new dress. When Flora looked up she was gazing into the dark, almond-shaped eyes of a beautiful black woman still gently holding her arm. Blinking a few times and feeling rather disoriented Flora stated the obvious. "You speak Gaelic."

"Yes, ma'am. My father was a Scot."

The sensation of being slightly disconnected from reality swept over Flora. After six weeks at sea to a new land, she found herself bewildered at the information the young woman was telling her. A woman whose skin was silky smooth and the color of good French chocolate. She looked down at her own sunburned hands as her mind wondered questioning where Allan and her boys were.

"Your father was Scottish?" she inquired rather bewildered.

"Yes, ma'am. A slave like my mother. But we free now. My mother and me were bought and set free by the Quakers. My brother too. I have papers showing

I'm free. I'm down on the docks today just to help out."

It was all making sense now. The prisoners of

war from Culloden and other battles were sold as

slaves in the colonies. Flora knew about that. It just did

not occur to her they would have had love, marriage,

and families. She wondered if any of them were still

alive. "And your father? Where is your father?" Flora

felt as if she were dreaming.

"He died when I was still young ma'am. Most all

the white slaves die way before their time. He left two

of us children. I have a younger brother." Then she

laughed. "He may be younger but he is three times the

size of me. Grew to be a good man."

Regaining her composure Flora held out her

hand. "I am sorry, my name is Flora MacDonald," she

announced. "Thank you so much for your help. You

have been very kind. I might have fallen into the water

I was so dizzy. I failed to pay attention wondering

about a silly basket of kittens."

When she smiled the face of the young woman

lit up like welcoming candles in a night room. She had

twinkling eyes and ivory teeth that reached from cheek to cheek. "My name is Lewa. It means beautiful in my mother's Yoruba language. If you need any more help you just ask for Lewa. You are going to be all right now." She patted Flora's hand, swung a basket on her back, and walked off heading toward the settlement.

Flora sat in thought watching the bustle of activity as the ship continued to unload and reloaded its contents into a variety of awaiting wagons. She thought that no one had the right to inflict horror on another, yet she knew from reading that for almost sixty years Britain had been transporting its unwanted population to the colonies for servile labour. She would learn later that the value of a black slave was twice that of a white. The reasoning was the white slaves were unable to work as hard or as long in the stifling heat and died too frequently. Basically, the plantation owners did not think whites were as good of an investment.

Flora also had read about slaves who had been emancipated in Edinburgh. She had read Lord Auchinleck's statement almost ten years earlier while in

Skye. He was freeing a black man and said, "It may be the custom in Jamaica to make slaves of poor blacks, but I do not believe it is agreeable to humanity nor to the Christian religion. He is our brother, and he is a man." More than one poor devil in bondage dreamed of Scotland and freedom.

Within a half-hour, Allan located Flora and ushered her to a carriage already holding Anne and the young ones. He had gathered their small clan together and near two wagons loaded with belongings from the ship's hold. His two prize horses, much thinner than when they left, were fastened to the back of one wagon, along with the milk cow. Arrangements had been made at several different homes where everyone could stay in Wilmington, including their livestock and Allan was wasting no time in implementing his plans for their future.

The entire party gasped when their wagons eventually pulled in front of John Burgwin's home where they were to lodge. The house itself was built up over an existing structure with a long, expansive staircase greeting and welcoming the guests. The second floor had a balcony the full length of the dwelling and on it stood a few folks waving a greeting to the MacDonalds. The style of the home was something that no one from Scotland had seen before. It was an impressive wooden structure where most, if not all their buildings in the old country had been made of stone.

Their host, John Burgwin, was a successful merchant in Wilmington, and also the private secretary to the North Carolina Governor. He too stood at the door welcoming the MacDonald party and all their trappings. As Flora MacDonald ascended his staircase John Burgwin held out his hand and introduced himself. Then he looked her over and said, "Oh, the little lady with the big reputation."

It seemed impossible for Flora to escape her past and she blushed as she and Anne were then ushered inside and upstairs to a lovely room overlooking the gardens. Two cradles had been thoughtfully placed in the corner to accommodate Anne and Alex's sons. The men were ushered into rooms located at the opposite end of the long hall and down a bit from the ladies.

Their collective servants were accommodated totally in another wing of the impressive mansion.

John Burgwin was thrilled to have them and announced that they were to rest and that on the morrow he was throwing a ball in their honor.

Flora groaned inside but kept a placid smile on her face. It was more than generous of Burgwin to throw a party on her behalf, however, she felt strongly she was not a trinket to be gawked at. It had been twenty-eight years now since her involvement with Charles Edward Stuart. Her hair currently boasted silver streaks and her once tiny waistline had grown thick. The notoriety was unwelcome as was parading her in front of a group of strangers. Flora was keenly aware, however, that Allan felt the opposite. He was excited to meet new, influential people and a ball was exactly an event that could accomplish this in short order, no matter what motivated the guests to attend.

She and Anne had brought ball gowns which were unpacked immediately and hung for the wrinkles to fall out. Anne looked just like a younger version of her mother, both being petite women and stunning with an air of autocracy and strength hanging about them like perfume.

On the evening of the ball Flora and her daughter descended the stairs arm-in-arm into a sea of unfamiliar faces staring at them. To add drama to the event John Burgwin had hired a piper who, upon seeing Flora and her daughter began playing the traditional song, *"Hey Tuttie Tatie"*. The crowd all clapped and made her feel uncomfortable, but acknowledging their need to celebrate something, she smiled and graciously joined them.

One of the gentlemen Allan was anxious for Flora to meet was the governor of the colony, Josiah Martin. Allan winked at her as he introduced them and stated that Governor Martin had been born in Ireland. He never missed an opportunity to tease Flora gently for stating that Betty Burke had been awkward because she was Irish. It had been a long-standing joke between the two.

The dancing started promptly at seven o'clock with a small group of musicians. Flora was moved from dance partner to dance partner with minuets and allemandes, everyone wanting an opportunity to touch the renowned heroine Flora MacDonald. She enjoyed hearing the cellos, hammered dulcimer, and violins playing together with the harpsichord, however, found the conversations tedious as she recounted over and over her adventures in Scotland and how they fared on their crossing. Even though accomplished at formal dancing, Flora was delighted when the rhythm picked up with familiar tunes and a reel giving her a sense of freedom in dance.

Around 10:00 that evening, much to everyone's relief, there was a seated supper. The table was laid out with casserole dishes filled with potatoes, several roasts, and a decorated tureen full of Hairst Bree, a traditional Scottish harvest broth. Flora was delighted to see Lewa among the servers and when the young woman ladled up her broth she leaned close to Flora whispering in Gaelic that she had made the broth, especially for her, and then she smiled. Lewa then spoke louder English and with mischievous eyes, as if she was answering an unspoken question, Lewa said, "I hire out to help for balls and such here in Wilmington."

Flora was tickled and smiled herself at the not-so-subtle advertisement. Then, before she left the table Lewa let Flora know that she had returned to the ship for her kittens and would bring them by Burgwin's home the next day.

Somewhere around midnight, the dancing resumed, with Flora and Anne making excuses and slipping upstairs. Flora was uneasy as one of the women at dinner had slightly upset her with an unkind comment. She had leaned over unsolicited and told her loudly, "It is your courage people admire Mrs. MacDonald, not necessarily the cause you represent."

Flora was cognizant of why she was the object of so much attention. They admired her tenacity or audacity as many would refer to it, of opposing the British King. Somewhat like standing in front of a tiger. What none appeared here to see clearly was that it was not her king, not the rightful king to the British throne. In addition, it was apparent that some also thought King George III did not possess the right to rule them in America. Could it be possible these people leaned toward the major Scottish opinion of the Hanoverian house?

Allan on the other hand appeared to be having the time of his life, talking and laughing with many influential people in the colony. He made quite an impression on the Governor and at last glance as the ladies retired, the two were engaged in conversation, drinking and smoking in John Bergwin's spacious library.

CHAPTER 41

Moving On—Oct-Nov 1774

Flora was grateful for the opportunity to sleep in a real bed, one which did not rock back and forth during the night. Additionally, she also was anxious to get to her sister Annabella's plantation. The wagons laden, with their furniture and belongings from Skye had been sent ahead with twenty servants to Annabella's Mount Pleasant. Allan wanted to stay longer in Wilmington and further his connections and when the two talked over their differing opinions the next day they compromised with two more nights and one more ball. Neither she nor Anne could take much more of their unwanted celebrity adoration where Allan was relishing every minute of it. Flora could see he was lapping it up like a thirsty farm dog.

North Carolina was beautiful Flora had to admit. Allan had hired a driver to take them to Mount Pleasant and the man was knowledgeable about the many plants and wildlife unfolding as a visual potpourri along the trails. The red maples were just hinting of autumn with a few leaves turning red. The river birches impressed her with their size, and the driver assured her that in the spring she would love the smell of their magnolias. He told her about the wild boars and whitetail deer and that there was always plenty of game to eat and then he continued on about the mice problem everyone encountered.

Flora patted the lidded basket that Lewa had given her and commented that was why she had grabbed onto a couple of kittens from the ship. The captain was just going to let most of them go on the streets of Wilmington and she felt she had a better use for them.

The boys, Sandy and James, followed the wagons riding Allan's two horses who were excited themselves to be out of the confines of the ship stable and able to move down the road grabbing a nibble of fresh green grass at every chance.

It took two and a half days of traveling to get to Annabella's home but was well worth the trip when it came into view. The curtain of trees surrounding the plantation folded back revealing an opening of Mount Pleasant standing alone and proud on a knoll. There was a clearing of several acres around the white-washed stately house, and it seemed to glow like a welcome beacon in the late afternoon sun.

The air was filled with dogs barking announcing their arrival and within minutes Annabella and Alex were running down the steps, as simultaneously Anne, MacLeod, and Flora were all running to meet them. It was a happy melee; simultaneous tears, laughter, and embracing. Allan took his time disembarking giving instructions to the driver while Annabella's two youngest children stood gawking at the display of affection they were witnessing. They were young when they first arrived in North Carolina and barely remembered their aunt, uncles, and collection of cousins.

The entire family was overcome with joy at being reunited after three long years. The extended greetings went on for some time outside before everyone felt comfortable enough to let go and enter the home. They just kept looking at each other and wondering if this was real. Had they really made it? Were they really together in this new land? Flora felt relieved, now she could breathe deeply again, practically worry-free.

Servants were scurrying about asking which room each trunk should be deposited in when Flora remembered the kittens and retrieved the basket from under the wagon seat. Once inside she let the tiny critters go to acquaint themselves with the home while Annabella's two youngsters took to chasing them across the polished wood floors.

In a short time the dogs once again announced company with their welcoming friend-is-approaching barks. The family gathered on the front covered porch just as a familiar figure appeared on horseback. Hugh MacDonald, on the other side of seventy, sat straight and proud in his saddle, shoulders held back as he came cantering toward the house. Everyone was thrilled to see him including Annabella whom he visited frequently. One of the servants took his horse as he dismounted and the hugging and back-slapping resumed all over again.

As the group of merry-makers stood in the yard relishing their reunion, and the sun began to slip behind the trees, the fragrance of chicken frying in bacon grease drifted toward them. It was the scent of home, of tradition. Their mouths started watering thinking of biting into the crusty battered herbs revealing the moist meat inside. Their senses filled with the aromas, the shared memories, and the bond of family and of clan.

A new beginning.

CHAPTER 42

Autumn 1774

Mount Pleasant & The Barbecue Church

Flora was more than happy to stay with Annabella while Allan took James and Sandy in search of what she hoped would be their permanent home. Anne had moved along within a few days to the plantation Alex MacLeod had purchased for them from a Duncan Buie a few years earlier. Flora smiled, pleased Anne and her husband had done so well. They had three wagons full of furniture and books brought from Scotland, where Flora had whittled her and Allan's down to one. The MacLeods promised to definitely be back in a month to plan a Yule celebration for the whole family.

Staying at Mt. Pleasant gave Flora time to decompress from the voyage and reacquaint herself with her beloved half-sister and family. During the second week of her stay, Annabella suggested that on the Sabbath they attend the Barbecue Presbyterian

Church. The church was only about a mile from her home and would be a pleasant walk through the forest. Flora eagerly agreed and took with her one of the small stones from Skye she had picked up before leaving.

As they walked Annabella chatted on explaining the congregation and its building. She told Flora that after finding a stranger frozen to death at the church door the winter before last, the congregation vowed never to lock it again. The poor soul was the first they buried in their churchyard.

The trees that had been cut to make a clearing for the church, were mostly the same ones that made up the plain log structure that came into view as they approached. Annabella told her that before the community had built this permanent place to worship they had met in what they called an Ordinary or a tap room. She chuckled when she said their first pulpit had been a whiskey barrel.

"Not unlike the Scots," Flora laughed back. She understood that an Ordinary would have been the largest place in the area to accommodate them. "I understand why it is named for the brook it stands by, but why was the creek named Barbecue?"

Annabella was re-tying her little one's bonnet. "One of the early seamen mistook the steam coming up from the creek one morning as smoke from a barbecue. Silly isn't it? And it held fast."

The question hung in the air unanswered as the party of women and children stood in front of the log building. It was quite plain and bereft of a fireplace or chimney for warmth. The doors were open exposing a sanctuary just as austere as the exterior, the pews made of split logs with legs. A great contrast to Saint Giles in Edinburgh with its carved columns and vaulted ceilings. This small kirk appeared dim, void of warmth, and without a musical instrument to be seen. There was a simple, small plaque at the entrance which was dedicated to James Campbell, their first Gaelic-speaking minister. Flora thought to herself there really would be no need ever to lock the door of this simple and unadorned structure.

Outside, not far from the entry was a cairn made of hundreds of stones brought from Scotland by other brave immigrants intent on making a new life for themselves in the colony. Flora reached into her satchel and placed her stone carefully on top of the others. She paused, holding her hand on the hard surface for a moment, and closed her eyes. She thought of the hundreds of souls who before her laid their stones here and in other cairns in this foreign country. She found herself wondering who they were and who would follow? How many hearts had crossed the wide water leaving their homeland on the other side?

The ladies entered the kirk just as the opening prayer was being led by Pastor John MacLeod in their mother tongue of Gaelic. The benches in the back were filled with a few black slaves and white indentured servants. Flora was relieved that her family had no need for slaves. She found the idea totally distasteful knowing that her own kinsman had been sold in such a manner. From what her sister had told her the church shared pastors, taking turns here on alternate Sundays; next week would be the Reverend James Campbell.

The singing commenced with a Presenter singing the first few verses in Gaelic. It was Psalm 100.

The congregation responded from their hearts singing the same melody and words, but each emphasizing their individual interpretations with dissonance. The result was an ebb and flow of voices not unlike the tides of the old country, a rhythm of the coming in and rolling out of the ocean, a natural movement within their very souls. There was some improvisation, however as the fluid voices sang sincere emotion swept over the congregation, and Flora's heart lifted with the lilt that took her back to the Isles, to home. When they got to verse seven she heard the words.

Make a joyful noise unto the Lord, all ye lands. Serve the Lord with gladness: come before his presence with singing. Know ye that the Lord he is God: it is he that hath made us, and not we ourselves; we are his people, and the sheep of his pasture. Enter into his gates with thanksgiving, and into his courts with praise: be thankful unto him, and bless his name. For the Lord is good; his mercy is everlasting; and his truth endureth to all generations.

There was an intimacy of connected souls in the humble churches she attended that eluded her in the cathedrals. Flora was unaware of the tear sliding quietly down her cheek or the homesickness overtaking her that was to become chronic.

CHAPTER 43

Late Fall 1774

Autumn with all its bounty arrived along with Anne to Mt. Pleasant and the three women sat around the table hand-peeling apples. Anne had come over to spend a few days with her mother and aunt bringing Flora some books from their library. Each lady had a small paring knife and would deftly spin the apple with one hand, slicing the skin off with the other. They joked and laughed seeing who could shave a whole apple without breaking the peel. They would sweep the apple scraps into a big bowl which later would be split evenly between the chickens and the compost. The finished apples were sliced thin and placed on drying racks.

Annabella was thrilled to hear all the gossip from the old country, things they had not exchanged in letters and she was doubly thrilled to have her beloved sister and niece sitting with her.

Ceitie MacDowel's name came up and what had become of her? Flora sighed a bit recalling her ginger-haired friend.

"Aye Ceitie, faithful as any dog she was. She set sail for the colonies years back with her husband and wee bairn." Bunching her lips together and frowning she continued. "We believe the ship was lost at sea. It, nor its passengers, were ever heard from again."

Annabella gave her a minute and then asked about their cousin Neil MacEachen and if Flora was still exchanging letters with him.

"He is still in France. He married a French woman and they have a son." Flora did not tell her that Neil had written saying he was so broke his wife was taking in laundry to make ends meet. Why strip the man of his dignity or violate his confidence? He never asked Flora for money knowing she too had little to give. He just wanted to let her know that for the time being things weren't going well for him. Prince Charles' promise of providing for him the rest of his life had never come to fruition. "I tried to persuade him to join us here," Flora told the girls, "But he is comfortable in his community there. It is filled by many expatriate Scots all seeking peace. Seems like we are leaving the auld country in droves." Flora knew that unless Neil and his family came as indentured servants themselves they couldn't afford passage to the colonies and that perhaps Neil couldn't bear that indignity. She wished her cousin had made a different choice.

Clearing her throat and wanting to change the subject Flora, in a tone more curious than condemning, inquired, "Annabella, none of the letters you sent gave hint to the troubles here."

Annabella put down her small knife and, wiping her hands on her apron shrugged, "We thought little of it at first. It was all too far away from us up in Boston." She started to giggle, "You did hear about the Boston Tea Party last year did you not?"

"No, we were busy packing, and the news always slow to reach Armadale. Tell us." Flora reached for another apple.

"It was just before Christmas when England imposed yet another tax on the colonies here. This one was on tea. People had been complaining off and on about the taxes, and that they were never asked or represented. They felt they were being treated as errant children and the tea tax put them over the edge. A group of men folk starting meeting in secret, of course..."

Flora interrupted Annabella's story, "Sounds like us in our youth joining with the Jacobites."

"There are some similarities. Anyway, they formed a band, dressed up like savages one night, feathers and all, and boarded three of the East India Company's trade vessels loaded with tea..."

It was Anne who looked alarmed. "Mum, isn't it the East India Company that my brother is with?"

Flora nodded and started slicing the apples on the wooden table with a wee bit more force.

Annabella continued. "From what I hear it was a great party. Everyone knew what was about to take place and there were thousands, maybe five thousand people from Boston, down on the docks cheering them on. It was the social event of the year."

The Scottish women all laughed heartily at the thought of five thousand people cheering on protestors of British rule and taxes. "Must have been quite a sight. I bet King Geordie is less than happy about that. Who is their leader?"

Annabella thought for a moment. "I think his name was Sam something." She picked up an apple and began peeling again. "Samuel—Samuel Adams is his name."

Flora thought for a moment. "I like his unarmed insurrection."

Twenty-year-old Anne suddenly smiled and put down her parring knife. "Oh!" she rubbed her belly. "I have a kicking wee bairn inside me." Then she laughed, "Maybe he is protesting his temporary captivity."

"Are you sure it is a laddie?"

"Aye, or a lassie with quite a kick like you mum."

The room lightened with laughter again as the women's conversation switched to babies, children and wondering what kind of farm Allan would be buying. Anne started describing where she and Alex were. They were going to name it Glendale. It was Annabella who asked with a smile. "I have tea ladies, Sassafras tea. We do not really need the tea from the East India Company." With that, she got up and put a pot on the wood stove and reached in her apron pocket and pulled out the key to the sugar chest with a smile.

Heating with wood was a different experience for all of the women having grown up burning peat. The smell of pine burning was not quite as sweet and earthy, yet remained pleasant mixing with the sweet smells of the apples blending with the Sassafras. The room was filling with a pleasant aroma.

CHAPTER - 44

Christmas—1774

It was Flora MacDonald's name that once again garnered great interest, this time it was among the colonist. Many called her the savior of the Bonnie Prince. Allan too attracted a great deal of respect with his carriage, his intelligence, and his general demeanor. There was a dignity about the couple that drew attention wherever they went, an attention that was not always welcomed by the privacy-loving Flora.

Their first Christmas in the new country found them again happily gathering with family at Anne and Alexander's Glendale Home. Annabella's older two children, a daughter and her son Donald had arrived from Skye earlier that month and everyone was looking forward to the family reunion at the Advent, hearing news from the Auld Country and exchanging small gifts.

The three women, with the help of their servants, baked and cooked for days spicing it all with gossip. There is nothing like women working together to share information from childbirth to politics. They roasted both a leg of beef and a pig, prepared Indian corn on the cob, and churned plenty of butter to go along with their clootie dumplings.

In the late afternoon, when the MacDonald family joined together in the parlor, they held their traditional reading of the Christmas story before the gift exchange. Flora, now the matriarch, opened her bible and began reading from the second book of Luke. She personally liked Luke's version better than Matthew's. The family arranged themselves about the room listening in rapt attention. Even Anne's little ones, curled up at her feet, sitting quietly as they listened to their grandmother read, her soft voice lilting with the passages and the story.

After the reading and gifts, the smiling group moved to the dining table where a delectable feast was laid out and waiting. Much of the furniture in this room had been brought from Scotland, but there were new acquisitions of finely polished chairs and a Mahogany Hepplewhite sideboard on which silver candlesticks reflected and glowed with the light.

Anne and Flora had made a duplicate table containing the same foods in the kitchen for the hired hands. They could plainly hear their laughter and conversations mingling with their own through the doors and it mattered little. Peace, love and joy spread equally over all the Glendale occupants. Their new friend, Pastor John MacLeod of the Longstreet Presbyterian Church was in attendance. The servants came into the main dining room and stood quietly as the Reverend MacLeod gave the Christmas blessing in Gaelic, giving thanks for the bounty before them and their great luck of all being together.

Allan was thrilled with his eventual land purchase which had taken place just a few weeks earlier and shared all the information during the Christmas meal. It was 475 acres in Anson County and strategically placed twenty-five miles southwest of Anne and Alex MacLeod's Glendale home. Glendale was perfectly situated halfway between Flora's and her half-sister Annabella at Mt. Pleasant. Hugh was just five miles from Annabella allowing everyone the opportunity to meet and enjoy frequent gatherings such as the one they were having.

Allan talked about the deal he had struck with Caleb Touchstone the previous owner, and bragged how he felt confident it was an outstanding investment. Seventy acres of their new plantation were cleared, along the bubbling Cheek's Creek and there was a heavy beamed building holding a gristmill. They would not only be able to grind their own wheat and oats, but they had potential revenue from grinding crops for the neighbors. There were approving murmurs and toasts through all of Allan's sharing.

.   Allan announced that he planned to move Flora and their servants to Cheek's Creek after the first of the year, right after Hogmanay, weather permitting.

CHAPTER 45

Cheek's Creek—Early 1775

The weather was cooperative that January with only a few light snow showers and temperatures hovering around freezing. The hard frozen ground made it easier to pull the heavily laden wagons down the dirt roads and trails. Had they waited until spring the challenge of muddy ruts would have presented a bigger obstacle. Flora, Allan, the two sons, and all their servants headed out early one morning with fond farewells and embraces, knowing their extended family was relatively close by. As Flora put it, "At least they are no longer on the other side of the Atlantic Ocean". Fannie and Johnnie were never far from her heartstrings and thoughts.

After a long day's travel they came into view of their new plantation, its imposing house and grounds. Flora was delightfully surprised. She could see the clearing then with orchards of bare trees, peaches, and apples. Separate but not far from the house was another smaller structure which could be used for laundry and summer cooking. It was more than she expected and she gave Allan an approving hug and clasped his hand. Both of them felt filled with promise and gratitude for their good fortune. It seemed like they had reached the pot at the end of the rainbow and Flora looked forward to the next year when she or one of them would return to Scotland for their children, John and Fanny. Right now there was no time to waste though and the entire party of MacDonalds began the chore of unpacking. Tonight they would sleep deep, filled with dreams of a bountiful future. Within days the house would be bustling with activity and cleaning while the men would be going to the fields hoping it was not too late to seed winter wheat and busy themselves cutting some of the perimeter dead trees to fill the woodshed.

Her mother's Spinet was reassembled in the parlor. Flora ran her fingers over the keyboard and anxiously awaited a relaxed time when she could play again.

Life took on a routine rhythm and before anyone knew it the air was filled with spring fragrances, apple blossoms mixed with a hint of peach. Looking out across the fields one could see a light covering of green so tender it almost looked edible. North Carolina came in bloom with blue day flowers, pink fawn lilies, and bright yellow wildflowers under the trees cascading in bunches down by the mill. Cheek's Creek was a fragrant bouquet of color and Flora loved it.

Periodically a rider would come through with mail along with the latest copy of the North-Carolina Gazette, which generally was a month old. Allan would read the papers aloud to the family in the evenings as everyone sat around the fire after their meal Flora frequently knitting while she listened. Then, they would discuss what had been read.

The latest issue of the Gazette that arrived that spring of 1775 spoke about the British Parliament and how outraged they were by the Boston Tea Party the year before. What the ladies thought so humorous earlier in the autumn was having dire consequences by a series of punitive acts. The Gazette referred to them as the Coercive Acts and closed the Boston harbor until restitution was made for the damage done to the East

Indian cargo of tea. The British Parliament had also instilled formal British military rule in Massachusetts and made British officials immune to criminal prosecution in the American colonies. This did not bode well with the populace as there would be no accountability for corrupt or unscrupulous deeds.

Both Allan and Flora agreed that the acts made sense requesting restitution, but they debated the immunity clause. Flora felt everyone should be held accountable for misdeeds. Acknowledgment of such would have satisfied her where Allan could rationalize some things.

He continued to read to Flora. "Oh," he said, "They have one listed as the Quebec Act. It extends freedom of worship to Catholics in Canada."

"What is wrong with that?" Flora questioned. "We have always tolerated other religions. Clearly, we all share the same God."

Allan grunted as he read on avoiding her question. "Oh, you know the British, they go to great lengths to stay Protestant." He paused as he read further. "Flora, the Gazette says here the people around

Boston in other colonies support the Bostonians." His voice then raised to an indignant and incredulous tone, "They are mobilizing in resistance to the crown. Good God!" Allan dropped the paper in his lap looking at his wife in the opposite chair her needles occasionally clicking. He read her the next line. "It says the Continental Congress met in Philadelphia and began orchestrating a united resistance to British rule in America. A resistance!"

Allan began muttering under his breath as he got up dropping the paper to the floor and poured himself a dram. He offered one to Flora and she silently shook her head. "I fail to understand Allan how the colonists are going to resist the British."

"War Flora! We have found ourselves in a tinder box here. We apparently have arrived just in time to witness an insurrection. Good God almighty! I need to write to Governor Martin. I will do that in the morning." Allan absentmindedly began blowing out the candles in the room without regard to Flora who was quickly putting her needlework in a basket before following him up to bed with only a single candle to light their way.

As promised Allan sat down the next morning and penned a letter to Governor Josiah Martin, one of many that had been exchanged between the two men who had become fast friends. Allan was decidedly supporting the British side of the troubles more and more and Josiah Martin was encouraging him.

Josiah openly requested Allan to gather loyalists and form a militia.

In late March Josiah, his wife, and children came to visit Flora and Allan at their plantation staying a few weeks. All had a lovely time watching the young Martin children play freely outside the confines of their yard at the fort. It seemed reminiscent of children playing on Skye, yet Flora was having feelings of foreboding which she kept trying to extinguish with logic to no avail. The saber-rattling as she called it was getting louder and a feeling of dread settled in her stomach like a brick.

CHAPTER 46

Late Spring 1775
Rev. James Campbell and the Barbecue Church

Spring in North Carolina continued its show of nature rejoicing. The babbling creeks were full, wildflowers in bloom, and trees leafing out. The great emergence from winter also brought about a new insurgence of hostilities, most of which the residents of Cheek's Creek were unaware of. Hostilities that seemed to have fermented over the winter months.

Anne arrived at Flora and Allan's in May with an armload of mail and old papers. Allan had chores to tend to and was too preoccupied to notice the collection on the table before he left for the mill with James and Sandy. Anne and Flora were alone on the porch when Anne pointed to the two-month-old copy of the Pennsylvania Journal and Weekly Advisor. That was one paper that had not arrived south before and the ladies were curious about a new fascinating publication.

"This man Thomas Paine certainly finds slavery an abomination," Anne said tapping her finger on an essay in the paper. "He thinks we should free them all and let them start their own settlement."

Flora looked at her daughter. "We own no slaves Anne."

"No, but my Alex is thinking if we clear those lower fields and plant tobacco we are going to need more help."

"Why can you not hire people? We have seen our own kin folk sold into slavery and you know that was wrong. Most all of those men and women died within months. It was a death sentence, not transportation—England got her pound of flesh." Flora felt the color rising up to her cheeks. "Good Lord Anne, surely you witnessed some of them being treated worse than coos. It is a horrible practice. There has to be another way."

Flora continued as she remembered reading an old copy of the Pennsylvania Gazette where Benjamin Franklin was opposing Britain selling thousands of her convicts in the colonies. Flora started to laugh. "You know what Mr. Franklin said about the slaves from England." Now laughing out-loud she could hardly get her words out. "He suggested that since the British thought that convicts could reform themselves in a new climate, that the colonies should ship them our rattlesnakes and it might change *their* nature in a new climate."

Flora glanced at the paper Anne had been talking about then picked it up and read aloud a column by Thomas Paine. He had written…"*That some desperate wretches should be willing to steal and enslave men by violence and murder for gain, is [more] lamentable than strange. But that many civilised, Christianised people should approve and be concerned in the savage practice is surprising… It has been so often proved contrary to the light of nature, to every principle of justice and humanity, even good policy, by a succession of eminent men…*"

She stopped reading as one of Anne's toddlers tumbled over a rocking chair and hit his head on the wood box. There was no real injury but the screaming and hurt feelings were only soothed when Grandma Flory picked up the wee one and comforted him with a soothing Gaelic tune as she softly swayed back and forth forgetting temporarily about the news.

When Allan came in from the fields Flora gave him a knowing smile that meant 'quiet'. The babe had fallen asleep in her arms and their daughter Anne had dozed off in a chair holding her newborn. With a long stride Allan gave his wife a kiss on her cheek and then began rummaging through the mail and pamphlets and newspapers laying on the table.

It was the letter from Josiah Martin that he opened first, dated April 25, 1775. Josiah stated his home had been attacked the day before by 'the Americans', the Whigs, the party for independence. Clearly, it was outrage and anger spilling over and fueled by the battles of Lexington and Concord earlier that month. Allan was not sure what he was referencing and continued to read. Martin, in his distress, had sent his pregnant wife and family to their relatives in New York. It was a short note, but requested Allan to come to Fort Johnston, his new headquarters, and that Martin, for his own safety was sleeping on the HMS *Cruizer* in the bay.

Picking up the old newspaper he read what Anne's husband MacLeod had already confided in him down in the orchard. There had been armed conflicts in Massachusetts between the American patriots wanting freedom and the loyal British Troops. The road to perdition and war was accelerating and the claymores rattling louder.

Allan again thought about what he signed, what he promised the King. That he promised to, *'maintain and defend His Majesty's Government and the Laws and Constitution of the Province of North Carolina, against all persons whatsoever who shall attempt to alter, obstruct or prevent the due administration of the Laws & the Public Peace and Tranquility of the said Province. So help me God.'* So help me God weighed heavy on his mind. His brother-in-law and his son-in-law were as deeply entrenched as he—but the women felt different, his wife, his daughter and his sister-in-law. If the men went off to war all they held dear would be left along to fend for themselves, all on their own.

Allan stood, the letter from the governor limply held in his hand. He was conflicted but knew he had to make a decision of which side to support. He no longer could remain neutral as some did, yet clearly saw the perils of joining one or the other side. He strode out the door to take a walk and think.

A week later word was all over North Carolina about the battles of Lexington and Concord. Few remained ignorant of the events and people were rapidly polarizing to one side or another. Neutrality seemed out of the grasp of those living in close proximity to others. Friends, neighbors, and family members were lining up on different sides. Allan called a meeting at his home of what he referred to as leading Highlanders. Both the two Alexanders, his son-in-law, and his brother-in-law attended. The discussions went on for hours, the women only hearing bits and pieces from the other rooms.

Finally, a consensus was made. The decision of this particular group of Scots was to remain loyal to King George III. Flora's heart dropped.

CHAPTER 47

Late Spring 1775

In May, Flora and Allan visited the family at Mount Pleasant with plans that all of them would attend the Barbecue Presbyterian Church together. It was the Reverend James Campbell's turn to preach in the plain log building, and they were looking forward to his sermon. Because North Carolina was a British Colony, the Church of England was only Anglican, and its head was King George III.

The King, well aware the Scottish Presbyterians had their own established philosophies, were allowed only to continue as a church as long as they subscribed to certain articles of the Anglican Creed. It was law, and in compliance James Campbell began the service reading the creed out loud to the congregation before he began their service the particular Sunday the MacDonalds were attending. Most of the membership found it a distasteful formality and ignored the articles while squirming in the pews waiting to get it over with and knowing the reverend couldn't legally preach without doing so or would be subject to arrest.

That was not the problem. It was what occurred after the service that disturbed many churchgoers, but for different, varying reasons. It was McAlpin Munn's threats against their friend Reverend Campbell that was upsetting. Munn's voice was angry and loud enough for everyone to hear both in and out of the building. Munn had started out after the service in complimenting the Reverend's preaching saying he enjoyed the sermon that morning and that they were getting better every sabbath. But then he shifted his weight and his voice took on a more sinister and threatening tone saying that if Campbell ever prayed again as he did for the American arms that he, McAlpin Munn had a molded bullet and powder in his horn to insert in Campbell's head!

Hearing this the color drained from Campbell's face and his knees almost gave out as Munn walked crisply away yelling back that he should let his young associate carry on and not return.

Flora had been standing close by and attempted to support her pastor by placing her arm on his, however, her words were not helping this time. He shook his head, "Aye lassie, I take your warmth to my heart but I canna allow another man to dictate the contents of my prayers. I know these people better than you and this was a sincere warning. I will not be preaching here again!" The twist was, that most of the older, established congregation agreed with Campbell's feelings for independence, they were just maintaining their silence as a traditional courtesy.

Campbell turned and Flora watched as he dejectedly walked back into the building, his head hanging low, intent on collecting his things that very moment. Flora had no choice but to turn and join her waiting family who were already loaded in their wagons. Allen's mouth was tight and he sat straight as he slapped the reins, the horses and wagon moving away in a silence so thick it could have been cut with a paring knife. The women, Annabella and Flora exchanged a full conversation with their knowing eyes and without word. They could read the other's face.

Neither woman wanted war with all its horror and risks. They could see the simmering emotions take over their new community and it was tearing it apart.

Arriving back at Mount Pleasant, Allan wordlessly walked into their guest room with Flora following closing the door quietly behind her.

"He should have known when to shut his gob!" Allan said.

"Who? Who are you talking about? Munn or Campbell?"

"Campbell of course. He shouldn't have taken sides."

Flora's eyes flashed. "I dinna believe we are talking about separate Gods here Allan and, if we are all using the same bible and we are, then they all contain the same ten commandments! You know the part that says, 'Thou shalt not kill'. It applies I believe to all—there does not appear an accompanying list of exceptions." Flora felt her jaw tightening.

Allan whirled around angrily and faced his wife raising his voice in frustration. "We cannot go against

360

King George! I took a loyalty oath! Campbell is praying and I might add, supporting the rebels!"

Flora stood staring at him for a moment then got quiet. They were, after all, not at home, even though she was sure Annabella and Alex were having a similar conversation in another room. Flora's fists started to tighten and she could feel the tension rising to her shoulders and up to her neck. Still, she kept her voice measured but her gaze steady. "I did not Allan! I did not sign a loyalty oath."

"I did!" He said again loudly. "I solemnly promised in the presence of Almighty God to bear faith and true allegiance to his sacred Majesty George III and at the bottom I signed, so help me God."

The two stood still realizing their opinions were as far apart as the isles they left and their new colony. In between these differing philosophies, there was a growing wedge of ice. They had agreed in the past on so many issues and argued so seldom. It was as if two strangers were standing facing each other wondering who the other hostile individual was.

Flora almost whispered her voice was so low. "Allan, like Ruth in the bible, I promised to go everywhere you went, lodge where you lodge and worship the same God. I did not Allan, promise to walk lock-step with you and your opinions. I have never believed for a minute that Geordie is our King and you know it. These people here, our people, know that. They want a new country, free from the Hanoverian house. They do not want to be beholding to a monarch clear across the ocean! And what does God have to do with that?"

The rap on their door temporarily broke the tension in the room. It was Annabella's servant announcing the afternoon meal. Flora reached up and kissed Allan wordlessly on the cheek. His eyes softened as he looked down at her and his tone turned to one of concern. "Flory—I'm protecting you and your pretty neck. We need to keep it in one piece. It isn't a matter of political sympathies. If you are thought once more my dear to be a traitor to the crown, you will certainly swing from the end of a rope. We have to stay loyal. Can you not understand that?"

Therein lay the challenge. Who would be loyal to a monarchy that had tried its best to squash their entire culture in the past? The Barbecue church's congregation was leaning mostly toward independence and the Whigs, but the Longstreet Presbyterian church near Anne seemed more loyal to George III. Was there also to be a split in the churches?

Flora's face visibly hardened. "So we switch alliances and go to mid-day supper," she sarcastically said raising her eyebrows. She looked at him, turned then flounced out of their room.

CHAPTER 48

June—1775

The men began arranging secret meetings, some held at her own Gristmill. And, Allan had not disclosed to Flory the letter he had received from his cousin in New York. The individual Flora thought was a peddler in the area, staying a night in their barn, was actually an officer sent by his cousin to inform Allan MacDonald of the unrest in New York. His cousin was requesting Allan and his brother-in-law Alex gather loyal highlanders together and form regiments of Scots that could be trusted. Allan would soon find out that Josiah Martin would make the same request.

From the talk at their mill and the local Ordinary Pub, Allan knew there were militias of rebels forming here and there, calling themselves 'Minutemen' because they thought and were preparing to respond to any hostility within minutes. The Minute Men appeared to be loosely organized and Allan thought their boisterous talk was simply the result of and paralleling their alcohol consumption. He dismissed them as a threat and thought them an ill-trained and ill-informed group. In his mind, Allan believed any insurrection against the King could be quelled quickly.

Later in the month, Allan was summoned to Fort Johnston by the governor again. Flora stayed back to manage their farm with the help of Sandy and young James. Allan would tell her later that the trip was more than challenging. The mosquito hatch was fierce along the swampy roads. If he wore his wool jacket they failed to bite through, but then he sweat, attracting as it seemed, more of the pesky creatures. When he took his jacket off they were able to bite through his shirt. His gelding too was miserably plagued and kept shaking his head furiously and blowing his nostrils. Between swatting mosquitos and trying to control his mount, Allan kept thinking about he and Flora's heated conversation before he left. Flora's words rang, like an out-of-tune church bell, over and over in his mind. He had signed the oath, but, being a woman, she had not. What good was a man if he could not keep his word? That commitment and trust were worth more than gold, yet he and his most trusted love, the one whose life he shared, and the children they created together, were at odds, both holding strong yet opposing beliefs.

The journey to Fort Johnston was over a hundred and twenty miles and became increasingly wretched with each step for both horse and rider. Later he would claim he lost twenty pounds in the two weeks. Allan would stop as often as he could at homes where he knew the occupants would be supportive and loyal sympathizers of the British throne. He knew he could sleep soundly in their beds and have a meal before he pushed onward.

Allan also was aware of his growing influence over the local Scots and totally cognizant that a portion of his sway came from Flora's hem and her fame with Bonnie Prince Charlie almost thirty years earlier. This knowledge in some respects empowered him, yet he also held a deep sense of responsibility for his kinsman. Allan sensed strongly that Governor Martin intended to use him as leverage to gain his support and gather more followers of the crown.

Governor Josiah Martin also needed to know from Allan what the mood was among the Scottish transplants in the Cape Fear area. Could he depend on them? So far most of the people were keeping tight-lipped as to which side they were supporting, but the rumors were clear as they too, appeared to be polarizing at different meeting houses and churches. In addition, Martin needed to get as accurate an account as he could about arms and ammunition, what would be needed by the loyal colonists in the way of weapons and what did they already possess? Allan MacDonald would be his intelligence source and quite possibly his ace in the hole.

It was Governor Josiah Martin that told Allan he suspected the French, who loved nothing more than to humiliate England, would be backing the rebels. Allan was silent for a moment, "They backed the Jacobite rebellion in '45. They still back the Scots. It was French ships that delivered Charles Stuart to Scotland, along with French gold and ammunition. It would be hard for many of us to shoot in the direction of a French soldier who fought next to us in the last battle."

The younger Martin eyed Allan. "I have procured some interesting information about you Allan MacDonald." He paused as if he should reveal it or not. "Is your family fully aware that you were a Captain in the British 84th Regiment in 1745? When your father was arrested? That you were lucky you were not there when your own father was brought to Fort Augustus where you were assigned?"

There were more than a few awkward moments as Allan's face reddened and his voice hardened. "Did your sources tell you that One-Eyed Hugh MacDonald was also arrested? Are you questioning my loyalties? You must know Hugh was also a Captain in the British Army." Allan slammed his fist down on the table, "I am a man of my word, always have been. I signed a loyalty oath to King George and I will stand by that, come hell or high water."

Governor Martin quietly poured and handed Allan a shot of whiskey dropping his loyalty questioning. "The British are short on everything here. They need more troops, more weapons, and more ammunition to put down this insurrection." He turned to Allan who had finally seated himself by a window looking out at the peaceful sea. Martin continued, "Those damned Whigs, calling themselves Americans scared my wife and children half to death attacking our home like that."

Allan took a sip of his drink. "What was their justification? Were there any? Did anyone say? Is it known?"

Martin sighed. "I had suggested the British give runaway slaves their freedom, and arm them with guns while enlisting them in the Loyalist army."

Allan stared at the man, letting that radical thought settle in his conscious. "A bold move. I'm sure the slaveholders are shaking in their boots considering their slaves would be armed and fighting against them. Arm the man you have beaten. Not a good plan." Pausing for his statement to sink in, Allan continued. "Imagine if you were a slave and your owner just sold your wife and child, moved them miles away, and then someone handed you a gun."

"I would shoot them dead!"

"Aye—Precisely! The problems here in the colonies extends far beyond the tax on tea Josiah. Besides, what about the slaves that look like you and me? The white ones? How are you to know who is who? Who is loyal and who would like to see you in the grave?" Allan cocked his head, raised his eyebrows then sipped his whiskey with a quizzical look at Martin.

Governor Martin was in a spot yet appreciated Allan's candor. He had a great deal to think about and was feeling an unnerving pressure from all sides. The British were short on troops and bought his idea to grant freedom to any slave who would join them, white or black. He did not tell Allan that Lord Dunmore in Virginia had already established an all-black regiment composed of runaway slaves.

Governor Martin, after spending time with Allan, sent him home confident that he had an ally. He also wrote to London requesting more troops and weapons. Neither would arrive until October of that year.

CHAPTER - 49

Late Summer - 1775

Flora, Allan, and their two sons most of the time attended the Long Street Presbyterian Church near Cross Creek. It was only when they visited Annabella that they found themselves at the Barbecue Church. They had become close friends with the younger Reverend James MacLeod who also was a Scottish transplant. This particular trip at the end of summer was combined with their need to acquire supplies which made them rather late for the service. Most of the congregation were already seated when the family entered the cool dark structure.

Reverend MacLeod started the service with healing prayer requests from the congregation and then proceeded with their traditional singing of a Psalm. He cleared his throat and announced whey would be singing Psalm 85.

"Lord, thou hast been favourable unto thy land: thou hast brought back the captivity of Jacob."

The congregation dutifully repeated the verse several times, including the darkies and other slaves in the back pews.

"Thou hast forgiven the iniquity of thy people, thou hast covered all their sin."

And so the call and response went, the distant tones and interpretations filling the North Carolina air once again with a decided lilt. It was clear though, when the reverend got to verse eight he was trying to drive a point home repeating the verse three times with a dramatic silence before each repetition.

"I will hear what God the Lord will speak: for he will speak peace unto his people, and to his saints: but let them not turn again to folly."

The collective congregation sang back in strong voices including the black and white slaves sitting on the back benches.

"I will hear what God the Lord will speak: for he will speak peace unto his people, and to his saints: but let them not turn again to folly."

The young minister looked out at the sea of faces, young, old, white, and colored then, for the third time said, *"God will speak peace unto his people—let them not turn again to folly."* Before anyone could react he quickly finished the final lines of the psalm.

"Surely his salvation is nigh them that fear him; that glory may dwell in our land. Mercy and truth are met together; righteousness and peace have kissed each other."

The lines came back in song.

"Truth shall spring out of the earth; and righteousness shall look down from heaven. Yea, the Lord shall give that which is good; and our land shall yield her increase."

The final line hung heavily in the air and then circled around the room like smoke from a fire. *"The righteousness shall go before him; and shall set us in the way of his steps."*

All was silent with the exception of people readjusting themselves awkwardly on the hard benches. The message from Reverend James MacLeod was clear. He wanted peace.

After the service, the young Reverend and friend of the MacDonald's singled out Allan. His message was simple and he spoke to Allan in Gaelic. "You are going to need a chaplain Allan MacDonald and I'll go with ye as that man."

CHAPTER 50

Allan takes a commission

Allan chose the time carefully to tell Flora he had taken a commission with the British Army. She had been suspicious for months this would be his decision and was not totally surprised when it at last came. They were alone in their parlor just before the family arrived to celebrate their successful harvest. It had been a good year, they had made a profit with the mill and were on their way to success in the colonies. Allan poured the two of them a dram and pulled up his chair next to hers in front of the fire.

"Flory my love," he began. Then, with a swallow he continued, "I have taken a commission with the Royal Highland Emigrants."

There was a moment of silence before she responded, trying desperately to keep the edge off her voice and failing, "How can you? How can you even consider for a moment to fight? You are fifty-five years old Allen and a grandfather. And what about our new

life here? Our starting over in a new country?
Everything is going so well. We have an abundance that
we have not seen before." She sipped her drink and
continued. "And what are you fighting for Allan?
What? Or should I say who? Reverend McLeod is
definitely preaching peace."

The two just stared at the burning embers for a
second or two. Allan lowered his voice. "You know who
we were fighting for, we wanted our Stuart King on the
throne. We fought for Bonnie Prince Charlie and lost.
Least you forget what Cumberland's men did to men,
women, and children in a six-mile swath across
Scotland. When they finished they burned homes to the
ground and left bodies laying in the dirt while they
took off with everything the poor people owned. We
cannot have that happen again me love. We cannot
allow ourselves to be victims again."

Flora detested arguing with Allan yet felt it
dishonest if she kept her true feelings silent. "And now
you have switched allegiances! You are defending the
same family that slaughtered us willy-nilly in our own
country and you are encouraging our sons to do the

same—to join you in defending the crown that beat us down." Flora's cheeks were reddening and her voice getting louder. "And what about our faith Allan? We are supposed to love our enemies. Jesus said that. I am positive that means not shooting them! There has to be a better way."

Allan measured his tone but retorted back between clenched teeth. "Flory, I am frightened, and only to you will I admit it. I believe we all are. Here we have a new life, we can speak our mother tongue openly, we can play the pipes, dance, and wear our kilts. We have our families here, your sister, our children, our grandchildren, and Hugh. It truly is a new start and a new Scotland and we are living without fear." He took a deep breath. "We have to defend our people again. Our way of life on this new shore."

Flora finished her drink. "I cannot see joining the British as defending our people Allan. I see it as betraying them. The British have been trying to stomp us out for centuries. They have objected and sought ways to undermine our very culture again and again. Have you thought laddie, as to what will happen if you lose? What were the results of Culloden? I dinna come all this way to die nor to be widowed."

Allan put his head in his hands and stayed that way for a minute or two before speaking. "Flora, a commission in the King's army will give us an income. I'm tired of scraping and struggling for every shilling and we have to think of the rest of the family. Our son Charles is employed by the East India Company and Ranald is in the Royal Marines. What will become of them if their parents are labeled as rebels? What future for him?" Allan looked at his wife of twenty-five years. "Oh Flory, I do not know what to do. I feel I'm being drawn and quartered here. If we lose it will be Culloden all over again just in reverse. If we win we will still be under the same royal yoke. Cannot you see —we are truly between two stones." He continued, "I remember well the thirty good men lying wounded in the barn by Auld Leanach's Cottage. Burned alive by the English you ken. Dinna think that could not happen here. Dinna think."

Flora could only think what a wicked wicked thing it was to take another's life. She got up and walked to the window. Staring out at the orchard she spoke softly. "I cannot back you in my heart Allan. I feel it is all wrong and for naught. Reverend Campbell is encouraging the established Scots, the ones that want their freedom and have been here for some time. Even our two Presbyterian ministers agree not. Do not picture me riding along on a white horse yelling words of encouragement to my countrymen. Unlike Joan of Arc, I refuse to lead troops for a cause and then be burned at the stake for my efforts. I cannot abide this decision, I simply cannot."

Flora turned again to Allan. "You know they will join you—all of them bonnie highlanders. They will believe that you and I are in agreement—and being loyal to me..." She almost sneered, *"The savior of the Bonnie Prince,* they will join you. Just how did those Sasannachs manage to pacify all of you like a flock of sheep?"

"Damnit Flory, I have no want to lose you."

"Nor I you Allan—nor I you. Neither do I want to see you injured in a swamp or buried in the churchyard. I do not want to be one of those poor souls standing sadly over the grave holding fleurs."

The two stood locked into each other's eyes in disbelief. They had experienced few disagreements in their lives together and now here they were clearly on opposite sides of this issue, both adamant on their positions.

Allan was silent. She was right and his guts were in a knot. Fearful of losing everything, including her, he quietly left the room—left the house and headed for the apple orchard where he could walk and think clearly.

What Flora had said about the two Presbyterian churches was true. The ministers had actually taken turns between three churches, yet since the rumblings of revolution had permeated their community, Rev. James Campbell, although never returning to the Barbecue Church, supported the Scottish families who had been in the colonies for over thirty-five years and openly wanted independence from the crown. The Reverend John MacLeod on the other hand was definitely a loyalist, wanted peace with all his heart, and was spending most of his time at the Longstreet

Church. Their different viewpoint did not affect their friendship though and they continued to correspond with each other regularly.

Allan shuddered at the thought of battling his kinsman, even though historically it was not anything new. He had hoped for so much more here in the colonies. He had prayed for peace and prosperity but instead, he felt trapped. Which way to go? Really, he had already made that decision. His head hurt as he heard these words. *Verily I say unto you, Inasmuch as ye have done it unto one of the least of these my brethren, ye have done it unto me. (Matthew 25:40)*

CHAPTER 51

Early—1776

It was in the first month, January of 1776, that Governor Josiah Martin, believing that the British army's General Cornwallis was on his way to North Carolina, gave the rallying cry to the loyal Scots being led by Allan and Anne's husband Alexander MacLeod. What they had no way of knowing is King George III had simultaneously ordered 120 ships holding 33,000 troops to quell the rebellion in the colonies, and they were indeed sailing across the Atlantic at that very same time.

The messages arrived, the MacDonald men gathered and by mid-February had assembled additional local Scots ready to march and meet the opposition under Cornwallis who, unbeknownst to them would not actually land in the Carolinas until May. However, preparations were being made, men and boys recruited and they were ready to march.

Allan held Flory tightly under the covered wood porch of their colonial Cheek's Creek home. It was mid-February, 1776 and quite cold. There had been a cloud cover for days making the descending gloom heavy as Allan embraced her longer than usual. She had custom fitted his red jacket and sewed all the buttons on both his and her son's uniforms. Flora had to admit to herself that Allan still cut an impressive figure even at fifty-six. He held himself erect, squaring his shoulders and without a sign of a fat belly or stoop.

Sandy, who had just turned twenty-one a week earlier and his nineteen-year-old brother James were holding the horses, impatient and eager to get on the move—to see action. Both boys were excited with visions of exaltation and proud to be with their father now leading the 84th Highland Regiment into battle. Their goal was to stop the rascal rebels at Wilmington, North Carolina, and thus end the thoughts of revolution there. Everyone was confident they would soon return glorious, the initial belief held by every soldier throughout history.

"I will pray for you all without ceasing," Flora's mouth quivered holding back tears. "Hold fast to what is good." Allan mounted his horse and she held up her hand as if to bless them. *"May your body and spirit keep sound."* That is all she could remember of Thessalonians to say to them. She wanted to leave them with something spiritual but felt woefully inadequate for the time. "God be with you."

Allan looked back as he mounted, smiling at her. "And with you my love, and with you."

Flora stood frozen, vacant, and cold as a marble statue, the sense of loneliness washing over her as her three men, her loves, each one holding a special part of her heart rode off. She watched for a long time as their red jackets appeared to be playing a game of hide-and-seek as they rode into the dense forest. A flash of red, then another, then the green eventually enveloping them until straining, she could see them no more.

She thought that the earth colors of the tartans and tweeds of the Scots were better suited in a forest and that her lads would not be sneaking around in the bright red coats they wore. They were so visible and unmistakable.

Flora turned and went into the empty house.

CHAPTER 52

Captured

By the second week in March, 1776, Flora began to worry. She could not shake the nagging, ominous feeling inside, the one she got so often got when something was terribly wrong. Anxious and lonely with her entire family somewhere else, she saddled up her bay mare and leisurely rode to visit her sister Annabella at home at Mount Pleasant. The bone-chilling cold of winter had moved on to a tolerable coolness and Flora was comfortable riding with a lighter plaid wrapped around her shoulders. Annabella of course was thrilled to see her, however, she too had not heard anything of the men, and was anxious for a letter or word of some kind.

After supper the following evening, when Annabella's collection of young ones were off to bed, the two ladies sat by the fire sipping cordials. As they were unwinding from the day there was a muffling commotion at the front door followed by one of the dog's loud barking. The door swung open without a knock and in the candlelight, the two ladies were shocked to see Anne's husband, Alexander MacLeod, holding up young James. Both women rapidly recovered their senses, jumped up, and maneuvered the two weary soldiers to where they had been sitting a few minutes earlier. Annabella tossed another log into the embers and the flames lept up with a crackle as questions began flying faster than the answers. The first tragic news was when Alex held up his finger as if to silence them, looked at Flora, and told her, "Allan and Sandy have been captured!" Then he looked at Annabella with sad eyes, "And your husband too ma'am. He is with them."

Flora felt her head spin and she put her hand down on James' shoulder to steady herself. "Are they whole?"

James patted her hand. "Mum, they were all right when we left them. Alex and I were lucky to escape. They were letting go most of the regulars and even Da's three men servants that had gone along. They freed them."

Flora looked quizzically at the door. "Are they with you? Shall we let them in?"

Alex shook his head and sipped the whiskey Annabella had handed him while he stared into the flames. "They have run off to God knows where. They knew we were coming, those Whigs, those rebels—they knew ahead of time and created a complete ruse. They had a couple of cannons already set up and it was all over in a few minutes."

Annabella put her hand to her mouth in shock. She knew many of the men were not adequately armed, the British had seen to that after Culloden. But here they were fighting for the British, some with only swords against muskets.

"We started to cross the stream at the Widow Moore's Creek Bridge, at dawn (February 27, 1776) but unbeknownst to us the rebels had taken up the planks of the bridge, greased them with tallow, and smeared soft soap all over before replacing them. There we were, looking proud and brave in our new coats and kilts, marching along with the pipes when the first horse started to skid across the bridge, throwing his rider into the creek. Someone yelled in Gaelic, and they charged right into cannon fire." MacLeod lowered his head and shook it in disbelief. "They even captured the Chaplain, John MacLeod from Skye."

"Better captured than shot!" Flora stated, sorrow changing rapidly to anger and her face reddening.

Alex shook his head, "Maybe. But there were at least fifty killed. Fifty loyal men lay dead in the swamp around the bridge within two minutes. Fifty families missing and grieving for someone. These rebels, calling themselves Patriots, are fighting with a fiery determination I haven't seen since Culloden—and possessing that same sense of fearlessness that we held back then.

Annabella got up, went to the kitchen, and fixed two plates of cold cuts and cheeses on top of thick slices of bread. The voices in the parlor had awakened two of her children who had come down the stairs and were gawking at their bedraggled cousins as she returned with the food. Handing over the plates to the men she rapidly shooed the young ones back upstairs, thankful they did not ask about their father. Then, as Alex began pacing she took his seat and sat down quietly.

It was Flora who broke the silence addressing MacLeod in her decisive and take-charge voice. "We will all get a good night's sleep, and in the morning ride together to your home Alex. You will not be suspect with clean clothes and fresh horses. We'll look like a family going to church in a wagon and young James can ride in the back between bags of goods."

"But Flory, they know you. Everyone knows who you are. You too may be in danger." Alex was exhausted leaning against the mantle when he glanced over. James' legs were stretched out his head limply drooped onto his chest—the boy had fallen fast asleep.

"Worry not about me." Flora answered, "We need to get to your home. I will be fine for now."

As Alex rose to go to bed and roust the young man, he turned to the ladies and told them that the regiment had started out with approximately 1,600 troops, however, half of them deserted along the way, their bravery fading as they marched. He shook his head thinking they were ordinary people, ordinary men, and boys who only wanted peace in their community. He could not conceive of ever applying the term coward or traitor to them. Their loyalties were to their families and the greater desire to stay alive. They had not left as a group, just a few here and there disappearing into the underbrush.

As planned, early the next morning, Alex MacDonald along with Flora and James set out for Glendale cleanly dressed in borrowed clothes, and driving a buggy. The journey would take them most the day, skirting a few small hamlets scattered here and there. He and James had taken off their red jackets and stuffed them inside one of the quilts which Flora had thrown in the back of the rig. In addition, Flora borrowed one of her sister's larger bonnets hoping to hide her face as much as possible in case they came across questioning eyes.

Before they left Mt. Pleasant Flora embraced Annabella. "Hold fast sister dear, they are alive. Hold that thought in your heart and pray they stay that way."

Towards evening their buggy pulled up to Alex's Glendale home to the welcoming arms of his beloved Anne. She was his life, his breath and he could not have been happier in her embrace and seeing his three young bairns. Little Norman had missed his father desperately. When Allan, at last, was able to sit down he had his two young boys, six and four sitting on both his knees. They did not want to let him go. Anne stood smiling, their third tiny son bundled in her arms. Alex too felt torn as he gazed at his most precious treasures, his family.

When the children were all tucked in bed Alex and James relayed the tale of Moore's Creek Bridge once again. Anne could only look at Flora and James sympathetically, now knowing Allan and Sandy were captives along with Annabella's husband. She worried about the future that was unfolding for all of them. Alex avoided telling her that he was planning on rejoining the troops in hopes of freeing his uncle and father-in-law—a decision that had not come easily.

CHAPTER 53

The Letter - 1776

A long month went by before Flora got her first letter from Allan through an unexpected route. She had wanted to check on Annabella and left her plantation in the hands of James and her servants one Friday. When she got to Mount Pleasant, Annabella handed her the letter which had arrived the day before by way of a member of the Barbecue Church. The man had recently returned from Halifax. He carried with him several letters from the captives in the area along, with the usual outdated newspapers and packages. With shaking hands she opened and read that Allan and Sandy, with over ninety other officers, had been marched a hundred and fifty miles to a jail in Halifax, North Carolina. He was unsure how long they would be there and thought they would be moved shortly. He told her that Chaplain MacLeod was with them and that the rebels had released all the private soldiers that survived the battle, including their indentured servants.

The letter was shorter than she wished, but it pleased her to know they could write at all, and grateful to hear from him. Flora planned on attending church Sunday next to let the Reverend Campbell know that John MacLeod was a captive along with her husband, reported to be alive and seemingly well. Campbell who was now preaching at a Presbyterian church in Guilford was scheduled to return Sunday as a guest speaker.

That afternoon, after returning from services, Flora sat on Annabella's porch grappling with events. She looked out over her sister's prosperous plantation then, pulling her cape tighter about her shoulders walked alone into the cleared field. She felt trapped in this new country. The surrounding forest felt like a platoon of green sentries standing shoulder to shoulder and not allowing her to peer over or around their broad branches. It was a different kind of prison. The cold walls of the London Tower were of stone and the interior constantly dark, but these walls of growing pine were beginning to close in on her. She couldn't see the horizon. There were no colorful sunrises or sunsets in this new land. Flora felt caged once again.

Her thoughts carried to her precious grandchildren, Anne's little ones. They would know no different. To them, this new land would be their place with the surroundings comfortably familiar. It would be their home always, but not hers. They would put down roots in this soil as many had almost forty years earlier. Flora realized she was the transplant and one that was not thriving in the new environment. It was closing in, this ruggedly beautiful forest and its brilliant flowers were choking her.

The Scottish immigrants who had been here longer, many second and a few third generation now, had a sense of the place, a connection. It was their home, their roots grew deep into the soil. They thought of themselves as Scottish, but many had never seen Scotland. Flora was rather astonished at her own revelation. For the most part, it was the more established Scots, the ones who had been here the longest that was in favor of independence from the

British. Of course, it was clear now. They held no connection to the British Isle, they felt connected to this land, these pine forests, and cultivated fields of tobacco, cotton and rice. This was never her home, however, it was truly theirs.

Flora shivered and turned toward the house keenly aware, deep inside her, that understanding a problem was not a solution. She would not be able to change Allan's mind nor the supportive men quickly lining up behind him with similar high passions. They too were prisoners in a way and couldn't comprehend the concept of self-government. They had, for centuries been ruled, told what to do; laws made by someone else with violations and punishments doled out by a higher authority. Many even held the very strong opinion that the monarchy was ordained by God himself. She would talk it over with Annabella, but the two ladies could no more stop the accelerating war than they could stop a landslide. Flora just wanted to go home and home was not Cheek's Creek, however neither could she leave with Sandy and Allan stuck in a jail somewhere. She would not abandon any of them.

CHAPTER 54

Early Spring 1776

The winter seemed longer than it should have, one gray rainy day followed by yet another and another. Flora could only pray futilely that the rain would not only sodden the ground but also dampen down the hostilities in the community. She hoped beyond hope for everyone's emotions to cool down and that she would see Allan and Sandy come riding through their orchard, returning home before the peach trees blossomed. In her misery, she fully realized there were other mothers out there who felt the same regardless of what uniform and side their loved ones had chosen. She knew that they too suffered in birth, fretted over their little sons as they grew, rejoiced in their accomplishments, and never, never considered using them as fodder for someone else's political ideals. She mourned collectively for all.

Eventually, what did arrive at her Cheek's Creek home, along with the mail and some dry goods was a printed pamphlet titled 'Common Sense'. Looking at the inscription Flora could heartily agree, that everyone should come to some common sense and stop what she considered to be nonsense. Instead, when she read the pamphlet the author was definitely pushing the colonists toward independence. He argued that the monarchy was evil and should be rejected as a form of government. Thomas Paine wrote and included a quote from the bible, *Judges 8:22-23: "The Israelites said to Gideon, 'Rule thou over us, both thou and thy son and thy son's son also…and Gideon said unto them, I will not rule over you… the Lord shall rule over you."*

Reading this Flora thought angrily to herself, 'good grief, our ministers do not even agree, and here is someone saying the Lord will take care of it.' She crumpled the pamphlet and threw it down and saying to herself out loud. "Someone has to herd the sheep—it appears they are all lost and there isn't even a good dog to show them the way."

By the time the peach trees bloomed what remained of her and Allan's servants had abandoned the plantation. Both sides of the war had promised freedom to anyone who joined their ranks. Black slaves, both men, and women were running away by the hundreds, perhaps thousands, joining the British and forming what they called the Ethiopian Regiment. The white slaves too were running, but blended in easier in the colonies and were able to 'disappear' within the cities and land. She and eighteen-year-old James were on their own to manage the work on the plantation and mill. They were working from dawn to dusk, planting a vegetable garden, feeding livestock and managing the food preparation and storage. They still had cows that needed to be milked twice a day and milk turned into butter and cheese. Flora's hands grew callouses, her dresses soiled and many a night she fell exhausted into bed with every muscle hurting from head to toe.

It was about that time that she received a second letter from Allan which she quickly tore open. He was fine, or at least wrote so, as was their son Sandy. He wrote that Reverend James Campbell, who was unabashedly in favor of independence from Britain, upon hearing that his friend Reverend John MacLeod was imprisoned with them in Halifax, had walked 150 miles from Guilford to seek his release. It was in Halifax that James Campbell implored the local congress to release his colleague to his custody. To appeal to their Christianity, Campbell stated that MacLeod was only with the 84th Highlanders in the role of a chaplain and that he had no particular political agenda or belief. Allan wrote that Campbell was successful and to everyone's knowledge, MacLeod was headed for Charleston where he thought he could get a ship home to Scotland. In short they would not be hearing from him again.

Flora's heart lightened and she was elated to hear everyone so far was alive, even though she worried if they were getting enough to eat. She decided not to write and tell Allan that the farm was struggling or that the servants were slowly abandoning them. She also would not tell him that she and James, along with Donald, Annabella's eldest, managed to do most of the spring planting, sewing the wheat and rice in the lower fields. He would simply have a pleasant surprise when he and Sandy returned home.

Additionally, her letters intentionally left out the fact that marauders and plunderers were in the area, frequently breaking into the houses looking for anything they could steal, sell or eat. She did not tell him of the little money left had to be hidden, nor that she had been sick with what she thought was just worry—a reoccurring fever that seemed to be sweeping the folks left in their small community.

Instead, Flora wrote him about how well they all were, that the plantation was productive, the fruit trees were bearing and they were anxiously waiting for his return.

CHAPTER 55

Summer 1776

Months passed before Flora heard from Allan, Sandy, or the others again, and then it was not in a letter, but a visit from Annabella. She had brought with her a collection of letters from Scotland and old newspapers that had finally gotten through to them, all accompanied of course, with scuttlebutt and the latest gossip with some real news of the auld country.

Apparently, the captive officers from the 84th Highland Brigade had been moved again, this time to a goal further north of the city of Philadelphia. They were still together, which the sisters agreed was a good thing as they could buoy each other's morale knowing they were not alone in their misery.

Flora had not attended any of the Presbyterian churches in several months. Her faith was not lost, she was just exhausted at the end of most days so, she and James would sit and read to each other from the bible in the evenings. Her hands, once so smooth, had the look of hard work etched on her fingers and nails. When she attempted to do fine needlework the rough skin would snag the threads and fabric. Annabella just blathered, filling her in on the church activities and thoughts. She told Flora the Presbyterians in the community were relieved that Reverend MacLeod had been released, and most still respected him regardless of his political viewpoints. A cup had been sent from Scotland and engraved, 'To the Presbyterian Congregation in Cumberland County under the care of Reverend John MacLeod.' Annabella told her that his congregation remained loyal to the man, believing he was an individual of eminent piety.

Flora quietly thought to herself for a brief second that she too would like to be heading back to the homeland when Annabella then handed her a newspaper. It was an old copy dated back to April of that year. The headline read *North Carolina is the First Colony to vote for Independence!* Flora's mouth fell open. She had no idea that this colony, the one she lived in was so strongly in favor of independence that they actually voted publicly on such a statement. This was the first she had heard of it. Apparently, they had titled it the Halifax Resolve. "Annabella, we are on the wrong side here and in the minority. The British are going to lose, they will not have a victorious war here. We are across the Atlantic from them and this is wild, wild country." Flora got up and walked to the window looking out to the bulging orchard. Her mouth tightened and she spoke slowly. "Our husbands are in dire straits. British soldiers will not be set free. Not released."

A few days later Annabella returned to her home at Mount Pleasant only to be met by her servants wringing their hands and telling her that her two youngest children were burning up with fevers. Neither child was eating in spite of the tempting morsels being prepared or the coaxing. The poor things were moaning, complaining about headaches, and unable to even hold down the smallest amount of clear broth. Her young son and daughter were gravely ill.

Without pause, Annabella sent her eldest son Donald back to get Flora immediately. He was instructed to tell his aunt to bring any tinctures or medicines she might have. The children's fevers were raging and they desperately needed her help straight away along with her herbal knowledge.

Riding hard it was a disheveled Donald who appeared back at Flora's door sobbing and saying his little brother and sister were deathly ill. Without thought Flora sprung into action, collected her bag of herbs and tinctures, and whistled for her bay mare who was in the nearby paddock. Slipping a rope around the horse's neck, Flory led the animal to a well-placed stump where she tied her, and went to fetch a saddle from the barn. By now Donald had regained his composure and grabbing the heavy saddle from his aunt set it up and onto the horse's back, pulling the cinch tight. Flora instructed her son James to stay at the house and tend to their livestock.

"I will be back here in a few days son," Flora told him, mounting up and pulling her long skirt between her legs. Her son was quite used to this maneuver knowing their mother was an accomplished rider and Donald had also seen his aunt do this. This was no time for her to ride side-saddle. Time was of the essence.

Donald also grabbed a fresh mount leaving his winded horse in his aunt's corral and the two rapidly rode off. Both knew the route well by now, along the beaten trail and through the dense brush growing along the river. Flora's mare was leading with Donald a short distance behind on a gelding. They were making good time. What Flora did not expect, nor did her horse, was the four-foot cottonmouth laying across their trail. Her mare instinctively threw up her head and reared, tossing the surprised Flora backwards and onto the hard-packed dirt. Donald reined his horse and dismounted running to her before either animal fully came to a stop. She lay dazed on the ground a shooting pain in her right arm. Stunned and wondering for a moment exactly what happened, she watched the equally startled brown-banded snake slither off toward the creek. Her mare also turned to see the results of her frightening reaction to the snake and was slowly walking back to her grounded mistress.

The situation left few options. As she regained her senses Flora knew her arm was fractured and was thankful the bones had not broken through her skin. It appeared to be a simple break, if any break could be called simple while you are experiencing it. She looked at her splayed legs and noticed part of her petticoat had also torn. Donald was next to his aunt while she explained as calmly as she could that her arm was broken. "Donald, we need to tear a strip from my petticoat and make a splint." It was her step-father Hugh that had taught her as a young girl how to set broken limbs and she had set a few for her sons growing up. She never expected to be setting her own in the middle of a dusty trail.

Donald found a few short curved bark pieces that would fit her lower arm in the underbrush. He was back shortly binding her arm with the torn petticoat strips and talking to her gently. "It is swelling. Do you want to go back to your home Auntie?"

It was hot and sweat was running in rivulets down her forehead and chest, leaving marks down the front of her dirty dress. "No, there is nothing to do there, we are more than halfway to your home. I can still be of some help to your mother and siblings. The bag of tinctures and herbs was intact tied tight to the saddle. But you are going to have to help me back up onto that mare."

Donald practically lifted Flora back onto her horse making sure she was firmly mounted and adjusted her stirrups before they proceeded on their journey. She fashioned a sling to cradle her broken limb and held the reins with her good hand. The incident slowed them down and was early evening when they arrived at the stately home on the hill. As they approached Mount Pleasant the wailing from the house was unmistakable. The two riders pulled up, then gasped as they heard and identified the sobs of grief announcing death in a crescendo of haunting cries. Even a small group of servants were weeping loudly together as they stood on the expansive porch, unaware of the approaching riders.

No explanation was needed. Donald slowly dismounted and then numbly helped Flora down before he tied up their horses. No longer was there a hurry to help. The two walked to the house and entered with heavy feet and hearts.

Annabella sat in front of the cold blackened fireplace slumped in her chair. The temperature both outside and in the house was stifling, the humidity oppressive and there was a sickly, stagnant odor in the air. She was gazing straight ahead at nothingness, seemingly unaware of anyone else's presence.

"Annabella dear, it is I, Flory." she looked into the vacant face and eyes of her sister. Patting her on the arm and kissing her on the forehead she whispered, "You just sit here, I will take care of everything."

The pain in Flora's arm could not be compared to the stabbing dull ache in her chest and stomach. The loss of the children was great and the anguish of her sister almost unbearable. It was a dark day, yet time and the season would not allow anyone to wallow in pain and anguish for long. She looked about the stricken staff to gauge who could help and settled on an elderly stout woman she knew from Skye. "Maggie put the kettle on and we need to get two caskets made quickly." She shook her head, "I dinna think we can

414

have a wake in this heat. These babies need to be buried right away."

Upstairs Flora pulled back the sheets covering the still bodies of the children and looked down at them. They looked so peaceful yet unnaturally still. They would need to be bathed, dressed and their bedding burned. She also had to tend to her own injury but, first things first.

She sent one of the servants with a wagon to the closest woodworker to order caskets and to bring a minister back with him. She was in the dark as to who was currently leading their churches with John MacLeod and James Campbell both gone. There had to be someone. She would have appreciated knowing who was coming, or where they were to bury the children, but these things would be approached one by one as needed.

Flora checked on Annabella who had been unable to budge from her chair in the parlor. After seeing there was a cup of stout tea next to her, Flora enlisted Maggie again to help her clean up. She herself was covered in dirt, her dress still torn and stained. She would find one of her sister's dresses but needed help to re-bind her swollen and broken arm properly and dress. Again Maggie came to her assistance, binding the arm and dressing her. Flora returned to the parlor, went to Alex's cupboard, and poured herself a stout dram, then filled two smaller glasses taking one to Annabella.

Pulling a chair next to her sister she handed her the drink without saying a word. The two sat there in silent grief as the house quieted and the hours slipped into the darkness like a shroud. Flora only got up occasionally to pour them another. She had no need to tend a fire, the weather was hot enough.

Exhaustion slowly overtook the two grieving sisters as they wordlessly sat lost in their own minds. Flora mercifully suggested she and Annabella go to bed, lit a candle, and led her grieving sister up the stairs, crawling into the comforting bed with her. There were no husbands to lend supporting arms. They and thousands like them were alone since the damn war started, including her daughter Anne. Alone to deal with grief, worry, and the simple task of keeping their family fed. Alone to manage the finances and what might be left of their employees. Alone to get the wood for fire and haul the water. And they would be alone to bury their dead children.

❋

The young brother and sister, whose lives were cut short by typhus, were laid side by side in simple graves not far from their Mount Pleasant home. Their final resting places were marked with stones and simple prayers were said. It was only the immediate family who stood saying their goodbyes at the side of the two small dirt mounds. Their grandfather, Hugh MacDonald had come and was practically holding up his daughter, the grief-stricken Annabella. He planned to stay with her until he felt she was strong enough to be by herself again and that was an indeterminate time. There were no words to describe the depth of sorrow everyone felt at the loss of these two innocents. So many hopes and dreams died and were buried along with their tiny bodies. Flora cleared her voice and then began to sing the Fleurs O' the Forest but her voice quivered and she could only choke out two verses.

I've heard the lilting, at the yowe-milking,
Lassies a-lilting before dawn o' day;
But now they are moaning on ilka green loaning;
"The Flowers of the Forest are a' wede away".
Dool and wae for the order sent oor lads tae the
Border!
The English for ance, by guile wan the day,
The Flooers o' the Forest, that fought aye the foremost,
The pride o' oor land lie cauld in the clay.

The devastated family walked silently back to the large house they ironically had named Mount Pleasant, Annabella tightly holding Fora's good hand and Hugh following close.

⁊

Flora returned home several days later to share the sad news with her son James. She would dictate a letter for him to write to Alexander MacDonald, Annabella's husband and father of the dead children they had just buried. He also would write one to his father. Her arm would slowly heal but it would take much longer to heal her sorrow.

CHAPTER 56

Independence!

Word spread quickly in late July of 1776. The Continental Congress had formally written a Declaration of Independence, a copy of which was printed in the Bradford Post, but Flora heard about it only when a copy of the Pennsylvania Evening Post made its way to her community.

She read it carefully and thoughtfully alone on her porch after the morning milking had been done. Then she read it a second time.

We hold these truths to be self-evident, that all men are created equal, that they are endowed by their Creator with certain unalienable rights, that among these are life, liberty, and the pursuit of happiness.

It was terribly hot and she mulled over the words while loosening the stays on her corset. 'The pursuit of happiness is not being bound up in these bloomin' corsets in the middle of a hot summer' she thought to herself. Change was in the air. The Quakers already had voted on the prohibition of owning slaves, and the idea of self-government was growing with the writings of Ben Franklin who openly admitted listening to and being influenced by the Six Nation people. They were The Iroquois Confederacy and he was looking at their successes with peace and prosperity. If the Native Americans could do it successfully he wrote, so could the white colonists.

There had been no news from Allan or either of the Alexanders in some time. At least she could share her fears and anxiety with her daughter and sister Annabella.

Cousins James and Donald were spending more time with each other taking on the responsibilities of their captured fathers. At some point, James talked Donald into accompanying him as he re-enlisted. Subsequently, the two lads left their grieving mothers to join the British troops shortly after the children's burial. Their rationale was to get their fathers home sooner.

Little by little Flora's remaining help deserted her, seeking their fortunes and freedom by disappearing quietly into the night and absconding with her milk cows and chickens. The dream of a happy new life and prosperity turned into a screaming nightmare and there was a meager pile left of her belongings. She had completely given up church attendance for multiple reasons. Many of the local women, some of whom she considered friends, blamed her for their misfortunes and their husbands following Allan's leadership. She knew in short order that alone and under these circumstances, she was in a dangerous situation once again. The pendulum had swung and Flora went from a revered heroine to persona non grata among her own people within a short span of time.

The final insult and injury was the notice that her house and property were to be confiscated by the rebels. She knew she had to leave. She stood running her hands over her mother's spinet, knowing it too would have to be left behind. Defeated, she loaded up the small wagon with her few remaining things, hitched up the last horse, and drove to Anne's Glendale home leaving Cheek's Creek and mill behind her forever. With head held high and face forward Flora forced herself not to look back. There would be no final glimpse of this place.

Anne had offered their home earlier as a sanctuary, emphasizing she could use her mother's help since she was pregnant for the fourth time. She had three small lads now underfoot and an addition on the way. Alex MacLeod, Anne's husband had put himself in an interesting position. He frequently was able to return to the plantation and check on her. For reasons which no one could explain, their servants, the ones they brought with them from Skye also stayed with the family. None had run off or stolen a thing. Alex did promise those who stayed a stipend and higher wages once the war was over. Only two men had disappeared and were barely missed as the Glendale plantation continued to be productive and an essential food supply for more than the immediate family.

Having experienced war and divisive opinions earlier in her life, Flora knew the situation and circumstances which they currently were in, were unpredictable. She felt that in essence, even though called a revolution, the unrest in the colonies appeared to her as a civil war. It was neighbors against neighbors with troops thrown in. The French in their blue coats sided with the patriots and the British red coats mixed with the loyalists. If an individual was not wearing an identifying uniform and you personally did not know them, it was impossible to tell by looking who was friend or foe. Flora had experienced a similar situation in Scotland where it made everything they did unnerving, right down to milling the neighbor's grain. She felt the only ones she could trust were her own family and those suspicious feelings were uncomfortable for her.

One afternoon, while Alex was home checking on his family and they were all sitting down for a meal, a rider came galloping up to the house. The man, familiar to Alex and Anne was urgently shouting as soon as he hit the ground and ran toward their entrance. "Run, you have to run!" Everyone jumped up from the table. "There is a vigilante group heading this way to burn you out." The man was red-faced and sweating and his horse panting and frothy. "They are on their way!"

In a whirlwind of ensuing commotion Anne and Alex jumped up from the table and started giving orders to everyone within hearing distance. Using pillowcases for bags they quickly threw in clothes for the children, grabbed their own and any food they could, stuffing the cloth bags with as much as they could carry. There was no time to lose. Flora already had a small casket of things, the locket with Johnnie and Fanny's hair, and the thin sheet Charles Stuart had used. She dumped the contents in an embroidered pillowcase along with her prayer book and a spare dress. Slinging the bag over her shoulder like a sailor she ran down the stairs. One of the servants brought a wagon around to the door and the family piled in. Alex picked up his now crying chorus of little ones and stuffed them next to the bags to minimize their jostling.

Anne too was crying and in between frightened sobs encouraged her servants to hide in the woods, that it was she and Alex the mob was after and not them.

Flora got in the back and with quick efficiency rearranged the small children between the bags. Alex slapped the reins, the drafts strained at the weight yet pulled the wagon up to a low hill speedily and just far enough away to see and hear the invaders running and screaming into the clearing surrounding Glendale and then up onto their expansive porch. Hoards were entering their house, pushing and yelling at each other for the advantage of plunder.

The escapees stopped breathlessly on the knoll where they stopped and gazed in disbelief as the so-called Patriots ran about their property below looting and burning. As they stood in shock watching, hidden in the trees, dark grey smoke rose up twisting in the sky with sickly yellow whips. They could see clearly the hot glowing embers hungrily consuming their home. The family watched stunned and helpless as their dreams of a future and treasures of their past were torched without impunity. It was unadulterated retaliation mixed with a celebration of independence. Destruction of what was perceived as an enemy home.

The light breeze pushed the acrid fumes in their direction filling their faces, crawling up their noses into their lungs, and causing their eyes to burn and water. The smoke mercifully allowed them all to cry openly at the sight that was shaking them to their inner cores. Alex's cheeks were streaked as he watched years of work go up in the all-consuming flames of hatred. The beloved home he had named Glendale was being burned to the ground and everything in it. His library of over 320 volumes, books on history, philosophy, and poetry that he had brought from Scotland. The beloved fiction that he read aloud in the evenings to Anne and his growing family. Gone! Forever gone to ash and he wondered what for? Flames fueled by men he once considered his neighbors, ones with whom he had sung psalms, ones with whom he had prayed and broken bread. They were burning up everyone's vision of a new country both his and theirs. And the books, his dear treasured books. Alex felt his body drained of its energy. He had to hold onto the side of the wagon for a moment realizing that in reality, he had saved his greatest treasures, his wife Anne and their precious children.

As the smoke blotted out the sun the afternoon took on an eerie cloak of yellow and grey, appearing as if it were late evening. The beleaguered group turned their backs and began to struggle on foot through the brush of an infrequently used trail. They would go to Annabella's Mount Pleasant, the only home left for all of them. The trip would take them a good eight hours on foot with the wee bairns in tow and sacks on their backs. Alex un-hitched the horses hoping they would follow them. He would try and send someone later to retrieve the wagon. Stealth was needed now as they escaped through the brush as evening fell.

Anne was mumbling over and over that they should never have allowed the recruiters set up their headquarters in their home. It had made Glendale a known and easy target. Flora's property was taken from her, but burning Glendale was a louder statement —a proclamation that stated the MacDonalds were no longer welcome in North Carolina.

MacLeod tried to console the sobbing young woman he adored, his emotions heavy with loss. "Aye, we only had two choices, my love. Either help assemble a troop of loyal Scots to back the King or support a revolution that is bound to fail." He paused a minute and put his arm around her. "We have each other my beautiful lassie and our healthy wee babes. We are all in one piece and together for the time being. Books and things can be replaced." In spite of his encouraging words to his wife, Alex MacLeod was devastated. His library had been his pride and joy.

Anne shifted her quietly nursing babe to her other breast, readjusting her tartan tightly around them both. MacLeod picked up the eldest child Norman and Flora grabbed the small hand of the youngest boy as they started off soundlessly on the footpath of the dense pine forest. The descending twilight made their trek barely discernible but also provided the cover they desperately needed to be undetected.

CHAPTER 57

Mount Pleasant 1777-1778

Hugh was still with Annabella at Mount Pleasant and thinking of turning his entire holdings over to his eldest grandson Donald. Annabella was slowly waking from the heavy cloak of grief but he felt strongly that she continued to need his shoulder and helping hand. So it was that the winter of 1777-1778 found them all under the ample roof of Mount Pleasant, at least the MacDonalds who were not incarcerated or in the military.

The non-stop activity brought on by Anne's young sons kept them all busy and when Annabella pitched in to help, she momentarily would forget the sorrow and heavy grief that her own loss tore at her. The daily activities of feeding the family and running the plantation kept all of them busy. Hugh made them laugh one evening when they were commenting on how infrequent they saw Alex MacLeod. Hugh, looking over at Anne's bulging belly got a wry smile and commented that Alex apparently had been "here long enough". His constant humor and alternate ways of perception brought them frequently a welcome sense of levity.

❋

The arrival of Anne's fourth baby was thankfully uneventful and a good thing. It was as if her body knew what to do now and did it with ease. The new addition was a welcomed little girl whom Anne named after her mother, Flora. When Flora held this granddaughter she would look into her innocent face and wonder which part of her was passed on. She recognized the dark curls about her face, but was that a tiny cleft in her chin? Will her eyes be the color of mine or Allan's? Part of her would continue with this one. She also wondered what kind of life and future this tiny little Flory would experience.

The three women attempted to keep up a routine that, even if monotonous, gave them some stability. Flora still did not attend church but instead, let Anne and Annabella go while she took care of the wee ones.

Even though Flora was happy the family had at last been left in peace at Mount Pleasant, she could not help but wonder why. The plantation seemed unscathed from marauders—an island of tranquility among the chaos. One evening she approached the subject after the children had been put to bed. It was Annabella's answer that totally caught her off guard

"Annabella, I'm curious, do you know why we are quite unmolested here? It is uncanny—not unwelcome under the circumstances. It just seems odd after all we have experienced. I keep thinking it is just the calm before the next horrendous storm."

Annabella looked at her with a wry smile. "Mount Pleasant is no longer owned by us. We are just living here for the duration."

"Not owned? You sold it?"

Annabella raised her eyebrows and grinned slightly. "My Alexander knew things were not stable in this colony. He sensed this war and all its possible repercussions. He dinna want to lose it all so, a few days before he left he conveyed this plantation to Donald Cameron. It is Cameron's now and has been for some time. This plantation is seen as owned by a Whig Patriot but inhabited by the wife of a captured loyalist. So far the ploy has worked. We have had no troubles." Then Annabella knocked on the wood table with her knuckles for luck.

Flora looked at her sister, covered her mouth, and started to giggle. "You mean to tell me you have pulled off a great deceit?"

Annabella smiled also and it was good to see after all this time. "Aye, that is exactly what I am saying," she paused. "Cameron is a dear friend and loyal Scot. He will give it back to us when this mess is all over—and it will be over at some point. We hope sooner rather than later. The British have been winning battle after battle." Annabella's eldest daughter had taken a position in Wilmington as a tutor and kept her abreast of much of the news. She had let her mother know that Fort Ticonderoga had surrendered to the British and was hopeful that by the end of the summer, the war would come to an end.

There had been a scarcity of letters and newspapers arriving at Mt. Pleasant. For one Flora had moved two times, and then there was a shortage of paper in general. News arrived orally as the riders were going back and forth between the towns, meeting houses, and plantations. Eventually, Flora received another letter from Allan, this one written on the back of a flyer advertising runaway slaves, three white and two black. He wrote as tiny as he could to squeeze in all that he wanted to say.

My Dearest Flory,

We are all well with the exception of lice, but there is no word on our release. One thing good to report is a man named Benjamin Griffith has been ordered by their Congress to provide us with blankets, clothing and fuel for the winter.

He said their goal was to treat us humanely and that would mark a reflection on the new congress favorably. So my dear, they are glazing the walls of the prison to keep us comfortable during the upcoming winter. Be well Flora.

Your loving husband,

Allan MacDonald

Flora took up the habit of walking out by herself in the afternoons and would sit in a shady spot behind Annabella's house where there was a bubbling spring. There she would pull out her petit tinder box, pack her clay pipe full of tobacco, and light it. She grew to enjoy this quiet time in contemplation away from the bustling house and children. At least there was plenty of tobacco and it seemed like it was one of the few things they were not rationing. Here, alone she could sit and reflect, nostalgically looking back at her life in Skye, Floggerty, and their home at Kingsburgh. She fondly thought of her own children recalling their antics, laughter, and occasional irritating rivalry and it was those halcyon memories that buoyed her spirits. She occupied her mind with visions of sunny afternoons and the additional rainy ones, where the family would sit around her mother's spinet and sing. Flora would focus on gratitude for what she had held, experienced, and endured. The family was still all alive and even though the future unknown, she had hope. It was hope that seemed to prevent the ever-present melancholy from taking a controlling role in her mind. More and more she accepted her current situation for what it was and sought to find some silver lining in the gray, oppressive political atmosphere. She knew if she focused on the negative and her pain it would have the potential of consuming her. She would not be able to give supportive strength to Anne, Annabella, or Hugh and she needed to keep encouraging them as their pillar, their ballast. In these quiet moments, sucking on her pipe by Annabella's spring, Flora could hear her mother's voice, "Lean ort lassie, carry on. As long as we breathe we keep going." Slowly she regained her vigor, her resolve, and rekindled her faith.

At last, good news reached Mt. Pleasant via a tinker and later followed by a short letter, written again on the back of a handbill from Alex MacLeod. The British were winning the battles around Philadelphia and released their captive troops in late August (Aug. 21, 1777). After seventeen long months cramped together, the three MacDonald men were heading to the home of Allan's cousin in New York. The note continued in minuscule writing that General Howe had outmaneuvered George Washington and the British had marched into Philadelphia without opposition.

(September 26, 1777)

The women were elated. Annabella ordered a few chickens to be butchered and apple pies to be made. They would have a small meal to celebrate their good fortune. With the British taking Philadelphia the war should be ending soon, perhaps before Christmas, and their sons and husbands would return. The ladies surmised that the men, Allan, Sandy, and Alexander would probably get a ship from New York and sail back down to Wilmington within a month or two.

Flora went into the parlor, uncovered Annabella's spinet, and began playing some upbeat tunes. Anne and Annabella were dancing with each other about the room as the children laughed, clapping their hands and joining in. None of them had felt such joyful abandonment in over a year.

CHAPTER 58

New York - Feb 21, 1778

The lightened moods at Mount Pleasant extended almost until Christmas when a long-anticipated letter from Allan MacDonald was received. Flora was dumbfounded as she slowly started sharing its contents aloud while she, Anne, and Annabella sat around the kitchen work table prepping for the evening meal. She was fully expecting to read their travel plans and approximation of an arrival time. Instead, Allan wrote that they arrived in New York safely and were staying with his cousins. It was the next line that she stumbled over and her voice dropped to a whisper. Only Annabella's Alexander would be returning to North Carolina as soon as he could. Annabella was smiling from ear to ear. Flora continued reading, however, her again her voice quivered in disbelief. Allan wrote he had re-enlisted with General Howe's 84th Highland Regiment! She sucked in her breath as if she had been punched in the stomach. Then, if that blow was not crippling enough he went on in the next sentence to inform her that Sandy had joined the Royal Marines like his brother Ranald.

Overwhelmed with mixed emotions Flora dropped the letter in her lap where it slid to the floor. In a mind-swirling stupor, she got up and walked outside unable to continue. Annabella motioned with her hands for Anne to stay put while she followed her sister out onto the porch. "I do not understand." Flora looked at Annabella, her eyes swimming as she tried to hold back her emotions. "Allan is almost fifty-eight years old. He is a grandfather for God's sake. Why does he want to keep fighting? Why does he not come home to me? I do not comprehend his reasoning."

There was no answer. Annabella just stood quietly by her sister putting her arm around her waist the two women supporting each other once again through their personal hurts and tragedies. Later Annabella would pick up the letter and joyously read again that her own husband was on his way home.

It was not Annabella's Alexander that arrived the following week, nor the month. Toward the end of February, Anne's Alexander MacLeod arrived at Mount Pleasant in the cover of darkness. He brought a mixture of news along with more letters for friends, neighbors, and the usual outdated newspapers to distribute. He was making quite a reputation for himself passing stealthily back and forth across military lines.

MacLeod gathered the ladies in the parlor in front of the fire after the wee ones were put to bed. He poured each of them a dram sipping his slowly before he began. "I've been made a Major," he announced quietly. "This is a great advantage to all of us. Governor Casewell has given his permission for all of you to sail to New York. And from there—home, back safely to Skye." He smiled.

The room went silent as his announcement sunk in and each woman in turn reacted differently. Annabella was the first to speak with a stricken face and practically stammering. "I cannot go Alex. No, the

now. My husband is returning to me here." She
faltered, "I cannot leave… my babies are buried here…
I cannot leave my Da Hugh, he would never survive
the trip. No—no the now!"

Flora was baffled and questioned openly. "Are
not the British winning the war? Why should we
return to Caledonia now? Why now?—Why now? We
have been through so much. I fail to understand." She
looked at Alexander imploringly looking for answers,
some of which were impossible for him to give.

MacLeod poured himself another drink from the
crystal decanter he had set on the mantle. "It is a gut
feeling, a knowledge I cannot explain. No one is
fighting during the winter. Everyone is hunkered down
waiting for spring and that is precisely how I am able to
get here and about. The colonists, the Patriots are
fighting for a different reason than the British. They
have more heart and more determination. You might
say a stronger reason burning through them like a fire."
MacLeod was not one to articulate much, but he was
uncharacteristically clarifying his reasoning, and
wanting the women to fully comprehend his

explanation. "The British troops are by and large fighting for a salary, security, and something to eat. The colonists are fighting with a driving zeal for freedom and self-governing. They want to make their own choices, beholding to no one, and definitely not those of a Monarch across the sea where they have no representation." He paused, "I think with their strong, resolute, and determination they will win and I want you ladies safely back in Scotland. All of you including the children!" He walked around to Anne's chair and put both his hands tenderly on her shoulders.

MacLeod, who had watched all his material dreams go up in smoke looked tenderly at Anne. "Aye, I want you to go home wife with our children and I've secured a safe passage for every one of you."

All through this Flora sat quietly listening with her hands folded tightly in her lap. She just simply stated that she would go with Anne and said nothing more, "I will accompany her."

There was one obstacle. MacLeod had secured their passage on a ship from Wilmington to New York, but they would have to get to Wilmington by themselves. There was continuing silence when he told them this. They would have to make careful preparations and plans. This time it was Flora who spoke first and firmly.

"Rest ye easy lad, we can do it. I can get us, Anne and your wee bairns, to Wilmington. Dinna fash I can do it."

There was no doubt that the small woman, her mouth pressed tight and eyes like burning embers could do just that.

CHAPTER 59

Wilmington, March, 1778

There was no time to dawdle. MacLeod helped Annabella's servants bring around a light wagon the next morning, filled it with straw so the children would be comfortable, and added their few bags and satchels. He placed his three young sons gently in the cushioned wagon bed, wrapped them in warm comforters, and kissed each on their foreheads. His insides were twisted and his feet felt heavy knowing that sending them home to Scotland and across the sea was full of perils, yet also knowing that keeping them here may be a far worse fate. Which was the lesser of the two evils? Either way, he was bidding his children and beloved wife goodbye, not knowing for how long or if forever. No one could even predict the next hour, let alone the future in this tumultuous time. MacLeod never could have guessed that the family's endeavor to start a new life in the colonies would have put them in such peril and dire consequences. His idyllic dreams had been shattered and smashed, along with many others, first by cannonballs and then burned to the ground in front of them. Now his central focus was to get his family to safety. He wanted to provide them with a future of peace and freedom from want, and at this moment Scotland seemed like their only option and their only haven. All this conflict and kaleidoscope of thoughts were going through the man's head as he lifted his precious Anne onto the seat next to her mother and then handed her their newborn tiny lass whom they had just named after her grandmother.

Between smiles, hugs, and tears Flora MacDonald, holding the horses' reins, gave the signal and the wagon jolted forward into the creeping dawn. They were headed for Wilmington, a three-day journey, however, they knew where friendly kinsmen lived on the route, ones who would proudly accommodate Flora MacDonald for an overnight and be trusted to keep a tight lip.

The journey went relatively easy and upon arriving at their destination of Wilmington, the city seemed more uncertain than their initial visit. It was still decidedly British on its face yet there were many patriots, the Whigs, Americans as they were now calling themselves, living and working in the city—and they all looked alike. Flora was heading their wagon towards John Burgwin's home when she spotted the lovely Lewa walking towards the market, an oversized basket balanced on her head. Both ladies smiled and waved recognizing one another and Flora stopped the horses and offered Lewa a ride, explaining where they were headed.

"You do not want to go there Miss Flora, no the now," Lewa told her in flawless Gaelic. "Mr. Burgwin has gone to England. He has rented the house to a Charles Jewkes."

"Who is he?" Flora asked.

"A businessman they say." Lewa squinted up at Flora then in Gaelic again told her that Jewkes sold rum, sugar, coffee, and—slaves. Lewa already knew that Flora was appalled by the sale of people—any people. Would she still want to stay at the Burgwin home?

Flora, trying to process the information realized that would not be acceptable and additionally not safe. Jewkes may be a Whig and that would not serve her nor the family well. She told herself to stay flexible and calm, but at that point, the boys all began crying at once as if they were dominoes falling in a line. The din of their hungry wailing was scrambling her thoughts and focus, and for a split second she felt irritated. Lewa was smiling at Flora now and she realized the young woman had grown into a real beauty since they met three and a half years earlier. Before she could formulate a plan, Lewa placed her basket in the back of the wagon, hopped in, and cuddled Anne's eldest crying lad which in turn seemed to settle all the children down completely. Then the smiling woman reached into her pocket retrieving a few hard biscuits. She broke them in halves and handed each a small piece. The little ones were looking at her in delightful astonishment.

"Turn to the right at the next street," she instructed.

Trustingly Flora flipped the reins, yelled out 'Gee' and the team turned right, heading up the dirt street. It was a short distance when they spotted a livery yard with a farrier out front. The big man was bent over with a horse's foot held tightly between his knees as he deftly leveled the hoof. He dropped the foot down when he saw them approach, wiped his hands on his leather apron, and came out of the shadows. Flora noticed the man had Lewa's eyes and smile.

Lewa introduced them to her brother who immediately helped the ladies down while at the same time slipping the two smaller boys onto his broad shoulders. She grabbed the infant Flora as he helped Anne down, then ushered them all into the modest house next to the barn. With the grace of a ballet dancer and in complete control, Lewa began fixing tea, handing slices of cheese to the hungry children, and providing a clean rag with a little sugar water for the teething toddler.

Flora and Anne both relaxed and enjoyed for a bit being comforted by this graceful woman who began talking to them while her brother expertly built up a warm fire in the corner. First came the questions. Why were they here in Wilmington? Where were they going and why were the two women traveling alone with all the babes?

Flora had become suspicious of everyone by now, not knowing their motives or which side they had taken. But Lewa made her feel different, comfortable, and at ease as she was with her own. She felt she could trust the young black woman with her life.

After listening intently and being satisfied that everyone in the room was in agreement, Lewa made them a modest proposal. "You know I am a free woman," she began. "I have a paper that says so, but when most meet me that is not the assumption." She smiled, "My pigment has put me in peril here. Most people, including some blacks, believe I'm a slave when they see me. That is, unless they know different." Lewa continued, "Some of the slaves and free folk like myself are being captured, kidnapped so to speak, by bounty hunters and then re-sold further down south. I do not know if you have heard, but New York is where people who look like us are going. Thousands have gone you know, literally thousands of escaped slaves, many of whom have joined the British." Lewa took a sip of her tea, "The British have promised freedom to those who enlist in their military."

Flora was amazed. First the British sold their prisoners of war to the colonies, along with their unwanted convicts and indigent individuals. The government then allowed privateers to actively trade in kidnapping more humans from Africa and selling those souls. Now they are promising the same people freedom if they fight on their side, maintaining the identical institution that got everyone there in the first place. It made her dizzy just thinking of the illogic. Somehow for years, she had been totally ignorant of the number of enslaved people, both black and white. She knew of course of their existence, but not the staggering number of human beings in captivity—used as a commodity. She listened carefully as Lewa talked.

"If I traveled with you two ladies to New York I could go as your slave and no one would be the wiser. It would be safer for all of us. If I went alone I would risk my life and liberty with marauders and kidnappers everywhere. With you I could help with the bairns and once we got to New York, I could find my husband."

"Husband?" Flora asked sounding astonished and wanting to take back the question immediately. Of course, the girl could be married and have a husband. Why not? She thought herself daft for even asking such a thing.

Lewa's face lit up, "Oh yes. I married a wonderful man, but he was not free until now. He escaped you see, and is in New York with The Black Pioneers." Then she added realizing the ladies knew not, "It is a whole British Unit of all black men and all are now free black men. It used to be called the Ethiopian Brigade." Lewa paused but kept smiling. "Black Pioneers is their new name."

There was a collective sigh of relief along with all in agreement. The women put their heads together and started laying out a plan. Lewa's brother would keep the wagon and team and eventually drive it back to Annabella's with a letter explaining what he was hired to do. Lewa would take charge of the two oldest boys, ages five and seven now. Anne would hold her tiny new daughter and Flora would handle the three-year-old. The boat on which MacLeod had made arrangements would be leaving the day after tomorrow and everyone had just enough time to wash their clothes, re-pack, and prepare scones and food that would keep for the journey.

In the meantime it was agreed that Flora and Anne would stay out of sight as much as possible while in Wilmington, Flora being known and the most recognizable. They thought it best not to draw attention to themselves or to Lewa. When the day came for them to board the ship to New York they formed a line and headed down the dirt street to the dock. Anne was first, Flora followed feigning a stoop with a shawl about her head, then Lewa with an oversized bonnet, a plain dress, and also face down holding the two boy's hands. She was playing her role as a slave well.

Lewa had already explained to them that her brother was safe in Wilmington—for now. He was essential to the city as the best farrier and blacksmith for miles around. The British and Patriots both needed his skills and his services. He was a free man and stayed totally out of politics while making a comfortable living constructing everything from rakes, hinges, and wagon wheels. If it was metal he could forge it, including weapons. Their plan was once she was settled in New York he would then close up shop in Wilmington and join her. It was risky, but the plan of the moment, and as with all plans, subject to change.

As their small parade walked to the docks and they rounded one of the corners in town, Anne gasped and her mouth flew open. Coming in the opposite direction was a red-haired woman wearing one of Anne's stolen dresses, the lavender one with the tiny flowers. Anne's eyes started to flash as she turned around to say something. Flora's hand darted out grabbing her daughter by the elbow. "Shush. Shut your gob. Do not react—keep going." Flora too had recognized the dress she helped make.

Anne realized that her mum was right. There was a good possibility she might spot more of her pillaged belongings before she got home to Scotland. She heard her mother say. "Lean ort lassie, carry on. As long as we breathe we keep going."

CHAPTER 60

New York

The March weather along the Atlantic coast was in the process of violently shaking off her winter coat. The sea was rough and the voyage to New York more than difficult. The unusually late winds and rain slicing sideways slowed the sailing north and instead of the normal few-day trip, the journey took the better part of a week. All on board got seasick, hanging their heads over the side to regurgitate what little they had eaten. The only exception was baby Flora who appeared to enjoy the pitching and rocking. There was no relief from the rolling and rain until they tacked into Upper New York Bay when the chaos of the ocean ceased and both the sea and the sky opened up to a tranquil blue. Anxious for fresh air and to escape the dark and stifling hull below, the three women ascended to the top deck with the children. At first, they could breathe in deeply and feel refreshed standing in view of the land however, as the ship sailed up the East River an hour later, they were overcome with a putrid stench. It was so repugnant the three ladies recoiled and instinctively covered their noses twisting their faces away from the land.

"What is that?" They choked, gasping from the nauseating smell.

One of the seaman, who had also pulled his scarf up over his nose, offered a muffled explanation through the layers, "Those are the British prison ships, ma'am. The British have moored their prison ships in Walkabout Bay."

Frowning Flora was the only one who completely comprehended immediately what he was telling them. They were ghost ships, the infamous death ships. The British were warehousing their American prisoners in hellish conditions, and most likely feeding them little or nothing. When the prisoners died they just threw them overboard. The stench was from rotting bodies, loved ones left to decay in the shallow muddy waters. She shuddered and suppressed a feeling of reoccurring nausea, gripping the handrail as memories of herself being on ships just like them many years ago still occasionally tormented her sleep. Flora, tears forming in her eyes, inquired about the names of the vessels.

"I'm not sure ma'am. One is called the *Scorpion* but the worst is the *Jersey*. There are almost sixteen of them moored in there. But no you worry, we will not be docking anywhere near there. We are up the river a piece."

Even though there was some relief and the rank odor dissipated as they sailed further on, the memory was branded in their minds. Flora was shaken and failed the remove the horrendous concept of man's inhumanity to man running through her thoughts. Looking at her grandchildren innocently running about the upper deck, she wondered what their future would hold. Would it be better? Would people be more kind? Would they live in peace as her church prayed? She reached down and tussled her grandson's curly brown hair.

She had a secret that she was yet to share with Anne, one that was additionally eating at her. She needed to pick the right time to tell her daughter and this was not it. They were pulling into the wharf and, if she was seeing correctly, Allan's cousin was the man on the dock waving a welcome.

❁

The women had grown quite close and Lewa was invited to the cousin's home for a stay, but she declined, intent and excited to locate her husband. With a quick hug and her memorable smile, Lewa left Flora, Anne, and the children at the dock. "Tapadh leat, thank you. Fare thee well and Gabh mo leisgeul, God bless you all." She told them in both their languages. They watched as the dark woman with a heart of gold disappeared into the bustling crowd of people on the wharf, confident in her security and freedom and searching for a specific young man.

Anne and her children, along with Flora were scheduled to leave for Scotland on the 22nd of March. They had one week left in the colonies, and what Anne was not yet informed of it was one week left together with her mother. Flora had made up her mind to join Allan and their son James, now both with the 84th Regiment of Highlanders stationed at Fort Edward near

Halifax, Nova Scotia. It had been an agonizing decision, however, it had also been slightly over two years since she laid eyes on her husband. Two years of daily and lonely struggles, two years of not knowing if she would ever see him again, two years of carrying everyone's burdens including her own. She wanted nothing more than to rest in his arms, and to lay down next to him in sleep.

She started the conversation when they were out walking together in the spring sunshine of New York. "Anne, I'm not off with the Fairies...."

Anne could not believe what she was hearing. She had never been far apart from her mother in her entire life. At a complete loss for words, all she could think of was distance—how far they had come, how far to return, and now an ocean distance of separation. Flora's intent was baffling, to join her father? "Mother, Fort Edward is almost nine hundred miles from here. What are you thinking? You will be no safer there."

Flora held her daughter's hand, explaining once again how strongly she felt she needed to join Allan, how torn she was and that as soon as the war was over they would reunite. She was not sure where, but she felt deeply in her heart they would be together again.

CHAPTER 61

Fort Edward, Nova Scotia

It was just a few days before Anne departed New York and indeed sailed back to Skye alone, still stunned her mother was not joining her. She took with her and Alex's four children, a bundle of letters from everyone who knew of her destination and bitter-sweet memories of North Carolina. Arrangements had been made for some time and Anne would be met by her Uncle Angus MacDonald who would assist her until Alex MacLeod could join her in Scotland at some point. Unlike the others, MacLeod had not sold his estate in Skye. Anne not only had a place to go she had a thriving track of land, a helpful family to lend a hand anytime she might need it, and a few servants. Anne would be in good shape.

Flora's journey to join her husband at Fort Edward was more than challenging and perilous than her daughter Anne's return to Scotland. Her mysterious, reoccurring fever returned and she could barely hold any food down. No one was sure of the cause and it mattered little but she attributed it to the heartache of separating from her beloved daughter and grandchildren. The illness did not deter her resolve though to travel north to Nova Scotia. It had just the opposite effect. Flora seemed more determined than ever to get to Allan. She booked passage as soon as she could on yet another ship traveling from New York to Halifax, a trip of 636 nautical miles and if she was lucky by catching the spring breezes to make it in just five more days at sea.

❖

It was late May when Flora, at last, arrived at Fort Edward on the Bay of Minos. Allan had been waiting anxiously for weeks not knowing how she was faring and ignorant as to the cause of her delay. He had left her a letter in New York with his cousin containing funds for her passage and was sure she had received it, yet so far there had been no word, nor had Flora arrived.

460

When the supply wagon eventually rolled into the fort Allan was thrilled to see one of the waiting soldiers lift the small woman down from the front seat where she had been perched like a bird next to the burly driver. After more than two years she was a vision for his blurry eyes. Allan strode over with quick steps and swept her into his arms. Both recalled immediately their other extended separation thirty years ago when he arrived at Lady Bruce's in Edinburgh to take her home and how he had swung her around then in the Bruce's entryway. As he held Flora now Allan realized how thin and fragile she had grown. He felt as though he was embracing a fragile feather and noticed her gossamer silver-streaked hair. Allan was a wash of guilt for leaving her in North Carolina for so long to fend for herself. Their life had not gone in the way he had hoped or could have predicted in this new land. However, she was here now, here with him at last. Allan pushed her bonnet back and leaned down to kiss her as their son James came into sight. It was quite a family reunion with the father and son surrounding and dwarfing Flora in their woolen red coats.

The men were equally delighted to show Flora the small cottage they had furnished as best they could anticipating her arrival. It was sturdy with two rooms, a big rock fireplace at the end, and a full stack of wood sitting by in a corner.

After she was shown the cabin, tea was made and Flora felt somewhat rested from what had been an epic journey from North Carolina. When she was alone with Allan that evening she relayed her and Anne's trip to New York, how Wilmington had changed, and the unexpected and welcome help from Lewa. Flora explained that her long delay in Halifax was because she was taken ill again and too weak to travel. Flora was honest with Allan and said she thought her fever had been brought on because of the grief of saying goodbye to her beloved Anne and the four little ones. She confessed how deeply concerned she was for Anne's safety crossing the Atlantic in the midst of a war and the potential perils. Allan fully realized then that Flora had never really been away from her daughter, the two spending so much time together that their parting made Flora feel as if a part of herself was being taken away and that a big part of Flora's heart sailed back to Scotland leaving him with her hollow body. Flora was worried about marauders and pirates everywhere with Anne's ship flagrantly flying the Union Jack.

Flora also explained to Allan how she felt about the town of Halifax. How it had refreshed her spirits and health and that she could finally look out at to the vastness of the sea, wind in her hair, and smell the salty waves just as if she were a bonnie lass again on Skye. She smiled and said she almost could have stayed there but he was on her mind and she strongly felt his call.

The bright spring sky promised a warm season. Winter had melted away once again in the North and small yellow flowers were poking up their noses here and there. Flora felt a great deal of comfort being with Allan and James again. She could barely take her eyes off either of them nor they of her. They were far from North Carolina and further from Skye, yet together. For Flora, her family was her most precious possession.

The ensuing summer was also pleasant with gardens providing the men of the fort with fresh vegetables and game. Flora was able to get out frequently and go for walks regaining her strength at Fort Edward. The fort itself was built up with earthworks, a palisade and a surrounding ditch. She had to smile as it reminded her of castle ruins in Scotland but a more recent construction. There were close to 170 men stationed here, many of whom were Scottish and had served in the Seven Years' War. It seemed they were far better equipped and experienced than those who had marched off with Allan to Moore's Creek years ago.

In addition, there were a few prisoners housed in their brig but not many and the conditions were remarkably better than those who had been held in the New York Harbor. The men in the brig at Fort Edward were mostly sailors who had been taken from the American privateering ships.

As seasons circulate in a pattern, autumn followed the halcyon summer of 1778 in Nova Scotia. The oddity was freezing temperatures descended on the land much earlier than normal and actually froze the apples on the trees before they could be picked. By December the temperatures had dropped below freezing and stayed that way until the end of February. The St. Croix and Avon Rivers along the sides of the fort froze solid and the relentless snow drifted up and over their cabin windows at the fort. The nights became longer and daylight shorter leaving the interior of the cabin not only bone-chilling cold, but now dark as a cave and they were using candles most of the day.

Unlike the radiant heat of the stone houses in Scotland, the wind whistled wicked through the exterior walls and the tiniest of cracks. The door frequently froze shut in spite of the fact they nailed blankets over the opening. The slightest moisture on the floors quickly turned to ice. Flora never felt get warm at all. She found herself spending most days wrapped in a blanket and propped up close to her meager fire. She would put on two pairs of knit wool socks, but still, the cold crept into her body and she felt her very bones were frozen. Allan shoved wood chips, paper and cloth into the cracks of the log building in an effort to keep the icy wind out, but his efforts were in vain.

It was her hands that hurt Flora the most. They were red raw, open and cracking between her fingers. At first they had just ached then stung, the last stage being when she ceased feeling them at all. The gloves she knitted failed to be warm enough. One day as Flora was the Fort's commissary, she took off her gloves for a few minutes to pay for some items. A Mi'kmaq woman also shopping looked at Flora's hands then gently lifted them into her own, turning them carefully over. Flora was delightfully surprised the next day when the same woman appeared at her cabin door and presented her with a pair of subtle leather mittens. Flora invited the native woman in where she took Flora's hand again and slipped it inside the mittens she brought and watching Flora's face intently. A soft warmth crept quickly into Flora's fingers and her face reflected the relief. Both women smiled acknowledging each other. The soft lining, of what Flora thought may have been rabbit fur, was providing relief to her hands that had felt frozen in pain for months. She was totally grateful for this woman and her artistic gift of colorful quill embroidery; stars and flowers sewn in a pattern of swirls. "Elles sont belles Merci beaucoup." Flora thanked her in French and told her how beautiful they were, knowing most of the indigenous people of the area spoke French.

The woman was not finished. She took Flora's shoes and rubbed a mixture that included bee's wax over the top to make them more waterproof, the whole time making tsk tsk sounds with her mouth.

Flora was speechless at such a kind gesture and wanted to reciprocate, but food was scant along with everything else that winter. The woman just smiled and waved to her as she went out the door. Winter will pass she said, "L'hiver passera."

But winter hung on for the residents of Nova Scotia that year. The days and hours would drag on endlessly and the icy fingers of the North were unforgiving. Chronic loneliness clutched hard on Flora's heart yet, what kept her going was the basic chores that could not wait. "Lean ort lassie, carry on. As long as we breathe we keep going." Those words became, once again, a life-saving mantra, as she put one foot in front of another in a rhythmic but boring routine.

On the way to get water particular frigid day, Flora read the mirror-like reflections on the smooth path to the well, knowing they were a warning of ice. Using her staff she moved carefully however, her left foot slipped on the slick surface, and in a flash Flora found herself in a heap on the hard frozen ground. As soon as she hit she knew she had hurt herself badly.

Pain tore through her wrist and up her arm and she could see her hand laying at a strange angle. Fortunately, Allan had been watching her from the fort and saw her go down. Rushing to her he helped her up and, with assistance from another soldier they half carried Flora between them to the Fort's surgeon.

The British surgeon examined her arm carefully and stated that she would heal, her wrist was dislocated and she had torn some tendons. He set her arm with instructions to keep it immobilized for at least two months while it improved. Healing would take the remainder of winter, two more long months before Flora could begin using it again.

Those two months seemed endless, and in many respects, Flora thought them worse than being in the London Tower. At least in the Tower she had Ceitie to talk to. Here there was nothing; no music, no company nor pets. Her useless hands sat unfamiliarly in her lap wanting to spin, knit, or embroider. All she could do was sit day after day in the semi-dark waiting for one of Allan's brief visits, consumed in her thoughts with only her worn prayer book to read over and over. Involuntary isolation like this was something she had never endured before and at times her imagination ran wild. At least she was cognizant of that fact and could discern between fact and fiction. Most days found Flora laying in her narrow bed, stacked with blankets and drifting in and out of sleep dreaming of Skye. She knew this was unhealthy and occasionally would try to walk around the cabin interior counting to herself, singing familiar songs, or reciting poems. Flora needed to maintain some strength, the sound of Caledonia calling her home was getting louder and louder in her mind.

Her mind drifted back almost thirty-five years earlier and she wondered if Allan would have arrested her had he discovered she was aiding the Bonnie Prince. It was such a long time ago, yet she pondered on those events repeatedly over in her head. He had always laughed when she would ask him that very question when they were young. But now, with nothing but time on her hands, she really wondered, her lonely imagination getting the better of her. Was that laugh covering up his true feelings? He was gone from his post in Scotland when Kingsburgh, his own father was arrested for being a Jacobite in '45. She knew that now. What would he have done if he had been there when his father was brought in cuffed with chains?

The melancholy winter crept tediously on with its short daylight hours and snow incessantly falling along with the temperatures. High drifts closed all the roads and trails in the surrounding area, preventing needed supplies to reach the fort. The men were extending what they had stored as long as they could however, the entire fort and hamlet were down to one meal a day with a bread they called 'fire-cake,' a tasteless mixture of flour and water cooked over open fires. The rest of the time they made thin soups and tea just to keep their bellies thinking there was food. Flora again began to lose weight along with everyone else in the hamlet. They were all slowly starving to death and knew it. The question of how long could they last was on everyone's mind. The winter days felt longer than they had in Skye even though Flora knew the actual daylight hours were longer if you could call it daylight. The drabness appeared only as different shades of gray, sometimes making it impossible to tell where the sky ended and the sea began. The very shape of the land appeared obscured many times, shrouded by a frozen fog.

Eventually, winter reluctantly gave way to spring. The roads opened in the warmth of the sun and the first supply wagon arrived through the thawing mud-filled ruts carrying the much-needed supplies. There was salted meat, flour, lard, and potatoes. A festive, celebratory mood erupted throughout the Fort Edward inhabitants realizing not only they would survive but tonight, for the first time in months, they would have a meal with the guarantee of another the next day. Hope returned and smiles broke out across faces too long grim. The wagons and horsemen additionally brought with them news and greetings from loved ones, letters, months-old newspapers, and military reports.

It was early May that Allan's routine was disrupted and he hurriedly made his way across the fort's grounds to Flory and their cabin. Looking stricken and his hands shaking he stood at their sun-filled door apprehensively. Flora's arm and wrist had healed well and she was doing some simple knitting by the window's light. When she looked up and saw Allan's face she shuddered, a cold knowing that a dark horseman just rode across her soul and she dropped the yarn and needles to the floor. Allan's voice shook as he stammered. "Sandy's naval ship is missing".
Allan crossed to the chair where Flora stared at him in disbelief and crumbled next to her on his knees, "Lost at sea," he whispered laying his head on her lap.

Flora heard the words he was telling her but felt like it she was mistaken. Had she heard him correctly? "What?"

"Sandy's ship went down Flory. He is gone."

For a minute Flora couldn't quite fathom what he was telling her and she sat stoically still. Her darling boy swallowed up in the dark frigid sea? She felt a stab in her chest, an actual pain as if it had been cut out yet she was alive, frozen in time, bleeding in horror. Sandy, the boy she saw waving goodbye to her and grinning as he turned in his saddle back in the North Carolina woods. Sandy, so young, full of promise and so loved, her dear son Sandy gone. The bitter reality of Allan's words slowly sank in.

Allan repeated the saying about death so often heard in Skye, "Ta se anois a staid na firinne, agus sinn-ne air staid na brèige." He is now in the state of truth, and we are in the state of untruth. "He is with God now Flora."

Flora screamed and Allan sat back on the floor shocked. "No - No! I dinna see him with God Allan. No! He is deep in the cold dark ocean and there is no reach to him! I cannot hold him. He is scared and I cannot help him!" With that, she gasped, screamed again, and staggered to her bed where she groaned as she rolled herself into a tight ball pulling the blankets over her head. Her cries of grief shook the room followed by a keening that sent shudders down the spine of anyone within earshot. Allan stood now, his hands drooping limply at his sides not knowing what to do, or how to console his wife. He was grieving too, but she was in her own private hell and would have to find her own way out. He was at a loss for how to help her. When he attempted to sit next to her and give her an embrace she pushed him away and pulled the blankets tighter, and in a fetal position shrouded herself.

The broken man pulled up a chair next to his wife's bed and sat helplessly there for hours. When the sun set he lit a solitary candle. At last, Flora was finally quiet and the room still. The first words she spoke to him came in a hoarse whisper from underneath the blankets, "I want to go home."

Clearly, Allan knew full well what she meant

CHAPTER 62

October, 1779

An Innis Aigh - Gaelic traditional song

Seinn an duan seo dhan Innis Àigh

Sing this song to the Happy Isle

An innis uaine as gile tràigh

The green isle of whitest sands

Bidh sian air uairean a' bagairt cruaidh ris

Though storms at times threaten severely

Ach se mo luaidh-sa bhith ann a' tàmh

It is where I love to be

Càit' as tràith an tig samhradh caomh

Where does summer come earlier?

Càit' as tràith an tig blàth air craobh

Where do trees come into bloom sooner?

Càit' as bòidhche 's an seinn an smeòrach

Where does the thrush sing more sweetly

Air bhàrr nan ògan 's an Innis Àigh

On the tips of branches than in the Happy Isle?

An t-iasg as fiachaile dlùth don tràigh

The most prized fish closest to land

Is ann ma chrìochan is miann leis tàmh

Wishes to live about its shores

Bidh gillean easgaidh le dorgh is lìontan
Lively youths hunt it early in the morning
Moch, moch ga iarriadh mun Innis Àigh
With line and net, around the Happy Isle
'S ged thèid mi cuairt chun an taoibh ud thall
And although I sometimes go to the mainland
'S mi 'n dùil air uairibh gu fan mi ann
And at times even think that I could stay there
Tha tàladh uaigneach le teas nach fuairich
A sad longing whose heat never cools
Gam tharraing buan don Innis Àigh
Always draws me back to the Happy Isle
O 's geàrr an ùine gu'n teirig latha
It is only a short time until the close of day
Thig an oidhche 's gun iarr mi tàmh
Night will come and I will want for rest
Mo chadal buan-sa bidh e cho suaimhneach
My eternal sleep will be so peaceful
Mo bhios mo chluasag 's an Innis Àigh
I lay my head in the Happy Isle

❧

That spring Flora withdrew tightly within
herself. What had passed earlier for socializing on any
scale ceased. She spoke little to anyone and her once
smiling face took on lines of severity. The wrist had

healed, but her heart was injured, a wound unseen, raw and tender. Most days she could be seen walking alone, head down along the river, then she would stand endlessly gazing east, across the sea. Flora even went so far as to decline attendance at the sabbath meetings. A traveling Catholic Priest coming through observed the bereft woman and referred to her in his journal as a 'Mater Delorosa', a sorrowful mother.

Allan had taken the unpleasant task of writing letters to the rest of the family informing them of their beloved Sandy's fate. It was Anne's response that began the slow assent for Flora to climb out of her depression. It was not Anne's usual letter with news of the children and home, but one reminding her what she told her the day they got on the ship from Wilmington heading to New York with Anne seeing her stolen dress and her reluctance to leave her husband behind. Flora told her then, and Anne reminded her in her letter. "Lean ort lassie. We carry on, as long as we breathe we keep going."

For Allan MacDonald there was the diversion of daily, routine duties at Fort Edward keeping him busy and his mind off the loss of Sandy. There was also James to consider and his own grief in losing his older brother. It was Flora who appeared to be moving about daily in an invisible fog. The MacDonalds had little to say to each other anymore with the exception of Flora quietly repeating her desire to return home to Scotland. "Wee Fanny is being raised by someone else, she needs her mother." Or she would add, "Anne needs her mother to help with the babes."

Allan would argue that he too needed her, but his words fell on bitter ears. Sandy's death drove a fat shim between the two. One day, attempting to reassure her he said, "He is with God now Flory. He is with God."

Flora stared at Allan for a few seconds. "I still do not see him with God Allan. I see him sinking into the cold abyss of the ocean, eyes open and terrified." She paused, "I see him reaching up for me and I no can help him. I cannot save him, and that image is what stays in my mind." Her eyes moistened and she bit her lip looking down. She blamed Allan also. She did not express it in words, but he knew. He should have sent

Sandy home after their time in the jails, the damp gaols of the freedom patriots in the colonies.

※

In the early autumn of 1779, Allan was able at last to secure a passage for his wife on one of Lord Dunmore's trade ships. The vessel would sail from Halifax to London and from there, her brother Angus could assist in bringing her back to Skye. Both he and Flora had gained back a few pounds after the winter of starvation, yet both remained underweight, malnourished in body and soul.

Allan's pride prevented him from securing passage for two. He was one to keep his commitments and his enlistment with the 84th Regiment was one. All their holdings in the Hebrides had been sold five years ago to facilitate their relocation to North Carolina. He congratulated himself knowing he paid off all his creditors at the time and Flora would have no that burden to face returning to Skye. However, he had bragged to no end about North America being a new world where he would once again hold a high position, be a respected landowner and successful businessman.

He was ashamed to show his face in Scotland again, let alone hold his head high until he had at least or at last, regained some dignity as a landowner. Allan had heard of land near the Kennetcook River in Nova Scotia he might be able to develop. The fact he had little money and less help to do so eluded his logic. He was driven to try. He suffered from the illusion that once successful his family would all return to him in Nova Scotia.

At the docks in Halifax Flora embraced Allan quickly, as if he was a stranger, then turned her back and walked up the gangplank carrying her bedding and small satchel tucked under her arm. He tried to speak to her but found himself at a loss for words. The chasm between husband and wife was already as wide as the ocean she was about to cross. One mind in Nova Scotia with wishful dreams and a damaged pride and the other whose heart lay on the Isle of Skye in Scotland.

He followed her onto the ship and stood on the deck, his arms hanging limply at his sides, his face crestfallen. "Write me when you get to the auld country so I know you are safe Flory," he said.

"Aye, I will be staying with me brother Angus. Anne has already collected Fanny so we will all be together—what is left of us."

Allan was running out of time. He leaned down, kissed her on the forehead, and told her he loved her, words he regretted not saying more often. She stared at his red coat again reminding her of the day she watched as he rode off with their sons into the thick woods of North Carolina, their coats resembling cardinals darting here and there among the green tree leaves until she could follow them no more. She did not answer him, the memory seemed from another time and different characters on the stage of someone else's drama.

Turning wordlessly he left.

�֎

Allan had been fortunate to procure her a berth having pulled a few strings to do so. It was but a humble bunk placed along the walls of the lower deck, not the fine cabin like the one she had arrived in to the colonies. There was a centralized common table to be shared by the other travelers with boxes and bales of

481

freight tied down in the darkened corners. To Flora's dismay there would only be one privy for all the passengers however, someone had graciously fastened a curtain in front. The hold was crowded with folks like herself whose single desire was to return home. She looked around, her eyes adjusting to the din, then placed her small satchel on a straw mattress along with her down comforter. These were all the possessions Flora had left. Yet she was content, thinking these simple accommodations would do nicely, better than hiding in a Corodale cave with a recalcitrant prince and she had to admit to herself she was thrilled to be on anything heading away from the Americas. A tiny birlinn would have done well.

The voices of men yelling heave-ho, ropes being loosened and the heavy foot activity of the crew above told Flora the ship was ready to depart. The vessel groaned and creaked, the sails unfurled and Flora MacDonald felt herself moving slowly away from this cursed land of broken dreams.

CHAPTER 63

Pirates!

The first evening Flora lay in her berth, relaxed to finally be heading home she gazed up at the thick planks overhead supporting the deck above. These had been her most humble accommodations on a ship thus far in her life, including those as a captive of the British. Someone prior to her occupancy, undoubtedly bored or wanting to leave their essence behind, had carved a Celtic cross in the wood beam above her. Their precision cuts exposed the lighter wood underneath and the carver, using the contrasting shades, constructed complicated Celtic knots in a circle around the symbol. She stared at it for some time finding it unexplainably comforting. It was almost the end of October and late to be sailing across the Atlantic. She had not felt herself in some time and referred to her own condition as being in a 'tender state'. What kept her going now was the drive to see her homeland. Her hope focused each day on seeing her native country of

Skye and the place she never completely left. She saw the Celtic cross as an omen of goodwill and good luck.

The initial three weeks of the voyage went without incident. The weather held cool and the trade winds were steady. The cargo ship was making good time and Flora found herself frequently joining the other passengers on the top deck stretching their legs, talking, and breathing the fresh ocean air while watching the whales and porpoise play. The bottom decks were full of pelts, dried, stretched flat, and tied in bales. They were a valuable shipment and would fetch a tidy sum in London.

One afternoon as the passengers walked on the top deck another ship came into view. It never was unusual to see another vessel, but this one was not running parallel to their direction but rather sailing right toward them. There was a moment of befuddlement as the onlookers stared in disbelief at the three-masted schooner headed straight in their direction when the warning shouts and the ship's bell rang out loudly. It was a pirate ship and was approaching fast. With the alarm sounded the top deck became awash of activity with seamen taking different positions, some loading their weapons and cannons being readied. No doubt the other ship's purpose was less than honorable and was clearly bearing down on them.

Two loud volleys exploded from the pirate ship's cannons, splashing precariously close to their vessel. Flora, suddenly alert, woke from her extended foggy doldrums and swiftly lept into action taking charge once again with a burst of energy. With arms flying and yelling she began herding the other women and children to the deck below and hopefully safety. She stood at the hatch door until each and every woman, along with their children, was in the hull, down from harm's way. As the captain ordered evasive maneuvers their vessel changed its direction with a pitch and yaw sweeping the deck with water. Flora was the last passenger ducking for cover, scrambling down the stairs when the ship shifted violently. She felt her foot slip on the side of the trap door and she plunged head-first down into the hold. She remembered none of it until she woke up hours later with the ship's surgeon's whiskered face hovering two inches above her own.

She winced as she turned in her bunk, and he told her to be still while he set her broken arm. All she could think was, '*again*?' It was not the simple break in the same arm she had in the colonies, nor like her wrist at the fort. This break was much more complicated and in two places. The surgeon had wooden slats cut to fit, then snugly placed them against the broken bones and bound them with a cloth. It would keep the bones in place while they mended, however, Flora doubted she would be walking freely about on the top deck for any more fresh air before the ship reached the Thames. And, that would be a good three weeks or more.

As she lay in her berth she thought that one's future will always remain unknown. Each day anew and every morrow remains forever in the shadows. No matter what plans someone holds, there is always the unforeseen—the unknown. Days ahead come for some and for others never again. Life was like the sea. Sometimes violent and angry and then, the beautiful tranquil halcyon days. Flora rolled over facing the wall, pulled up the quilts to almost cover her head and let the tears fall silently. She had lost Sandy, she feared she would never see Allan again, and hoped Fanny and Johnnie would forgive her for leaving them in Scotland and going off to the Americas. The Americas had become a decision she most certainly regretted. She thought of it as five years in hell. She allowed herself, for a minute or two, to wallow in self-pity, then she fell asleep thinking that God did not protect us from the daily challenges, the heartaches, or our own foolishness. He did, however, unexplainably sustain us through it all. As she whispered the Lord's Prayer, the gentle swaying of the ship rocked her to sleep.

Flora was unaware of how long she slept when she was awakened by a skinny young girl with ginger hair. She was the same age Fanny was when she left her years ago. "Miss Flory, Miss Flory..."

The child held out a bowl of soup and sat down on the side of the berth. "My mum said to bring this to you. We are so grateful you helped us all to safety, and sorry you hurt yourself."

The soup was steaming and smelled divine. Flora tried to sit up but found that simple action challenging with her arm bound up as it was. A quick thinker, the girl set the bowl down at her feet and pulled on Flora's good arm helping her onto her side. Then, being very practical she held the bowl in her two hands while Flora took to spooning the soup into her mouth with her good arm.

With piercing hazel eyes the child chatted endlessly as Flora ate. She told her about the pirates and how the ship they were on had returned one or two volleys and then, outmaneuvered the other vessel. She explained not only her family, but included lengthy descriptions of each, the personalities of her brothers, and how they too had given up on peace in the colonies and were sailing back to London. Flora found her ceaseless blithering difficult to follow, but a welcome diversion. When her soup was finished the young lassie smiled, excused herself, and thanked her again telling her in Gaelic she would return with another meal in the evening.

"How old are you dearie?"

"I'm nine ma'am and have as many brothers and sisters." Then she threw back her head and laughed aloud.

"Aye, just the age my daughter Fanny was. I am quite eager to see her again."

"You will ma'am. You will." The girl patted her good arm reassuringly.

The young one scurried with the empty bowl to the galley, then returned shortly lugging one of the ship's cats in her arms. She placed it near Flora's stomach where it immediately started kneading the quilt before rolling contently into a ball purring. Flora reached down touching the warm animal and broke into a smile as she stroked its fur.

"Thank you," she whispered to the child. "Thank you. Have you heard the story of Puss and Boots?"

"No ma'am. I do not believe I have."

"I will tell it to you on the morrow."

❂

489

It was a week later in their journey that they hit an Atlantic storm. The gales came in forceful gusts tossing the vessel like a toy, with the passengers and crew practically tying themselves down along with any loose barrel or trunk for safety. Flora sat, as most all the other passengers did, with her back against the hull and her feet braced straight out against the side of her wooden berth. She wrapped her arms around her pillow with the ship's cat tucked safely between the folds of her skirt. All aboard were exhausted by the endless hours of pitching and heaving trying not to fall from their perches.

At last, the vicious assault ended and one by one conversations began again as folks were unfolding themselves and checking for bruises. Flora managed to get herself to the upper deck when it was all over and there she was met by the most magnificent sunset. The clouds were dissipating and appeared overstuffed in gentle folds of color laying snug against the fading blue of early evening. Part of the sky was streaked with a fire orange melting into yellow then rays of brilliant red

490

and magenta shot from the horizon. All of these hues were reflecting and undulating on the seawater in a magnificent dance to silent music. It seemed as if the bow of the ship was crossing a painting of exhilarating color. She found it hard to take her eyes off the scene as it drifted in front of her face, and she was mesmerized by the sheer beauty of nature doled out after such a ferocious storm.

As she gazed at the marvel Flora MacDonald could see, off on the darkening horizon, the rising shadow of land, the shadow of The British Isles. Her journey back to her roots was coming to fruition. She lifted her good hand and felt she could almost reach and touch the Isle of Skye. Scotland was just a wee bit past this crepuscular light.

CHAPTER 64

Home to Milton

At the end of November, 1779 when the vessel carrying Flora and friends docked in London. Her arm was not completely healed and she had taken ill, yet again. It was the reoccurring fever so many from North Carolina at that time were experiencing. Her illness, along with early winter weather prevented her from traveling further north until spring. She would have to find a modest room in London since her friend, Lady Anne Primrose, had passed away four years earlier. There would be no difficulty finding Scottish sympathizers who felt it a privilege and not a burden to house the still-famous Flora MacDonald for a few months.

In early spring, as soon as there was a break in the weather, Flora, feeling stronger, traveled north to Edinburgh by coach. Once in Edinburgh, with the last of her money, she obtained passage on a small schooner, just like the one she and Allan had sailed on over thirty-one years earlier. It carried her north under full sails, up and around Aberdeen, Peterhead, and then headed round and through the Pentland Firth. Flora could taste and smell the life-giving sea air of home. Taking deep breaths with her eyes closed she could feel its life healing her body and soul. One more day and she would actually see her home, the Hebrides, and knew, at last, she would be reunited with her family. A deep sense of contentment and anticipation permeated her very being and she felt joy for the first time in way too long.

❁

The MacDonald clan had gathered at the Milton Farm on South Uist, the home where Angus and Flora had been born. The anxious group had been waiting excitedly for her return. Her daughter Anne had reclaimed Fannie from the MacLeods soon after had come home over a year earlier. In the absent years, Fannie had grown from a gangly-legged nine-year-old to a tall young woman of fourteen who now wanted to be called Francis. In the crowd was Flora's brother

494

Angus who had been watching the shore for several days, ever since he had received her note from Edinburgh telling him of her arrival.

At last, the small boat hired at the port came within eyesight and shouts went out. Rambunctious children came pouring out of the doors and barns screaming in excitement as they ran to the landing waving greetings. They were quickly followed by a passel of dogs barking, Anne on their heels and Fannie close behind. As soon as Flora disembarked she fell into a gleeful collection of embracing arms which almost knocked her over. Angus stood at the back of the crowd, with arms folded contently across his chest and grinning radiantly from ear to ear. Everyone was speaking at once in this scene of happy chaos.

Flora was home.

EPILOGUE

Flora MacDonald stayed with her brother Angus at Milton for more than four years, until Allan eventually returned from Nova Scotia. Rumor was during that time he returned to London for business but failed to travel north to Scotland to see his family before returning to Nova Scotia.

After the 84th Regiment was disbanded Allan had been awarded a grant of 3,000 acres near the Kennetcook River in Nova Scotia. Again, unable to make the land profitable he went home to Skye in 1783.

With the help of their sons Charles and John, both with close ties to the East India Company, Flora and Allan were able to lease a small estate at Pendiun on the Isle of Skye where they lived their remaining days.

Flora MacDonald stayed on Skye for almost ten years to the day when she passed away on March 4, 1790, at the age of 68. She was attended by the doctor who had taken care of Donald Roy's foot after the battle of Culloden.

It is claimed that her funeral procession was over a mile long with three to four thousand people attending. The heroine of Scotland was escorted to her final resting place with dozens of pipers. It is also told that the funeral procession and burial were held during a vicious lightning storm.

Reports state mourners at Flora MacDonald's wake consumed three hundred gallons of whiskey.

January 31, 1788, Charles Edward Stuart died in Palazzo Muti, Rome in the same room he was born in. He lived to be 68 years old and fathered three illegitimate children.

Neil MacEachen died in Sancerre, France that same year, 1788. He had stayed loyal to Charles Edward Stuart, however, was never financially compensated for his efforts. He married, had children, and changed his surname to MacDonald.

Annabella, true to her word, stayed in North Carolina until her father Hugh passed away in 1780. A year later she, her husband Alexander, and their surviving children also returned to Skye, lucky to leave the area before the British forces evacuated the colonies completely.

Anne's husband, Alexander MacLeod also returned to Skye and she bore him a fifth child, a daughter whom she named Mary.

Fourteen or Fifteen years after Flora died the Skye Boat song was written by Robert Louis Stevenson.

'The Lyon in Mourning' by Rev. Robert Forbes remains one of the most vivid accounts of Scottish history, precisely because it told the tale of everyone involved from his many first-person interviews.

I hope you enjoyed reading Misneach, The Story of Flora MacDonald. If you enjoyed the novel and perhaps learned something new, please recommend it to a friend or leave a review where you can.

Thank You,

K. L. Huntley

BIBLIOGRAPHY

A MacDonald for the Prince by Maclean, Alasdair   Inverness, Scotland   Acair, Ltd., 1982 https://www.ncpedia.org/anchor/anchor

A Woman Nobly Planned by John J. Toffey - Carolina Academic Press, Durham, North Carolina   Copyright 1997 ISBN 0-89089-957-6

Flora MacDonald, Her Life in the Highlands and America by Elizabeth Gray Vining   1967 Geoffrey Bles. London SBN: 7138 0184 0

Flora MacDonald in America by J.P.Maclean, Ph.D. Scotpress, Morgantown, West Virginia 1984 ISBN 0-912951-20-6

Flora MacDonald, The Most Loyal Rebel by Hugh Douglas Alan Sutton Pub. Ltd 1993 ISBN 0-7509-0348

Johnson & Boswell: *A Journey to the Western Islands of Scotland* Edited by R.W. Chapman Oxford University Press -

North Carolina Quakers in the Era of the American Revolution by Steven Jay White Master Thesis. University of Tennessee - Knoxville March, 1981

Scotland, A History Edited by Jenny World Oxford University Press Published 2005 ISBN 0-19-820615-1

Scotland, The Story of a Nation by Magnus Magnusson Copyright 2000 Harper Collins Publishers, Hammersmith, London, England

The Autobiography of Flora M'Donald: Volumes I & II Leopold Classic Library Edited by 'Her Grand-daughter' Printed by Ballantyne & Co, Edinburgh, and London

The Oxford Illustrated History of the British Monarchy by John Cannon & Ralph Griffiths Oxford University Press, New York 1988 ISBN 0-19-822786-8

The Timetables of History, New Updated Edition. by Bernard Grun
A Touchstone Bon: Published by Simon and Schuster, NY ISBN 0-671-24987-8 and 0-671-24988-6 Pbks

Tower of London By Christopher Hibber and the Editors of the Newsweek Book Division Library of Congress No 70-136436 1971

White Cargo: The Forgotten History of Britain's White Slaves in America By: Don Jordan & Michael Walsh: 2007/2008 Published: Edinburgh: Mainstream Publication and in USA New York University Press. Washington Square, NY NY 1003 - ISBN #978-0-8147-4296-9

101 Scottish Songs selected by NormanBuchan Scotia Bookletts 1962

VIDEO: Rough Crossing - BBC

Online: Digital

From Caledonia to Carolina: The Highland Scots Written By: Kathryn Beach

ANCHOR: A North Carolina History Online Resource
Beach, Kathryn. "From Caledonia to Carolina: The Highland
Scots." Tar Heel Juniors

Historian, Spring 2006. Republished with permission.
https://www.bbc.co.uk/scotland/education/as/jacobites/
std/?p=facttl1

Museum of the American Revolution
https://www.amrevmuseum.org/big-idea-5-opposition-to-
independence

North Carolina Museum of History
https://www.ncpedia.org/history/usrevolution/reasons
19

https://www.smithsonianmag.com/arts-culture/the-food-
that-fueled-the-american-revolution-25701053/

History of the Barbecue Presbyterian Church, Harnett
County, North Carolina: Digitized by the Internet Archive in
2013 http://archive.org/details/historyofbarbecu00jame
State Library of North Carolina/Raleigh

Google books: https://book.goggle Digitized Jacobite
Melodies: A Collection of the Most Popular Legends, Ballads
and Songs of the Adherents to the House of Stuart from 1640
until the termination of the Rebellion in 1746. With Historical
and Explanatory Notes. Glasgow: Published by Richard
Griffin & Co. 75 Hutcheson Street. MDCCCXXV (1825)

https://www.thenational.scot/news/14947786.scotland-back-in-the-day-loyalties-of-scots-were-divided-in-americas-revolution/

Oath of Allegiance to the King George III | DocsTeach
www.docsteach.org › documents › document › oath-of

https://southportnc.org/wp-content/uploads/2017/08/The-History-of-Fort-Johnston.pdf

Journals of the American Congress from 1774-1788: In Four Volumes

https://en.wikipedia.org/wiki/Act_of_Indemnity
By United States. Continental Congress

https://www.newenglandhistoricalsociety.com/how-scottish-pows-were-sold-as-slave-labor-in-new-england/
https://www.nationalarchives.gov.uk/education/resources/jacobite-1745/9128-2/   Sept 16, 1745
Act of removing arms from Scots...

Convict Labor: https://encyclopediavirginia.org/entries/convict-labor-during-the-colonial-period/

https://en.wikipedia.org/wiki/Dress_Act_1746
https://www.blackhistorymonth.org.uk/article/section/history-of-slavery/scotland-and-slavery/

https://thefireonthehill.wordpress.com/2014/11/12/the-jacobite-mary-and-ann-drelincourt/

Look up Prisoners in Walkabout Bay Prison Ships - Possibly NY University Press, Washington Square, NY NY 1003   s

https://www.hebrideanconnections.com/people/108995

History of American women/Women in the American Revolution. womenhistory.com

History of Barbecue Presbyterian Church Harnett Co. North Carolina by Rev. James D. McKenzie
Digitized by the Internet Archive in 2013 http://archive.org/details/historyofbarbecu00jame

https://www.history.com/this-day-in-history/british-parliament-adopts-the-coercive-acts

Presbyterian Historical Society - The National Archives of the PC (USA)

https://www.history.com/this-day-in-history/the-boston-tea-party

http://wightonfamily.ca/genealogy/essays/weddings.html (wedding traditions)

Skye Pioneers and The Island https://electricscotland.com/history/skye/pioneers12.htm

History of the Presbyterians in North Carolina: https://docsouth.unc.edu/csr/index.php/document/csr05-0362

Thomas Paine: https://alphahistory.com/americanrevolution/thomas-paine-calls-end-slavery-1775/